Letters from Ellen Tollet 1

Edited by

Mavis E Smith and Peter Smith

"…the idea that it was a pleasure to the writer to write it as well as the reader to read it…"
(Ellen on letters in Letter 35)

I

Published by Inniemore
p.smith.crewe@gmail.com

for
Betley Local History Society

To Claire and Ethan

ISBN 978-0-9538151-6-6

Printed by
Johnsons of Nantwich Ltd. (Est. 1827)
01270 625207   www.jprint.co.uk

CONTENTS

PART V: Marriage of Annabel, 1851 onwards *218*

Postscript

Acknowledgements

The authors thank Betley Local History Society for their financial support in the publication of these letters.

We are most grateful to Sally-Anne Shearn, the Rowntree Project Archivist, of The Borthwick Institute for Archives at York University, who first informed us of the Milnes-Coates Collection of letters from Ellen Tollet to Annabel Crewe, and kindly gave us permission to photograph the documents. Extra help was given to re-copy some unclear letters.

To Sue Baxter, archivist at the Claydon House Trust, Buckinghamshire, we are grateful for allowing us to quote from letters in the Verney-Nightingale Archive. Similarly Sarah Davis of the Shropshire Archives allowed us to quote from the diaries of Ellen Tollet with the smaller loose page diary of Georgina. Helen Burton of the Special Collections at Keele University kindly provided us with references.

We are particularly indebted to Paul Anderton of the Newcastle Guild of Historians who read through an early draft and suggested valuable additions to the text.

Especially helpful was Judith Bettley-Smith who checked a draft of the book and made constructive comments. We are also grateful to John Miller for his help with an earlier version.

Thanks are also due to Jerry Park, Graham Dodd, Gregor Shufflebotham (the BLHS archivist), Shirley Kennerley, Philip Smith, and members of the Betley Local History Society.

Wikipedia, Google and other search engines and archives provided valuable sources for initial information on historical data for the period of the letters, and we are grateful for this internet help.

Illustrations

The cover of the book is a reproduction sepia wash drawing by Cornelius Varley (1820) of Betley Hall from Dominic Farr of the William Salt Library Trust, Staffordshire Record Office, who generously gave us permission to use it (ref: SV1.180).

The numbered illustrations in the book have been included by courtesy of the following holders of copyright or with their permission.

- The National Portrait Gallery for the photograph (1861) of Annabel Crewe (Mrs Monckton Milnes) by Camille Silvy. [*Illustration 28*]
- The National Trust for the mezzotint of Mrs Foster Cunliffe-Offley with a dog by Louis Busiere (after Sir Thomas Lawrence), and a photograph of Powis Castle. [*9,19*]
- Clare Griffiths of the Brampton Museum and Art Gallery, Newcastle-under-Lyme Borough for the water-colour of Madeley Manor by William Callow (1843). [*2*]
- David and Annabel Stacey and the Trustees of the Bridgeman Family Archives for the photographs of Broad Road Welshpool [*18*], Minny as a child [*21*], Archdeacon & Marianne [*29*], Vicarage group [*30*], Georgina [*31*], Ellen [*32*].
- For the illustrations from the Tollet Sketch Book we are indebted to Sarah Davis of the Shropshire Archives, who allowed us again to reproduce, on the title page, the silhouette of Ellen Tollet with the words "Ellen aged 16, 1828", ref 4629/11/2/1, and other sketches from the notebook of Georgina or Ellen Tollet, (ref 4629/11/2); Georgina [*3*], Charles and Mary Wicksted [*4*], Eliza [*5*], Carry [*8*], Fanny [*11*], William Clive [*12*], Church [*15*], Ship [*22*].
- Philip Crocker for the engraving of Lord Hungerford Crewe from the tenantry of Crewe Hall. [*13*]
- The family of the late Edward Watkin for the postcards of Betley Church and Vicarage, and the Entrance to Betley Hall. [*23,24*]
- Claire August for the drawing of the early Welshpool Vicarage from an old photograph belonging to the Parish given by Rev Roger Brown. [*10*]
- John Lovatt for the drawing of Madeley All Saints' Church. [*26*]
- Gregor Shufflebotham for the water colour of a distant view of Crewe Hall by either Georgina or Ellen Tollet.[*20*]
- Crewe Hall Hotel for the photograph of Lord Hungerford Crewe's Coat of Arms.[*33*]
- The Borthwick Institute for the inside front cover [*cat: 149*], and the envelope.[*17*]

Some sources have been difficult to verify or locate. If we have inadvertently omitted any acknowledgement, we apologise.

General References

Bostridge, Mark (2009) *Florence Nightingale: The Woman and Her Legend*, Penguin.

Clive, Mary (1948) *Caroline Clive*, Bodley Head, London.

Gladden, Ray (2011) edited by Jerry Park, *The Crewes of Crewe Hall - a Family and a Home*.

Gladden, Ray (2014) edited by Jerry Park, *Come and Build it Up Again*.

Hinchliffe, Edward (1856) *Barthomley: In letters from a former rector to his eldest son*, Longman, Brown, Green and Longmans.

Kennedy, J (1970), *Madeley, A History of a Staffordshire Parish*, University of Keele, Dept of Adult Education.

Seacombe, J T, Crane, J T, William Crane, William (1836) *Comicalities of Travel: For the Tarvin Bazaar*, Chester.

Shearn, Sally-Anne (2017) *Milnes Coates Archive*, Borthwick Institute at University of York.

Smith, Mavis E (2005) *The Tollet Family of Betley Hall*, Betley Local History Society.

Smith, Mavis E (2008) Editor, *Ellen Tollet of Betley Hall: Journals and Letters from 1835*, Betley Local History Society (referred to as *Journals* in this book).

Smith, Mavis E (2010) Editor, *Diary of a Betley Governess*, Betley Local History Society.

Tringham. Nigel J (2014) Editor, *The History of the County of Stafford*, The Victoria History, Vol XI.

Williams, Jean M & Williams, L (1999) *The New Madeley Manor House*.

Preface

In the summer of 2017, Sally-Anne Shearn from the Borthwick Institute for Archives at the University of York contacted us with the information that a large collection of letters and documents had been donated to the archive. The gift included the particular correspondence of Annabella Hungerford Milnes, née Crewe, received from her friend Ellen Tollet of Betley Hall in Staffordshire. The contact was prompted by the discovery of three books by the first author about the Tollet family, which included a diary written by Ellen Tollet.

Most of Ellen's letters to Annabel (the name she was often known by) were written over a 20 year period starting in 1832. About 80 letters have survived, many are quite long and, in total, contain over 80,000 words. Annabel was the daughter of the 2nd Baron Crewe of Crewe Hall, and Ellen was the sixth daughter of George Tollet of Betley Hall, a noted lawyer, land owner and a leader in agricultural development. Annabel was also closely connected with her aunt Mrs Cunliffe who lived for a time in Madeley Manor. The three properties were within a few miles of each other. Ellen was born in 1812 and Annabel in 1814. Ellen never married and Annabel eventually married in 1851.

In 2008 Mavis Smith edited the book *Ellen Tollet of Betley Hall: Journals and Letters* (Betley Local History Society), which contained Ellen's daily observations on her life. The detailed diary runs from 8th January, 1835 to 11th October, 1836, followed until 1846 by occasional notes on the Tollets. After 1841, the latter was more of a journal than a diary mainly about the upbringing of her niece Minny – which was of particular significance to Ellen in these letters.

The correspondence shows Ellen writing about the concerns of leisured, cultured ladies. The letters cover opinions on literature, religion, politics, the arts, and the position of women in Victorian society. She socialised with a large number of members of this stratum of society with her comments on marriage, suitors and gossip. We have tried to transcribe and identify names, and their relevance, but sometimes we have been unable to decipher the handwriting.. Often Ellen cryptically does not explain indiscretions and scandals for us. Perhaps readers can help us? Was Miss Rathbone poisoned in Bath? What was the scandal of Lord Melbourne? What was the amazing story of Miss de Salis and Captain Greville? What was the outcome of the Harper court case? What was the court case that William Clive had to attend in Shrewsbury? What was Mr Clayton's self–sacrifice?

The letters narrate Ellen's life over twenty years which include her close contact with her niece Minny, and the joy that gave, but also the sadness of the deaths young people which were ever present in that time.

We enjoyed the lengthy process of transcribing the handwriting, notwithstanding faded letters, illegibility and cross-writing. The digital camera and computers made the task easier. Our acknowledgements to many individuals and organisations who helped with this project are listed separately.

Mavis E Smith
Peter Smith
Madeley, January 2019

Introduction

Letter writing in the 19th century

Letter writing probably reached its peak during the 1800s. It was also helped by the introduction of the penny post in 1840 which was the beginning of a national method of communication. Prior to this date there was a postal system which was run by a variety of organisations. It was expensive and arbitrary with many different charges for letters based on number of pages, locations and distance. Often the cost was charged to the recipient. The postal cost, together with the high cost of paper, explains the use of cross-writing covering every inch of space. Interestingly, Ellen Tollet stopped using cross-writing after Letter 21 which was written in October 1839.

Who had the education, interests, spare time and contacts to indulge in the writing of long letters? Principally the main writers were women who were the daughters or wives of aristocratic birth, of the landed gentry and of others who had substantial wealth. The daughters were usually educated by governesses with the occasional period spent by some at a ladies' college, unlike boys who would be sent away to public schools from an early age unless they had a private tutor. Girls' education could be of a high standard including arithmetic, composition, Latin, French and possibly other European languages. It could also include leisure activities such as drawing, painting and dancing. Of course, this was mostly in preparation for marriage.

Many ladies, spared of any household duties and even the bringing up of children, would spend their mornings writing letters to other women in a similar situation. Unmarried daughters particularly would exchange gossip within a network of contacts. For some ladies this letter writing developed further into novels. Often they chose to write anonymously, like Jane Austen, the Brontes and V (Caroline Wigley Clive) who was related to the Tolletts through Charles Wicksted. Other discussions did arise in correspondence such as feminist issues, women in politics, and interests in science, but all indicating some deference, at this time in mid-nineteenth century Britain.

Ellen Tollet (1812-1890), writer of the letters

Born into the gentry on 29th May, Ellen Harriet Tollet was the seventh child of George and Frances Tollet of Betley New Hall in North Staffordshire. She had six sisters and one brother.[1]

It was a wealthy land-owning family. Their father George Embury, a barrister, showed great promise by becoming a young Recorder of Newcastle-under-Lyme from 1792-1801. A polymath, he was a Whig politician, standing as an MP for Tewkesbury, near his home town, but he later withdrew his nomination. The previous Betley Hall was bought by the first George Tollet in 1718; he had a senior position in the Government as Commissioner for the Navy but he died in 1719. Subsequently Betley Hall was inherited by Charles Tollet. He rebuilt the hall in 1783. After Charles Tollet died in 1796, George Embury, a distant relative, inherited the sizeable estate in Betley on condition that he changed his name to Tollet. He later became a JP and Deputy Lieutenant of Staffordshire: he was a significant figure in North Staffordshire and South Cheshire. Towards the end of his life he was offered a baronetcy for his service to the Whigs by Lord Melbourne in 1837, which he declined.

Perhaps he was most renowned as an agriculturalist, for which the Board of Agriculture awarded him a gold medal for a 60 page report "On the means of converting portions of grass lands into tillage and returning the same to grass after a certain period, in an improved state." Currently being renovated, the model farm, which he had designed on the site of the black and white Old Hall across the road, was the envy of his landed friends from far and wide. When Ellen was born her father was the Lord of the Manor, owning substantial property in the village and holding the advowson of the church.

George's wife, Frances (née Jolliffe), was the daughter of a merchant from Sculcoates Hall in Hull. She was an heiress. Her mother's family were Wicksteds from nearby Nantwich. George and Frances married in 1795 and the eight children were born over the course of the next twenty years. Frances, too, was well connected in society. Her closest friend was Frances Nightingale, mother of Parthenope and Florence. The Nightingales had two main houses at Lea Hurst in Derbyshire and Embley Park in

---

[1] For a history of the Tollets, see Mavis E Smith (2005), *The Tollet Family of Betley Hall*, Betley Local History Society.

Hampshire. This family friendship lasted for a century with Florence Nightingale's last known letter to Ellen in 1888. The Tollet family made a mark on local society and their fame spread into other wider political and literary areas. Their closest friends were the Wedgwoods of nearby Maer Hall. Their list of other acquaintances was extensive including the Davenports of Capesthorne, the Clives of Powis Castle and Welshpool, the Tayleurs of Buntingsdale, the Wilbrahams and Tomkinsons of Dorfold (at different times). There were many house parties where politics, literature and gossip were discussed. Also, in the same context, finding husbands for seven daughters, like Mrs Bennet in *Pride and Prejudice,* must have been a daunting task for poor Mrs Tollet.

Charles (1796–1870), the eldest child of the Tollets, had to change his name to Wicksted in order to inherit a fortune from his uncle, who had estates mainly in South Cheshire. He was educated at Eton and Christ Church, Oxford and was renowned for his hunting prowess and known for his poems on the subject. In 1822 he became a High Sheriff of Cheshire and later was a JP. In 1834 at the age of 38 he married Mary Meysey Wigley, herself an heiress of the Shakenhurst estate in Worcestershire. They had three children, George, Charles and Mary. Later the two boys succeeded to the Betley Hall estate.

All the Tollet children were well educated. It was a lucky circumstance that there was in Betley Hall a famous library containing many rare books from the first George Tollet and his successors, including the poet Elizabeth Tollet. From the Letters, we learn that many books were bought or borrowed immediately they were published probably through a Book Society. The daughters had easy access to learning! We know that four girls (Frances, Elizabeth, Marianne, Georgina) were educated at home, at first by governesses supervised by Mrs Tollet, where the strict and regimented style of those days was encouraged. In their teens they were sent away to colleges for young ladies to complete their education. They could write and draw with style and knew several languages. They were well known by the gentry of North Staffordshire.

The eldest girl was Penelope (1797–1882). She was rather shy but concerned with philanthropic work of improving conditions in schools and women's prisons.[2] Little is known of Frances (1800-1862), who was a semi-invalid, and cared for by Penelope as she grew older. Elizabeth (Eliza)

---

[2] Claydon House Archive, Penelope to Mrs Nightingale, 1843, bundle 217.

(1802–1836), was a devout Christian and regarded as a knowledgeable geologist. As a child she was acknowledged by the governess, Miss Martin, to be a very intelligent scholar but also stubborn, by not paying sufficient attention to her lessons, when in fact she was ill with a bad chest.[3] She died probably of TB, aged 34. A bright and lively child, Marianne (1804-1841) was the first of the sisters to marry. Many of her drawings, done possibly when she was on a grand tour, still survive. Her husband was the Rev William Clive (1795–1883), who was the brother of Lord Clive of Styche, and a relative of Lord Powis. They lived in Welshpool, where they were regularly visited by her sisters who kept her company when she was pregnant. Unfortunately she had many miscarriages and stillbirths, before she successfully produced a daughter called Marianne but also known as Minny (1841–1930). A few days afterwards the mother died.

The next three girls were very close. Georgina (1808-1872) was the great favourite of the governess and friend of Ellen throughout her life. It is possible that the two girls were sent away to school in their teens to a ladies' college near Liverpool where Ellen made a strong friendship with Jane Lawrence. Sadly in 1826 Georgina developed an abscess on her lower arm, which was amputated to save her life. In her convalescence they went to a coastal resort on the Mersey so that Georgina could bathe in the sea. It is evident from the letters that she was a popular person who had poor health, causing her to feel depressed. Fortunately she had the family to support her, especially Ellen. After their father's death in 1855 they lived at various addresses in London or close to their niece, Minny.

Georgina later was regarded by Charles Darwin (1809–1882) as a fine stylist. Thus he engaged her to proof read his *Origin of Species*. Later she wrote a popular, amusing book called *Country Conversations* (1886) – mainly using remembered stories from the villagers of Betley. Even today some of the paintings of Georgina and Ellen, usually of countryside scenes, are occasionally sold at auction. Ellen, the next sister, was the diarist and writer of the following letters. The youngest daughter was Caroline (Carry) (1812-1840). Like her sisters she was attractive and was loved by all. She had the good fortune to marry a popular young man, Thomas Stevens, formerly the assistant Poor Law Officer in North Staffordshire. By the time of their

---

[3] Mavis E Smith (2010) Editor, *Diary of a Betley Governess*, Betley Local History Society.

.

4

marriage in 1839 he had changed his profession by becoming the curate of Keele. A year later, Caroline too died in child birth. Of the seven daughters, five never married and two died in child birth. Sadly, there was only one child surviving to adulthood from the seven daughters, Marianne (Minny) who features extensively in Ellen's letters.

Ellen was intelligent, bright, sharp–witted, kind and very well read. She could understand Latin, French, Italian and German. When she was young, Ellen was quite boisterous and certainly annoyed Josiah Wedgwood II when she was laughing rather loudly in Maer Hall.[4] Caroline Clive on a visit to Betley Hall in May 1844 observed, "The Tollets are so many and various and so given to talk that conversation scarce ever goes down."[5] However, Ellen had spells of feeling low. Ellen's *Journals* in 1835-6 indicated that her closest friend was Emma Wedgwood from Maer.[6] However there were frequent references to the Crewe family. Like Georgina, Ellen was asked to help Henrietta Litchfield (Emma's daughter) and Emma Darwin in 1873 to proof-read a new edition of *Coral Reefs,* first published in 1842 by Charles Darwin. Ellen said the first sheet was "perfectly clear" although Darwin felt the whole book was "atrociously written". Much later Darwin changed a sentence about monkeys in *Origin of Species* so that Ellen should not be offended.

It seems that Ellen was a prolific letter-writer. In addition to these 80 known letters to Annabel, we know from various records that she wrote frequently to others. It is evident from surviving letters that there was a circle of correspondence between these ladies: Ellen and Georgina, Annabel and Henrietta, Florence and Parthenope Nightingale, Emma Darwin and Charlotte Wedgwood. Their letter-writing too seemed to be shared so that all the family news could be seen from different points of view, even though they might diverge as with Annabel and Henrietta.

How Ellen first met Annabel Crewe can only be surmised. They were of a similar age and shared backgrounds with similar political views, although Annabel's family was of a much higher social order. A letter from Annabel to her sister in 1850 declared that she had known the Tollets from

---

[4] F Burkhardt & S Smith (1985) editors, *The Correspondence of Charles Darwin, Vol 1, 1821-1836,* Cambridge University Press.

[5] Mary Clive (1948) *Caroline Clive,* Bodley Head.

[6] *Ellen Tollet of Betley Hall: Journals and Letters from 1835,* edited by Mavis E Smith, Betley Local History Society (2008) [referred to as *Journals* subsequently].

childhood. Ellen probably knew her as a family friend, because Annabel may have been staying with her aunt, in Madeley Manor, after her mother died. The house was only about three miles from Betley Hall. Ellen wrote regularly to Annabel, who was abroad for long spells. Regrettably we do not know her replies.

George Tollet was regarded by the first Baron Crewe as his neighbour, probably through his legal, political and agricultural connections. Both families kept houses in London as was the fashion then. Annabel's opinions were mentioned in Ellen's *Journals,* and it was clear that these two young women shared secrets. What is more, Hungerford, Annabel's older brother, frequently called upon the Tollets as he passed the hall, and at one point in Ellen's *Journals,* it seemed as though he was paying her the attention of a suitor, which clearly she did not like.

By the 1830s Ellen was aware of "the emptiness occasioned by idleness" that women of her status were expected to accept. Her entry in her *Journals* for 29th May 1836 records her response to this experience. Though wishing for "more stirring scenes, more active employments" she could see no opportunities for them in the future. A similar fate faced Annabel, which she managed to avoid by marriage.

The Hon Annabella Crewe (1814–1874), the recipient of the letters[7]

Annabel was born into an aristocratic family. Her grandfather, John, became the first Baron Crewe in 1806. He had inherited from his ancestors the grand Jacobean hall, about 4 miles from Betley, which became a centre for gatherings of lavish house parties arranged by John Crewe and his wife Frances (née Greville), with guests of prominent Whig politicians like Edmund Burke and later Charles Fox. They had two children John and Elizabeth who married Foster Cunliffe-Offley, the MP for Chester. (His wife is referred to as Mrs Cunliffe in these letters.) The grounds of the hall had been landscaped by William Emes and later by Humphrey Repton. Paintings by Sir Joshua Reynolds and Sir Peter Lely adorned the walls of

---

[7] An extensive article about Annabel Crewe can be found in the Milnes-Coates Archive of the Borthwick Institute at the University of York. Many of the personal details of Annabel were put together by the Sally-Anne Shearn, the Milnes-Coates Archivist.

the house, and there were literary connections too, such as Sheridan who dedicated *School for Scandal* to Frances Crewe.[8]

1. Crewe Hall, the family home of the Crewe Family [from Hinchliffe's 'Barthomley'].

John Crewe, the second Baron, inherited his father's extravagance. As an army officer, serving in Peking on the staff of his mother's cousin, he married Henrietta Maria Walker Hungerford. Her fortune had been wisely restricted, so that it could not be used by her husband. They had three surviving children - Henrietta (1808-1879), Charles Hungerford (1812-1894) and Annabel. Their father was a gambler who accumulated vast debts. The first Baron Crewe gave his son the money to pay them off, but he supplied his friends with the money instead. In the army he had been promoted to the rank of Major General in 1808, Lt General in 1813 and much later to General. Unsurprisingly his marriage failed. In 1820 he arranged a bogus marriage with his pregnant mistress in the chapel of

---

[8] *The Crewes of Crewe Hall – a Family and a Home* by Ray Gladden, edited by Jerry Park (2011).

Crewe Hall. This took place before his wife died in the same year. (Bigamous and bogus marriages by the aristocracy were deplorable, but not uncommon at the time.) His children were then made wards of court on two occasions with the result that the first Baron Crewe and his daughter, Mrs Cunliffe Offley, took control of their education.

Until 1830 it is not clear where the three siblings lived. Court records in 1822 show that their mother's dying wish was that Mrs Cunliffe should care for them. She and her husband lived in Madeley Manor, a fine Regency hall below the Bryn. The children probably stayed there until the governess was appointed by their grandfather, when they moved to Crewe. Letters from the children's mother indicated that she wanted Hungerford to be educated by a tutor so that he could be close to his grandfather, but she died before this could occur, resulting in Hungerford being sent away to school.

As a child, life for Hungerford was unsettled and probably undisciplined. He was an eccentric boy, spending too much time with the servants. For instance, he was allowed to go to one of his grandfather's farms and shoot chickens. Hungerford was sent to Eton, where he witnessed his tutor commit suicide.[9] At Oxford he did not excel academically and Mrs Tollet in Letter 35 made comments about his state of mind, acknowledging that he was improving with age. With his great wealth he seemed to be a target for ambitious society mothers to provide a marriageable nobleman as a son-in-law.

From 1822 the girls were taught in Crewe Hall by the novelist Sarah Burney (sister of the more famous Fanny Burney) on an extremely high salary of £300 per annum.[10] She was there about five years. Clearly the children would have had contact with their aunt in Madeley Manor too during this period.

After their grandfather's death in 1829, Mrs Cunliffe became the main beneficiary of the Crewe estate and not a penny had been left to her brother, John, who brought a second judicial ruling against his sister about the girls' future. Henrietta chose to live with her father in the Belgian chateau of Bois l'Évêque in Liege, and it was decided that Annabel, who was under age, should stay with her aunt in Madeley Manor. Her father

---

[9] Ray Gladden (2011) *The Crewes of Crewe Hall* (edited by Jerry Park).

[10] Lorna J Clark, (1997) *Letters of Sarah Harriet Burney*, University of Georgia Press.

complained that mixing in London society with Mrs Cunliffe was not a suitable background for one so young, but he lost the case and never saw Annabel again.

The Cunliffes were sociable people, fond of the arts, as was the first Baron Crewe. Mrs Cunliffe was witty, knew how to organise a good salon, and she had a remarkable singing voice, according to Edward Hinchliffe, a distant relation.[11] She had married the eldest son of Sir Foster Cunliffe of Acton Park, Wrexham. Like their relations they were collectors of art. There were no children of their own, and they lived in Madeley Manor and Upper Brook St, London.

Life for the children had been unsettled because of their parents' failed marriage and probably by the consequent instability in their childhood. They had lived in a number of places. They stayed either abroad or with their mother in the south of England, in London, or in Crewe Hall or Madeley Manor.

2. Madeley Manor painted by William Callow (1843).

[11] Edward Hinchliffe (1856) *Barthomley*, Longman, Brown, Green and Longmans.

Because Henrietta had converted to Roman Catholicism whilst she was living abroad with her father, Mrs Cunliffe dissuaded her from discussing religion with Annabel in her letters. Annabel was very attached to her older sister, whom she held in awe, calling her "my dearest dear, Henriett".[12] In fact the three siblings remained close throughout their lives, even though they were far apart, and they were all friendly with the Tollet family.

After her husband died in 1832, Mrs Cunliffe spent some time with Annabel abroad, as did another relative, Sir Stapleton Cotton with his daughter, Caroline.[13] From 1833 to the summer of 1836 Ellen directed her letters to Annabel on the continent. Until 1850 Mrs Cunliffe was Annabel's mother figure, guiding her through society.

In 1835 the second Baron died, and Hungerford became the third Lord Crewe. Two years later he succeeded to Crewe Hall thereby becoming a very wealthy owner of vast estates, mainly in Cheshire, and nearby Madeley and Mucklestone. He set about improving his property at enormous expense, employing notable specialists like William Blore, the architect, and William Eden Nesfield, the landscape designer. He was eccentric in appearance and manner, but he was kind, shy and lacking in confidence. Caroline Clive, writing in 1841, met Hungerford at Betley Hall and described him rather unkindly as, " …. both silly and sick. He is very courteous and good-natured, but nervous, shy and weak."[14] Fortunately, however, he took advice from his close relatives and an excellent estate manager, Edward Hall Martin, who had also worked for Mrs Cunliffe on the Madeley Manor estate.

Henrietta came back to this country, living at various times in the Crewe house in Hill St, London, Tiverton, Devon and in Prior Park, near Bath. The siblings remained very close to each other and the two sisters were always there to help Hungerford, to offer advice in arranging public events, where he was ill at ease. The letters of Ellen Tollet offer a more endearing quality to Hungerford's personality than hitherto recorded.

Mrs Cunliffe's death in 1850 made Annabel desolate. Eventually she received the gift of a book of poetry from Richard Monckton Milnes, and

---

[12] Henrietta's name was often shortened to 'Henriett' in letters.

[13] Stapeley Cotton (1773–1865) became 1st Viscount Combermere of Combermere Abbey in 1827. His daughter Caroline by his second wife Caroline Greville was born in 1815.

[14] Mary Clive, *ibid.*

this was the blossoming of a friendship with her future husband. In Madeley she spent considerable time planning the monument to her aunt. About the same time Ellen was caring for her elderly mother, who died in the same year, and the two friends were naturally separated.

It was during the 1830s and 1840s that the majority of Ellen Tollet's letters were written, when they were commenting about the lives of the upper classes, during periods of social change. Just as the relationship between Ellen and Annabel was intense, the friendship between Annabel and Henrietta was deep and life-long.

The Crewes had a large number of relations and friends who are mentioned in the letters. They include the Grevilles, the Williams-Wynns, the Heskeths, the Blackburnes, the Moriers, the Hinchliffes, the Willoughby-Crewes, the Cottons of Combermere and the Offleys.

On 30th July 1851 Annabel married Richard Monckton Milnes (1809-1885), whom she had first met years before in 1835 in Rome. He had been a rejected suitor of Florence Nightingale, whom the Tollets knew well. He was a member of the Apostles' Club in Cambridge, originally a Conservative MP for Pontefract, later becoming a Whig supporter in 1846. He was well connected in political circles, renowned as a poet and biographer of Keats, a friend of Clough and Tennyson, and a patron of talented writers. A man of influence, he was elevated to the peerage in 1863 as Baron Houghton – hence Annabel's new title of Lady Houghton.

After her marriage, Annabel's close friendship with Ellen Tollet naturally declined. Annabel was then living in Fryston Hall in Yorkshire and in Upper Brook St, London. Sometimes she came to Crewe Hall to see Hungerford. Only occasionally did the two friends meet, when they now had a mutual source of conversation because Annabel had three children: Amicia (b 1853), Florence Ellen (b 1855), and Robert (b 1858); Ellen Tollet had her niece, Minny.

The social setting

Two bright, well-educated young women of different social classes were writing to each other for twenty or more years from the 1830s. This was a time of change during the Industrial and Agrarian Revolutions with the growth of science and engineering. The advent of the railways revolutionised the mobility of people and especially wealthy women who were now able to move more freely. It also meant that there was more social interaction.

Ellen's family were wealthy, active Whigs with a social conscience. It was a time when the majority of the population were poor. Thus there would be considerable discussion about political events in the country, during their family and friends' country house parties - which contrasted with the lives of ordinary people. The letters had passing references to the Reform Bills, the Corn Laws, Education Acts, the Poor Laws and the Anti-Slavery Bills. To keep abreast of topical events Ellen read *The Times* daily, but she never developed her thoughts to Annabel.

Both the Tollets and Crewe families were involved with the Church and religious philosophy - hence the many references to the Oxford Movement and its effects. The Tollets were of the Anglican High Church, attending St Margaret's in Betley regularly. Ellen strongly recommended Annabel to read published sermons, but whether she followed the advice is unknown. While Ellen could tolerate the Methodism of the Bloomfields and the Unitarianism of the Wedgwoods, she showed some prejudice against Catholicism. She quickly came to the defence of Thomas Stevens when it was suggested that he was Popish, and seemed alarmed that Henrietta Crewe was trying to convert her sister Georgina to Catholicism. In contrast she was delighted once at a dinner party at Powis Castle when she found herself with twelve Anglican clergy – she chose to chat to the brightest one.

What is rarely mentioned is the work done for the poor in the villages of Betley and Madeley by the two major families and their daughters. Regrettably it was hardly a topic for two young ladies' letters: Ellen's *Journals* specify her contact in Betley with the Sunday school, the Poor House and her encouragement of Mary Gater, the deaf child. However, sadly there is little reference to the many governesses, servants, coachmen and estate and farm workers who sustained this lifestyle for the wealthy: those are to be found in the correspondence between Annabel and Henrietta.

The other hall in Betley was the Court, which still remains. It was the home of the Twemlows, related to the family of the same name, at Peatswood which was visited by Ellen. There seemed to have been little contact between the families during this period. In the letters there was one small passing reference to Betley Court. However, Ellen did acknowledge their presence a little more in her *Journals*.

The letters show what life was like for upper class young women at the time of early Victorian society. Their family problems are evident, as well as their personal relationships with each other. The development of their characters as time progressed is noticeable. For young ladies life seemed to be a round of country house visits in a search of suitors. Before the coming of the railways, country houses were often used as hotels for the wealthy as staging posts for travel about the country. However, rail travel changed this: it became possible, for example, to reach London from Betley in the same day. By coach travel previously such a journey would probably have taken at least three or four days with overnight accommodation.[15]

Ellen and Annabel both had artistic and literary interests. It was expected that the polite lady of the upper classes would be able to discuss the latest literature and comment on the art seen in the newly built galleries in London. To be artistic was a bonus – they each had art masters, and Ellen also was proud of her patchwork, to be handed down to her relations.

It was important for the Crewes that there should be heirs to the wealthy Crewe Estate. All Annabel's close family were relying upon her to marry and to have children. There could not be three unmarried heirs in the family, and it seemed highly unlikely that either Henrietta or her brother would marry. The reader is made aware of Ellen's attempt to influence Annabel into her way of viewing marriage, and especially eligible suitors. This dominating aspect of Ellen's personality was less evident in her *Journals*. Here she tried to manipulate Annabel's feelings about the opposite sex in these letters, but she did not succeed. Mrs Cunliffe, Henrietta and later Mrs Blackburne played far more important roles in Annabel's life than that of a close neighbour.[16]

The development of science was only just beginning to affect medicine. Anaesthetics were in their infancy and the relationship between cleanliness and health not always understood. Infectious diseases such as cholera, smallpox, whooping cough, etc were rampant. Inevitably correspondence between two women would include matters of health. Ellen spent considerable time in writing about Marianne's misfortunes in childbirth and Eliza's death, probably to the point where Mrs Cunliffe made some

---

[15] George Tollet wrote to William Nightingale in September, 1836 that, "Betley will be as good as town house" in London because of rail travel, Claydon House Archive, bundle 34.

[16] The Blackburnes are referred to frequently in these letters. Emma Hesketh (1795–1886) married Rev Thomas Blackburne (?–1847) in 1819. Annabel and Emma (often called Mrs Blackburne in the Letters) were cousins. After her husband's death Emma became a close friend of Mrs Cunliffe and the Crewe family (see Milnes-Coates Archive, Borthwick Institute).

comment to Ellen about not discouraging Annabel from marriage. The physical contact between sick people was made abundantly clear in the letter about Hungerford with the 'hanky' over his mouth, when the deaf Duke of Sutherland stopped by to see him. Ellen's casual remark about having a vaccination against smallpox in 1841 was a reminder of this illness. The 'cures' of bleeding, blistering and leeching were still being practised, as Minny experienced.

In the *Letters,* Ellen Tollet was revealing a different aspect of her life with Annabel whom she had known from childhood. As they were of different levels of the upper class, they were mixing in two different circles of friends, who had similar political views. Always there was the feeling of superiority of the aristocrats, with their ability to travel overseas, to have servants to cater for their needs, to have a doctor in attendance, to entertain on a grand scale and to be known by royalty. The upper gentry were in a group below, and Ellen did seem envious of Annabel attending a royal ball and spending winters abroad. It seemed significant that at Annabel's wedding in 1851, only Miss Duncombe and Ellen were neither aristocrats nor of the Crewe family. In one newspaper list of guests, 'Miss Tollet' was at the end of the named list before the 'etc, etc'.

Once she was reprimanded by Mrs Cunliffe for not giving Hungerford a formal invitation to meet her aristocratic friends, the Clives. Ellen responded that he did not require one as he was a friend of the Tollets. Ellen was always wishing to make a good impression on the Crewes, and to present a more upper class view of her family.

Some notes on the text

The letters are wide ranging in content of society and family matters. The majority are well written, sometimes humorous and sparkling with wit, and varying moods. Some letters are gossipy, with terse sentences and sometimes they are difficult to comprehend. The vast store of Ellen's knowledge is reflected in her capacious vocabulary. What is particularly pleasing is the lack of repetition. The continuity of family events gives them a semblance of structure.

It is difficult to publish letters where no obvious pattern emerges except by chronology. As is usually the case with archives of letters, only half the story is available. Unfortunately about a quarter are undated: we have attempted to place them, either by clues of topical events and family information or by reference to the other letters. The reader may not always agree with the sequence given here. To group them thematically would give little flavour of the writer's feelings or the way they developed.

We are aware of ethical issues connected with the publication and dissemination of private correspondence even after families have given their permission. In the case of these letters, the bulk of them were written over 160 years ago and it seems unlikely that the content would upset current families. However, letters throw an invaluable light on the attitudes and prejudices of the period which should be judged at that point in history.

Transcribing these letters has been a pleasant experience because the reader never knew what would be on the next line – Darwin may be lying on the couch in the next room or the deaf Duke of Sutherland could be at the front door. It is also frustrating because the recipient's answers to questions posed by Ellen remain unknown.

The work proved to be a fairly difficult task, despite the help given initially by Sally-Anne Shearn, whose summaries of the letters were quite detailed. Words were not always easy to transcribe because Ellen Tollet did not clearly differentiate between certain letters. Names of individuals often presented a particular difficulty, unless there was a context. She tried to fill up every last piece of blank paper so that words sank into the inner margins, and spaces were filled even on the inside flap of the envelope and near the address of the first page, with the result that a sentence seemed inconsequential. Sometimes the reader will note she coined words, for example, 'chatteracious', 'invalidish', 'babymania' or 'steadified'. Sometimes words are obsolete like 'chay' or 'gulph'. Many of the early letters were cross written to save paper which was expensive. Ellen Tollet's vocabulary was immense and spelling accurate. Despite weaknesses in places, her style at times is remarkable: for example when she described a local vicar: "I know he was light; I knew he was not always too true; I did not know he was vulgar. Did you?" (Letter 15)

The sentence structure and spelling of Ellen Tollet are those of an educated person. Her punctuation is difficult, often non-existent. At the time informal punctuation in letter writing was not unknown. Even the work of Jane Austen lacked modern punctuation. By comparison, the writing of Georgina, and her mother seem up–to–date in this feature. To make the letters more intelligible and easier to read, we decided to add punctuation, particularly to long rambling sentences with links of hyphens and "&s". There are some characteristic epigrams and witticisms which are buried in the text which have been scattered among the titles.

We have aimed for an accurate rendering of the letters, but there could be the inevitable mistake in deciphering words. Square brackets have been used to include dates or words that are editorial, and occasionally to guess at missing words to improve the meaning. In addition the letters have been given topic headings to summarise the content and context. All italicised words in the letters are editorial with the exception of Ellen's lapses into other languages and book titles. Additional correspondence is also in italics.

The reference, *Journals,* is an abbreviation of *The Journals and Letters of Ellen Tollet of Betley Hall from 1835.*

A list of abbreviations used by Ellen

A – *Annabel;* C – *Caroline or Carry;* CW – *Charles Wicksted;* E – *Eliza;*
G – *Georgina or Georgy;* H – *Henrietta or Hungerford;*
M – *Marianne Tollet or Marianne Clive (Minny or Minnie), Ellen's niece;*
(R)MM – *Richard Monckton Milnes;*
Mrs C – *Mrs Cunliffe;* MW – *Mary Wicksted;* My Lord – *Hungerford;*
V – *Caroline* Clive, *Mary Wicksted's sister;* WC – *William Clive*

Tollet Family

George Tollet (1767-1855)): he changed his name from Embury to inherit the Tollet estate.
Frances Jolliffe (1775-1850)), his wife: she was from the Wicksted family of Nantwich.
Charles Wicksted (1796-1870), son, changed his name in order to inherit from his mother's relatives.
Penelope Margaret (1797-1882), daughter.
Frances (Fanny) Elizabeth (1800-1862), daughter.
Elizabeth (Eliza) (1802-1836), daughter.
Marianne (1804-1841), daughter, married to Rev William Clive of Welshpool, brother of Lord Robert Clive of Styche, and cousin of Lord Powis.
Georgina (Georgy) (1808-1872) daughter.
Ellen Harriet (1812-1890), daughter, diarist and letter-writer.
Caroline (Carry) Octavia (b 1815-1840) daughter, married Rev Thomas Stevens.
Mary Wigley Wicksted, from Shakenhurst, wife of Charles Wicksted.
Caroline Wigley, elder sister of Mary, later married to Rev Archer Clive, cousin of William Clive. She became a well-known Victorian novelist and minor poet using the pseudonym 'V'.

Crewe Family

John Crewe (2nd Baron) (1771-1835).

Henrietta Walker-Hungerford (1772-1820), his wife.

Henrietta (1808-1879), daughter.

Hungerford (1812-1884), son.

Annabel (1814-1874), daughter, married Richard Monckton Milnes.

Amicia, Florence and Robert, children of Annabel.

Elizabeth Cunliffe-Offley (1780-1850), sister of John Crewe, married Foster Cunliffe-Offley.

Willoughby Crewe (1792–1850), nephew of 1st Baron Crewe, Vicar of Mucklestone.

Family Trees

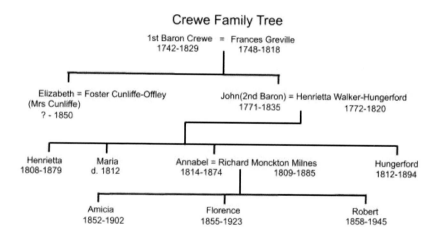

Tollet Family Tree

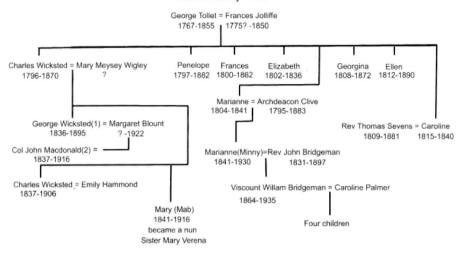

George Tollet = Frances Jolliffe
1767-1855 1775? -1850

Charles Wicksted = Mary Meysey Wigley
1796-1870 ?

Penelope
1797-1882

Frances
1800-1862

Elizabeth
1802-1836

Georgina
1808-1872

Ellen
1812-1890

Marianne = Archdeacon Clive
1804-1841 1795-1883

George Wicksted(1) = Margaret Blount
1836-1895 ? -1922

Rev Thomas Sevens = Caroline
1809-1881 1815-1840

Col John Macdonald(2) =
1837-1916

Marianne(Minny)=Rev John Bridgeman
1841-1930 1831-1897

Charles Wicksted = Emily Hammond
1837-1906

Viscount Willam Bridgeman = Caroline Palmer
1864-1935

Mary (Mab)
1841-1916
became a nun
Sister Mary Verena

Four children

Transcripts of Letters

PART I: Early Letters, 1831–1836

"I think this great misfortune of single women ..... is that they have a great lack of useful employment"

"Better, say I, to marry for situation or money, than for neither love nor money"

At the time of the first letter, Betley Hall was a busy household with seven of the siblings still living at home. The remaining daughter Marianne was married to the Rev William Clive who was the vicar in Welshpool. George Tollet IV was active in the church, he supervised his model farm across the road, and was a prominent member of the local Whig party (as was Charles, the master of the hunt). His wife, Frances, organised family house-parties for the local gentry and the girls were employed in the village with visits to the poor and in providing amusing and intellectual conversation for their guests, as befitted their role in society.

From the 1830s the family was experiencing health problems with Eliza and Marianne. The letters to Annabel understandably reflect their concern. Politically there was considerable upheaval nationally with the Reform Bill, the Corn Law Acts, Education Bills, and in the church, the Oxford Movement. As Ellen Tollet grew older, they figured more strongly in her correspondence. At the age of twenty her first extant letter was written to reveal a happy relationship with Annabel, where they could write freely about their thoughts and emotions. They clearly knew each other well and referred to their families and past events in their lives. It was a time when they could both look forward with optimism and joy. Clearly finding a suitor was of prime importance.

Of the twelve letters in PART I, ten were sent to addresses on the Continent, which suggests the girls rarely met during this period. How often they met subsequently is unknown but is probably very little because generally their social groups did not overlap.

Over the twenty year period 1832–1851, of those which are known to exist, Ellen wrote about three or four letters a year to Annabel.

Letter 1 [*cat: 276*]

Marriage at Maer; ladies' fashion contrasting with Islamic dress; the John Crewes at Calais; house party in Betley; Marianne's stillbirth; cholera in London

[*Betley, May 1832*]

Dearest Annabel,

It was my intention not to have written to you till next week after we had been to the wedding at Maer,[17] as I should have been able to make my letter so much more entertaining, but if this is so dull that you find yourself under

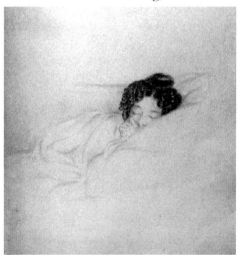

3. A sketch of Georgina by Ellen.

an irresistible impulse to leave it before you get to the end, you might lay the blame on Georgina who, little rogue that she is, has written a trick letter to a friend on her intended marriage & is advised to get it franked so I have ventured to enclose it.

What in the world have I to say? I fear I must have recourse to mention, but no, the marriage of Mr Wilbraham & Jessie Brooke will do for a handsome paragraph. You never mentioned it but of course it is true. Mr Harry Brooke confessed to Charles that the man had offered & everyone says of course she would not refuse him.

Mr H B is coming tomorrow & we will try to get more particulars. It is a very proud match for her. I believe he had a good character & has long been in a marrying way – I believe — falling in love with every pretty young lady going. It is very curious that both the others should be married before Harriet & as Jessie who is so much the least pretty has a better *parti*[18]

---

[17] The wedding at Maer of Richard Wilbraham & Jessie Brooke occurred on 24 May 1832 (obituary in *Law Times* May 11th 1844). Jessie Brooke was a member of the Wedgwood family from Maer Hall.

[18] (French) eligible person.

than Mrs Warburton, I suppose the beauty will end in making the least match of the three. Her old love Dr Molyneux is coming today to give us a week of his company. I hope he will be in a good humour. I have heard it said that a match is likely to be made up between him & Lady Louisa Craven his cousin.[19]

I wrote a long letter to Henrietta this Thursday. In her last to Georgy she had amused us by telling us that if she was sure our natural good taste would soon convince us how much more higher & ladylike it is to wear high gowns all day long & how that Mademoiselle Evelina would be shocked at English young ladies' necks. [20] To all of which I replied that custom is everything, & that some excellent girls I know, who are followers of Mahomet, would be quite as much shocked at Evelina's boldness in shewing no face to every one she meets.[21]

I am going to Welshpool in a fortnight or so. Our going to London is just as uncertain as ever but I think as cholera continues, it is more 'no' than 'yes' as to our going- not that I should be the least in the world afraid, but our friends may not like to have us & may leave at Easter & not return.

I suppose you have heard that the John Crewes are to live at Calais. I wonder whether they will visit Bois l'Évêque.[22]

The trial comes on next week & Edward Clive is subpoenaed & much to his annoyance. Our wicked brother [-in-law] William is going to Shrewsbury to hear it.

Marianne has ordered *Eugene Aram* into our society & we expect it every day.[23] We are harrowing up our souls by reading *St Ronan's Well.* [24] I think it

---

[19] Louisa, Countess of Craven, originally Louisa Brunton (1785?–1860) was an English actress.

[20] *Evelina* is a novel by Fanny Burney (1778). She was the more famous sister of Annabel's governess.

[21] Ellen was commenting on the Islamic dress code for women in 1832.

[22] Meaning Bishop's Wood. The second Baron Crewe was living in the Château de Bois l'Évêque in Liège, Belgium until his death in 1835, which explains a possible visit. The Baron was described as 'eccentric', but he created a beautiful garden. The Château was destroyed by fire in 1944. (Source; *Histoire de Liège*).

[23] *Eugene Aram* (1832) was a novel written by Edward Bulwer-Lytton (1803–1873). It was based on the real life of Eugene Aram (1704–1759), a schoolmaster

is the most affecting book almost ever read. I am very glad you get so well through your dinner parties. I should like of all things to see you enacting the young lady complete.

We are going to have a week of the Messrs Tomkinsons, Brooke, Blackburne, Hammond, Mainwaring, Sir T. Boughey & Lord M. Then next week we go to Maer on Monday & I believe they marry on Tuesday, home again, fasting on Wednesday morning. I am sure we shall never help crying at the wedding, for the bride, I hear, is getting very low spirited but my tears had such an exhaustion at Marianne's execution that they never have recovered it & flow with great difficulty ever since.[25] I really must finish this dull letter but I will send a much better next time if possible. Thank you ten times for your last & with best regards to Mrs Cunliffe. I am

Your very affectionate,

Ellen Tollet

PS: Carry [*Ellen's sister*] does not add, as news is so scarce.

Letter 2 [*cat: 337*]
Before Annabel goes abroad

[*after April 1832*][26]

To: The Hon Miss Crewe, Madeley Manor

Dearest Annie,

Alas! I fear we shall not meet again so I send you dear Mrs Cunliffe's night cap which I am sorry to say is not quite of the right wool & when I get any better I will make her another.

Carry also sends the parcel you were so good as to promise to convey. Goodbye, Farewell, Adieu! All these words are unfortunately now to be applied – pray remember the poor creatures in the country who have to

---

and renowned philologist. In a notorious case, he was eventually hanged in York for the murder of a friend Daniel Clark, which had occurred some years previously in 1744. Probably 'society' refers to the Book Society of which they are members.

[24] A novel by Sir Walter Scott (1823).

[25] An unusual expression: did Ellen mean she was crying at the birth of Marianne's stillborn child? Mrs Tollet arranged a rota for her daughters, so that Marianne always had company during her pregnancies.

[26] Mrs Cunliffe's husband, Foster Cunliffe–Offley died on the 19th April, 1832, and it is presumed that Annabel and her aunt went abroad after this date.

shiver thro' the months of February & March before one bit of hope of summer comes to cheer them, so write often & tell us all your gaieties. How heartily I wish for you a long enjoyable season & if you are doomed not to escape from the fate your friends have planned for you, may it come to you under every <u>ameliorating</u> circumstance. Once more with 100 loves from all,

Your most affectionate friend,
Ellen Tollet

Letter 3 [*cat: 15*]
Gossiping letter; Ellen and Georgina staying at a house party in Madeley; a short break for Eliza on the Liverpool coast; the Bloomfields; Hungerford's 21st birthday; Paganini; the new vicar in Madeley

Betley, Aug 17 1833
Mademoiselle A Crewe, Poste Restante, Aix la Chapelle

My dearest Annabel,

I do hope this will reach its destination in safety & find you comfortably established at Aix. I have directed it without the Prussia at the top for certainly [*it*] is not in the dominions of that country according to the map, tho' perhaps it may belong to His Prussian Majesty. Your continental scheme certainly did astonish me but you will be surprised to hear that yours was not the first announcement of it when your letter arrived.

Penelope & I are staying at Madeley[27] – yes, staying at dear Madeley where we met the Twemlows of Peatswood. She had heard it from Mary Hesketh. My news was not fresh to you either. I suspect very much the greater whence you had it, I fancy. Lady Lucy gossiped a little to Mrs C Wynn – very naughty of her as she was Marianne's first confidante. I will now begin a regular history of ourselves since I last wrote from W[*elshpool*]. We left Marianne after a month's visit much better than we found her - her ailments gradually subsiding. On our way home we spent 2 days with the

---

[27] During the early part of Ellen's *Journals* from 1834–6, Madeley Manor was tenanted by the Egertons, while Mrs Cunliffe-Offley was abroad with Annabel.

Everard Feildings[28] at Stapleton. She was Anne Boughey – you know – she lives in a very pretty parsonage with a very kind, dull husband who certainly does not look as if he were of the imperial family of Germany. However she is very happy & not at all fretting because she has no intentions of a family.

When we came home we found dear Eliza[29] certainly better but still looking so ill as to make us feel anything but quite comfortable about her, but 2 or 3 days after our return Marianne, Papa, Eliza & Carry set off for the Egremont Hotel on the Cheshire coast nearly opposite Liverpool in the hope that sea air would be beneficial.

P F G & I were left at home & we had the happiness of hearing of considerable improvement & that they found the place very amusing. We led very quiet lives during their absence, our solitude only broken by going to a horrid dull, wet, low meeting at Cloverly & 2 days' visit at Madeley.

It is quite impossible to describe to you what I felt the first evening finding myself a visitor in that house. It was with greatest difficulty that I could exert myself & not sink into a reverie (a very painful one) all the evening. The party consisted of Lady & Miss E Charles, E & son & poor Tom a cousin, the Twemlows & Mr & Mrs Broughton & daughter. We all like Lady E[gerton] very much & Miss is a good-natured, cheerful girl but still she is quite a Miss & she was not at all seen to advantage with Miss B with whom she has a silly hollow friendship & who is this most say-anything sort of damsel I ever saw. Penelope & I had amusement & I may say interest in matching & reflecting on a sort of cousinly flirtation between Miss E & Tom. He is an interestingly agreeable young man whose health has been ruined in India & who is now returned thither as, since his return, the English climate has disagreed. I could not help feeling sorry for her, for after having him as a constant companion for a year, she must feel his loss very severely. It was a dangerous situation for the poor girl for, of course,

---

[28] Hon Everard Feilding was the Rector at Stapleton, a village about 4 miles south of Shrewsbury. He married Anne Boughey daughter of Viscount Feilding and Lady Powis. Uncertain why there is a mismatch of names, but there is a connection with the Powys family which explains Ellen's link with the Rector.

[29] Eliza had developed a bad cough and had been taken to many doctors to try to cure it. TB was a common illness at the time.

he has not a farthing & could not marry yet being of susceptible nature, was sure to get into a sort of love with him, tho' if she had been sensible, she would have struggled with it & never have allowed herself to think about him. Of course these remarks are all quite private. I should not indulge in these remarks on our neighbours if I thought they would ever be repeated.

I am thankful to say that Eliza returned from the sea very much better indeed. Her appetite & strength are good but her thinness & cough are still very tiresome tho' those are better & I hope & pray that, as the improvement as continuous though sadly shows, we may see her in time restored to her former health & looks.

I also hope that you will be able to send me a good account of the effects of the change of air & scene on dear Mrs Cunliffe. I am glad you will have a little society among yourselves as otherwise I am not sure that you would like Aix, as I fancy is rather dull. I was so very sorry to hear from Mr Willoughby Crewe who called a short time ago that you had been disappointed by Mr Morier as an escort but he did not know exactly how it was. He also told us that Capt Greville has quite settled upon Monteux as a residence. Poor dear man, I hope he will find it tolerably pleasant – certainly it is a great advantage everything being so cheap there that they may afford to have luxuries & advantages which would be quite impracticable in England.

We had a letter from Henrietta the other day. I do hope she will come to England. She tells us of Fanny Hayman's intended marriage. I hope it will be a happy one. Charles knows Captain Somerville & says he is a very nice man. There is a great disparity between them – 20 years at least, but still that does not matter much. Indeed, I think the happiest marriages are often in this way.

What a shocking disparity between Lord Barham [*1781–1866*] & his newly married wife – 33 years & a fourth marriage too![30] You know, I

---

[30] Ellen was scandalised by the fourth marriage of Lord Barham to Lady Frances Jocelyn. He was 1st Earl of Gainsborough who became the 3rd Baron Barham in 1823.

suppose, that Captain Somerville's brother married Charlotte Bagot[31], the black drawing man's sister. Do you remember telling me how terribly low Miss Hayman was at one time? I fancy she has had some love passages in her life so she will be much better off comfortably married.

Hungerford's coming of age was celebrated at Crewe by plenty of eating & drinking by the tenantry, at which I believe Mr King presided. We heard dinner gong & Barthomley bells ringing & *voilà touts*.

Next week we are expecting Lord & Lady Bloomfield & their daughter. I have never seen him & have a curiosity to do so. He is most delightful character & his history is a very interesting one. He was got out of the King's favour by Lady Conyngham[32] & Sir W Knighton & the final cause of his *congé* was his opposing the King's giving some jewels to Lady C which he had no right to do.

On Saturday we are going to hear Paganini[33] at Newcastle & in about a fortnight we shall have the delight of seeing Marianne & William & during their stay, we hope Lord Clive & Lady Lucy will join our party.

Marianne tells us she is a wonderfully slender figure – indeed Mamma says it is quite odd. However there is no sense to doubt the happy fact & to make the matter more certain I have set about a baby's cap & Mamma has bought two for her, so you see we begin in good time, however, the little clothes take so very long in time to make that it is really quite necessary. I saw Sir Philip Egerton's little son & heir yesterday & a very fat, healthy tho' not a pretty child – he is 4 months old.

---

[31] Rev William Somerville (1789–1857) married Charlotte Bagot (1800–1865) in 1830. She was the daughter of Rev Walter Bagot (1731–1808), Rector of Blithfield, Staffordshire. According to records he was married twice and fathered 15 children, including 8 after he was 60. The meaning of 'black drawing man' is a mystery.

[32] Elizabeth Conyngham, Marchioness, (1769-1861), alleged to be the last mistress of George IV. She had Whiggish sympathies. William Knighton was Keeper of the Privy Purse, and he succeeded Benjamin Bloomfield (mentioned in these letters). Lord Bloomfield, a Methodist, was a family friend,

[33] Niccolo Paganini (1782-1840), celebrated Italian violin virtuoso, was making a tour in 1833. He performed at Stafford in August, and in many other towns.

We have all been reading a book called *Le Mie Prigioni* by Silvio Pellico.[34] If you have not read it you really must. It is perfectly charming, interesting to a degree & what I think is a great advantage – it is such delightfully easy Italian that even I can read it without a dictionary.[35]

I was quite shocked to hear of the death of Mrs Brooke Cunliffe tho' I do not know her, poor thing, leaving her young family!! There have been as many reports as to who is to have the living of Madeley as Scheherazade told stories; now we are told a Mr Daltry. I confess we're glad Mr Hulme had it not, as neither he nor his wife are at all nice people & I am sure it is of great consequence to the poor dear parish. Another report that your aunt intends coming to the Hay House in about 5 months' time.[36] How I wish this may be true. Is there such a hope?

What a long letter I have written upon looking it over. I think, dear one, the fact is I have had too much to tell which always makes a letter too matter-of-fact & newspaperish. Pray write to me soon & tell me of your doings. I think you will find yourself in the same state as I am with too much to tell but you won't like.

Carry sends most especial love. She is grown quite a young lady & very much improved in looks. She has now quite an air. Fancy the change: however is only external, I am happy to say! Some travellers describe all your dinners at the different inns. Tops, bottoms & corners.[37] I suppose you have been John Bullish enough to get some relics at Waterloo, a military button or two or even a bullet. [38] We have a good many that Charles, innocent man, bought & now farewell, dearest Annie, with our united love. I am your most affectionate,

Ellen Tollet

---

[34] Silvio Pellico (1789-1854), Italian writer, poet and dramatist.

[35] Interesting to note that Ellen also had a working knowledge of Italian.

[36] Hay House in Madeley, an important house belonging to the Crewes.

[37] Ellen was stating that every piece of writing paper was being used.

[38] Note the collection of memorabilia from the battlefield at Waterloo, after 18 years. The Tollets also collected newspaper reports and portraits of Napoleon (Tollet Album, Newcastle Museum).

Letter 4 [*cat: 283*]
Delayed post; Eliza's illness & faith; Ellen in Welshpool for Marianne's pregnancy; Henrietta's Catholicism*; Hungerford's personality; Mr Sneyd's marriage*

Welshpool, Wednesday, Nov 23, 1833

Mademoiselle Annabel Crewe, Poste Restante, Naples, Italy

My dearest Annabel,

It so very long since I wrote to you & I have so much to tell you that to sit down to address you is quite a formidable undertaking. Before I begin on any other subject let me thank you for the letter from Munich & in Marianne's name for the very curious & pretty addition to her baby's wardrobe. I should have done this much sooner had the packet arrived in due season, but I did not get it till more than 6 weeks after date, which proves that tho' the conveyance thro' which you sent it was a very cheap one, it was not very expeditious. Before this reaches you, you will have seen so much that is new & interesting that you will have had time to forget that Ellen Tollet exists, but the sight of this will remind you that here I am, still your anxious & loving friend & quite fidgety when I reflect that the number of miles between us must be counted by 4 figures.

I am sure you will be truly sorry to hear that the time which [has] elapsed since I wrote to you has been a season of great anxiety & occasional wretchedness. You may have perhaps heard through Henrietta to whom I wrote a short time ago that my darling sister Eliza has continued a great invalid & tho' she is, thank God, not in a state to occasion us any immediate alarm, her complaints are still such as to make us feel very sad on her account. We are assured that the lungs are not affected yet, but with a cough & very high pulse there is much cause for serious alarm. It is quite impossible for me to describe to you either our anxiety & sorrow or her beautiful cheerfulness & happiness. Not only does she never murmur but she never complains unless when forced to do so by our anxious enquiries. She appears utterly [*unconcerned*] as to the termination of her disorder & the only grief she sees but little of this for, as her illness is not attended with active suffering, we are enabled to be almost as cheerful as ever outwardly, though within there is a great change in our feelings.

The last 4 or 5 years of my life have been entirely years of happiness, so uninterrupted by any real trials or almost without annoyances that I have always felt it could not last very long & now tho' the comfort of hoping is still left, extreme lightness of heart & freedom from care gone, but with long sorrow. Mercy is so wonderfully mingled that I think one feels the presence of a unifying Father more in adversity than ever in prosperity & the manner, in which Eliza is comforted & supported under her trial, is what I could not [have] imagined if I had not seen it. Hers has been a state of constant preparation for sickness & death & now that one at least of these trials is come she is enabled to bear it with resignation & even with cheer, cheerfulness & enjoyment, as coming from Him whom she did not neglect in health & who will not forsake her now.

I hope, dearest Annie, you are enjoying your Tour & that it is producing good effects on your dear Aunt. Naples must be a charming place in Winter & I suppose not so gay & full of English as Rome. I do not understand whether Lord Combermere & daughter stop at R[ome] or came on with you. I quite long for your next letter: pray let it be very soon & tell me what acquaintances you make and all about every thing. You will see by my date that I am with Marianne. I have the comfort of finding her extremely well in very good spirits but as I shall leave her on the 6th of December, I hope to escape the actual groaning.[39] Penelope is to succeed me in my office & will be head nurse. The real monthly nurse comes today which seems very like the near approach of the enemy but I think she will have to wait for some time. I judge by appearance. We might be thought safe for 2 months.

You can't fancy what a fine stock of baby linen she has, much of it made by herself. I brought 5 caps with me from Betley including yours. Imagine the finest cambric shirts with open hems all round, & such frilling & fudge you would laugh to see the drawers which contain it all. However she has nothing sensible than worked muslin frocks. M, like other Mammas expectant, wishes for a boy, but we wish a niece more particularly as the boy, if it is one, is to [be] called by the very ugly name of Richard which is a

---

[39] 'actual groaning' – Marianne's cries in child birth.

great offence to us all, but it is William's doing out of respect to his deceased brother & therefore we do not like to oppose it. I have never yet thanked you for the very nice letter from Aix-la-Chapelle.

Marianne has seen Mr Wynn since his return & was glad to receive a very good account from him & and was quite surprised to hear of Henrietta's visit to you there. It shews that her interest & affection for you & your aunt are all alive. Indeed I think with her, absence does (not) [*Ellen's parenthesis*] make the heart grow colder. I am afraid you found her reserved & Catholicky! A person who lives so much alone must alter a good deal & get very wrapped up in themselves. I fear there is now no chance of her coming to England this winter. I suppose Madame Biolley[40] is still the reigning favourite unless indeed some young Monsieur Biolley or Augustean or *quelque chose* has taken her place in Henrietta's affections. Of course, you have read that charming book *Le Mie Prigioni*.[41] Was there ever anything so interesting? I think it has been as much read & admired in England as *I promessi sposi*.[42] I heard, though how I do not know, that you had been at Manheim seeing the Grevilles. Of course pray tell me how they like their *séjour*. I was much amused by a para I saw in the paper giving an account of a fracas the Captain had had with some Germans. It was very likely incorrectly told but still I could imagine it all true as I know the dear man is a wee bit peppery.

Since writing the former part of this letter I have received one from Georgina enclosing one from Henrietta which, to my surprise, I found was dated London. Georgina also says that Hungerford had just spent an hour at Betley having arrived at Crewe the night before & was coming to dine the next day. Was not this very affectionate? Georgy says he is greatly improved indeed. She says his oddities were not the least observable & appeared very polite & pleasant. This, I am sure, you will be delighted to hear.

---

[40] Madame Biolley was a close friend of Henrietta. Her husband was the Belgian politician Raymond de Biolley (1789–1846).

[41] *Le Mie Prigioni* (1832) was an Italian novel by Silvio Pellico (1789 – 1854).

[42] *The Betrothed* (1827) was an historical novel by Alessandro Manzoni (1785 – 1873).

Henrietta talks of going to Bath, but I hope she will not return without visiting Betley. We hear that she has made a convert of Mr King's son & Georgy very maliciously observes perhaps she may confer an additional kindness on him by visiting that fate with his. But this, I need not tell you, is only a joke between ourselves. Hungerford is going to spend the winter at Paris. I think it is a great pity he does not stay in England & endeavour to make a few good acquaintances.

Georgy, among other news, tells me that there is a report that Mr Sneyd of Keel[43] is going to be married to Lady Harriet Ryder - but it is not from a good authority indeed - if it is true. I don't admire her taste for tho' certainly agreeable, when he chooses, I think a more affected, heartless piece of goods than he is I do not know, & his wig & dress altogether give him such a patched up appearance. He told me he had seen you at dinner in London. He thought you very pretty. Voila! Mr Ralph Sneyd! By the bye, he thought me very agreeable so he is very condescending to the young ladies. I hope you will soon write to me & tell me all your news.

Marianne sends her very best love to you & Mrs Cunliffe. I will let you know as soon as I can when I am an aunt. I would have delayed writing until after the event but I thought I flattered myself you would be growing impatient. The account of dearest Eliza tonight is very much the same as ever. I trust my next letter may have better news to tell.

God bless you, dearest Annabel.

I am your most affectionate friend,

Ellen H Tollet

Annabel's family too were having problems. Her sister Henrietta was dissuaded by her father and others from entering a convent. For the next few years she seemed deeply troubled: Ellen could have been more understanding.

Letter 5   [cat: 284]
A gloomy letter about Marianne's confinement; Eliza's fortitude in her illness

---

[43] Ralph Sneyd lived at Keele Hall, and was a neighbouring friend of George Tollet.

3 Jan 1834

To: Mademoiselle Annabel Crewe, Poste Restante, Naples

My dearest Annabel,

I sit down to write to you without one feeling of pleasure & this is saying a good deal, but really my news is all of a gloomy nature. As such one can feel no pleasure in communicating now I had anticipated the delight of telling you that I was so proud & happy aunt of a flourishing baby! But every fond hope that we have cherished has been destroyed just when about to be realized. After continuing quite well till Saturday 14th December, dearest Marianne was taken ill & continued in a state of great danger & suffering till the following Thursday when she was delivered of a dead girl. The anxiety about her was so great that those who were with her (William & Penelope) could hardly feel the loss of the darling child, they were so completely filled with gratitude for the preservation of the mother after such a protracted & extraordinary suffering. The sweet creature was a very fine & uncommonly fat baby & Marianne's fortitude was quite surprising & she bore up all through in a way that astonished everyone.

You may imagine the disappointment & sorrow this has been to us all, but we must bear it & every other trial as a means used by our heavenly Father to bring him nearer to Him & which will have that happy effect if we make a right use of it. You may imagine what a serious affair M's has been, when I tell you that Sutton from Shrewsbury was sent for & that tho' she has improved gradually for a fortnight it is only the last day or two that she can move herself in bed. Dear creature, she has endeared herself to all by the way she has [*illegible*] all. She says the loss of her child is a trial sent by her God to show her the sinfulness of too great a desiring & longing after any one earthly blessing.

The Clives have been all kindness to her – Lady Lucy[44] tho' *en famille* herself coming to see her every day till she got too bad for it to be safe. That dear woman, the Duchess of Northumberland has written her the sweetest letter to W[*illiam*] making touching allusions to her own similar

---

[44] Lucy Herbert (1793–1875), Countess of Powis.

misfortune. Poor Will[*iam*] has been in sad distress on account of Marianne but is now getting quite happy.

I wish my bad news has come to an end but I must tell you that poor dear Marianne has been thrown out of her Jersey carriage & tho' not seriously hurt, was much bruised & shaken & is not yet recovered from its effects - tho' considerably better. This with our anxiety for both M & Eliza has made our Xmas anything but a merry one. Indeed if we did not thrive against it we should be very, very gloomy but we try to remember that mercy is mingled with all our chastisements & that both M & Mamma's misfortunes were very near being much worse & Eliza's state is a constant source of gratitude as well as of sorrow, for never was any one supported thro' a long illness. She is exactly the same - only slight variations in the cough. She bore the disappointment about the baby beautifully. Oh! It would have cheered us so to have had Marianne blessed in the way she has so long deserved, but all is for the best.

Now dearest Annabel, let me talk of your affairs. I fear from your account that your dearest aunt's health is very indifferent but I hope when you are stationary in the shocking climate of Naples that she will improve. I did not understand from your letter whether the Cottons accompanied you on to Naples or stopped at Rome. I hope the former. I hope if you return in the Spring, you will come all together for I do think the journey would be very anxious for you alone in case Mrs Cunliffe is liable to these attacks but, trust be, that since they will have disappeared.

When shall I see you again? I do hope & trust you will not be tempted to stay longer than the winter in foreign parts but I know Italy is very enticing – Henrietta in England & wishing to come here & [*we*] are doubtful whether we can receive her! This is unfortunate but I have still hopes Marianne may feel equal to seeing her as we should enjoy her company very much. You may imagine that with 2 invalids we lead very quiet lives! We see no company except an occasional man or two etc, saving one Ball to which Carry & I have been. This is all. Carry liked the Ball better than she expected but it was not likely she should feel in very good spirits under all circumstances & as for myself I was never so flat.

Two of us are going to Madeley on Tuesday. We find them very good-natured neighbours[45] & we do very well together. I long to hear from you now that you are settled at Naples, you must tell me all about your society etc. Pray do not marry an Italian Count or we shall be sadly separated, but if Lord Etherington should by lucky chance be travelling on the Continent & wintering at Naples of course I can make no possible objection. Is your sister being engaged or married provided you come to England very soon?

I have never yet thanked you for the very nice long letter you sent me from Rome. I hope you have received mine from Welshpool written a few days before yours arrived. I hope this will not cross one from you on the road but if it does you must write again in due time after receiving this.

I suppose it is no news that Emma Bullock is going to marry Mr Biddulph. Mrs Parker's brother saw her & him at the Liverpool Music Meeting. He looks old enough to be her father but both the Miss Parkins & that damsel herself are highly pleased at the match, so a little disparity will not signify.

We have been reading Caspar Hauser's melancholy history[46] – of course you have seen it & now the newspapers tell us the poor youth been cruelly murdered by an unknown man in the gardens at Anspach. It is a curious history.

I have, I see, entered into no particulars about dearest Eliza but that I did in my former letter & her symptoms continue so exactly the same there is little to tell you. I think as soon as ever spring comes we shall migrate somewhere most likely to the sea for her. I hope Marianne will either come here or go somewhere with us when she is got well & only wants a little change, for her spirits will sink sadly when she begins to go about again & has no darling baby to solace & to suffer so much & all for nothing is, I have always heard, most peculiarly trying to a woman & having waited four years makes M's case much more disappointing. However with such a

---

[45] Madeley Manor had been let to the Egertons (see Letter 6 and footnote).

[46] Kaspar Hauser (1812–1833) was a German youth who emerged having spent years of isolation in a darkened cell. He was stabbed and killed in 1833. This notorious case was made into a film in 1974.

husband she is still a highly favoured person, for he is one who will be such an assistance to her in leaving her to bear her trials with submission.

I have exactly nothing more to tell you, dearest Annabel. Caroline, dearest, tells me to give you her most affectionate love & the same you have from me & from all. Pray say everything that is most affecting to your dear aunt for us. G remembers that we are particularly anxious to hear how Naples agreed with her. I know her kind heart will feel for our Marianne & for all our other anxieties. Farewell my darling, I am your most affectionate,
Ellen H Tollet

Letter 6 [*cat: 370*]
Eliza's health improving; Marianne & William's happy visit; the Egertons in Madeley Manor; Henrietta entering a convent; gossip

Betley
13 May 1834

Mademoiselle Annabel Crewe,
Poste Restante,
Naples
My dearest Annabel,

I hasten to begin a letter to you because I am so anxious to have no news crossing your last nice letter, though Mr Dick did not reach me perhaps so soon as expected; it is now 2 days since I received it. Thank you for it & for all your & Mrs Cunliffe's kind expressions of sympathy in our anxieties & in our rejoicings. We had indeed much to be grateful for & though we cannot consider ourselves yet out of that troubled water, we are nevertheless far, far more happy & comfortable than is our right we had the slightest hope we should be, dearest.

Eliza is gaining her strength & health so very slowly that her recovery is not one of those sudden delightful resurrections you sometimes see but this was not, I suppose likely after so very long an illness but she does gain strength for she is now down stairs & has been out in the carriage & in a wheel chair many times without suffering from it but her walking capacities are very, very small & this must be so, while she has so wonderfully little muscle & flesh.[47] Her appetite is very poor & she has no cough or any bad

---

[47] Catherine Darwin wrote to Charles in November, 1833, "Poor Eliza Tollet is thought to be in a consumption. She has had a cough now for 9 months and is

symptoms except now & then deranged stomach. As soon as she is well enough I hope she will be persuaded to go in the sea & this will do good too. We have had almost as great a trial in her as Miss Eliza for tho' her bodily health is quite as good as usually her nerves are so weak from less or rather great diminution of sleep which she has had ever & even her fall from the pony chair that she has suffered from depression of spirits & many nervous symptoms which are very painful both to endure & to witness & I hope & pray she will continue to improve, now that she is able to be so much in the open air.

I have a very good account to give of Marianne, when William paid us a short but happy visit of 3 weeks; we had the comfort of seeing her in really very good health & only for her not being so active as usual on her legs. She has perfectly recovered from her disastrous confinement. She is in very good spirits & looks forward with hope and joy to the time when she may again have the opportunity of going through the same <u>tortures</u> over again. A singular task truly! But it is explained – what William calls that dreadful disease – <u>babymania</u>.

Caroline returned to Welshpool with them about a fortnight ago & is, I hope, enjoying herself a little after our melancholy winter & spring.

What a loss you must have had of the Cottons. It must make a great difference to you. I had heard in a roundabout way that you were like to stay the summer & winter abroad. I must confess my selfishness led me to be very sorry when I heard it but I am sure if, as you say, you are better & happier where you are, I could not for a moment wish for your return indeed. I do hope & trust that when (if ever) we do see your dear aunt & yourself again in this country we shall find you both improved in health & spirits by your busy séjour in foreign parts. There are never more affectionately interested for you both than these, this house contains.

I have been a little visit at dear Madeley lately. Mister Mainwaring & a Mr Knox were the only company & we were very cosy. William Egerton who is going into the church is a particularly nice youth & I like all the family I have seen except a very dull one named Charles.[48] I have been very

---

getting gradually weaker" F Burkhardt & S Smith (1985) editors, *Correspondence of Charles Darwin, Vol 1*, Cambridge University Press (1985) p.261

[48] When Mrs Cunliffe and Annabel toured the continent, Madeley Manor was let to Lady Egerton (c1780–1870) and her family of Oulton Park, Cheshire. Ellen became a close friend of Mary Anne Egerton from March 1835 (See *Journals*, p 26).

sorry to hear of the sad state of poor Mrs Daltry. I should fear there was little or no hope for her; it is most melancholy!

Old Mrs Sneyd of Keel is dead after a long illness. Keel is going to be quite renovated - preparatory, I suppose, to Lady Angelina's arrival.

Of course you have heard of Lord Molyneux & Miss Hopwood.[49] She is very plain & they say like Fanny Hinchliffe only no squint but, of course, agreeable. He wrote a very funny letter to Charles & insinuated that she had been deeply in love with him for years! Is it not an odd match but I say she has a better chance of happiness than if had married her for beauty alone? I believe Mrs Ireland Blackburne gives it out that Molly is marrying *nolens volens*[50] & Miss Fox Blackburne cries in her dressing room all day. I am glad you like the Wortley so much I only wish she did not write that terrible poetry about bulbuls & roses.[51]

We had a long call the other day from Miss Parker & Emma Nuttall who was staying at Muxton & anything so entertaining you cannot imagine as Emma was. She is the happiest bride elect I ever saw. She imagines herself deeply enamoured with her Henry & her little head is so full of silks & satin veils, chariots & britzkas, rectories, favour & wedding cake all in entertaining confusion. The great event is to be next month. Mr Turton[52] is to tie the knot & then they go abroad for a short time in a britzka[53] with cupid the courier & the graces and muses in attendance on the happy Mrs Henry Biddulph.[54]

You will be amused to hear that I was gravely visited the other day whether Henrietta had not taken the veil.[55] I said I believe not for she had not mentioned in her letters which, I thought, she would do. Nothing that Henrietta could do that was not actually wicked would surprise me except

---

[49] Notwithstanding her looks they did marry in 1834.

[50] Whether willing or unwilling.

[51] Refers to Lady Emmeline Stuart-Wortley (1806–1855) where the line "…. as the *Bulbul* o'erpowered the young rose of the dell …." occurs in the poem *The Frown*. The *Bulbul* is one of about 140 species of birds of the family Pycnonotidae (order Passeriformes) mainly found in Africa and Asia.

[52] Mr Turton was the vicar of Betley.

[53] A britzka was a horse–carriage with 4 wheels pulled by two horses. It had a folding top over the rear seat and the rear–facing front seats. It was possible to lie in it.

[54] Wife of the Rev Henry Biddulph (1786–1867).

[55] Another reference to Henrietta's possible entry into a Catholic convent.

this, for I have always thought she would end in marrying, but if she continues single till about the age of forty she may turn her mind towards a convent.[56]

We are now reading a very entertaining novel called *Village Belles*[57] something in Miss Austen's style & *Crabbe's Life* which is most interesting.[58] Georgina & I amuse ourselves by sketching & colouring out of doors, but it is sad 'Danby' work at present. [59] I have such a horrid cold in my head that I am dull to a degree. Pray forgive it & with our muted kindest remembrances; believe me ever.

Your most affectionate friend,
Ellen Tollet

PS: Pray write before long & tell me all you do & all your most intimate acquaintances & then I shall see whether I can pick out Lord Etherington or Mr Gooseberry figure among them.

PPS: I heard the other day in a letter from London that the D of Wellington had been making himself quite ridiculous by his attentions to Giuletta Grisi.[60] Trentham is being so altered & 10 acres laid out in [a] flower garden.[61] (*Additional material on the envelope*)

The first entry in Ellen's Journals *was made on January 15th 1835; it was a retrospective view of past events in the lives of Eliza and Marianne, and gave a description with a different aspect of the wedding of Charles and Mary.*

---

[56] Ellen was not being tactful in writing like this about Annabel's sister – 'her dearest dear'.

[57] *Village Belles* (1833), a novel by Anne Manning (1807-1879).

[58] The English poet George Crabbe (1754–1832) was noted for his realistic portrayal of people and events. He was an admirer of Walter Scott. *The Life of Rev George Crabbe LLB* (1834) was written by his son George Crabbe.

[59] Was the painter Danby noted for landscapes too?

[60] Giuletta or Giulia Grisi (1811–1869) was an Italian opera singer. She was a soprano and performed internationally. She made her first appearance in London in the Spring of 1834. Ellen seems to be observing the absurd behaviour of the Duke who was 65 in 1834.

[61] Ellen alludes to the changes probably instigated by Charles Barry (1795–1860), working with William Sawrey Gilpin (1762–1843), on the vast improvements being made at Trentham (N Tringham, *Victoria History, Vol XI*, p 238).

Letter 7 [*cat: 21*]
Wedding of Charles Wicksted and Mary Meysey Wigley of Shakenhurst;
Ellen staying with Marianne at her confinement; gossip about Hungerford;
books

Betley, Nov 2 1834

To: A H Crewe, Poste Restante, Florence

Dearest Annabel,

I have delayed writing to you much longer than I otherwise should, from
knowing that Papa had written to Mrs Cunliffe & informed her of the
happy event which was going to happen to our family. I can now tell you
that the wedding is actually over. It took place on Tuesday the 28th the
same of the month as Marianne's, 5 years ago. But before I say a word

4 Charles and Mary Wicksted.

about any of our proceedings I must give Papa's message to dear Mrs
Cunliffe. He thanks her very much for her very, very kind letter & all her
expressions of friendship towards us all & he goes on to say he certainly

understands her wish not to pledge herself to any future arrangements at present, only he would esteem it an additional kindness if she would let him know as soon as she had finally made up her mind on the subject, tho', of course, he is fully aware this may not be for a long time.[62]

I am sure you will require to hear from my own pen that our new sister is in every way likely to prove a sister indeed. She is very sensible, very clever & very sweet tempered & what more can we wish? She is also very fascinating in her manners & extremely pleasing in appearance; she is perhaps not what everyone would call pretty. I think I understand female curiosity so I shall tell you that her hair is very glossy auburn or chestnut, eyes ditto, nose good, but mouth not at all good as she shows all her gums when she speaks. She has a light airy figure & is particularly graceful & elegant. We have known her nearly all our lives and always thought she would suit Charles exactly & often told him so & when she came to stay 3 weeks here the same thing struck him so he offered & was accepted & very happy they both were & are now each thinking the other a perfect demi-god or goddess & I believe only wishing they had married years ago. She has the solid advantage of a good fortune, which was almost romantic enough to please Papa.

Carry & I went to Shakenhurst for the wedding. It is a very pretty place with very fine timber in the very fine county (Worcestershire). There was only a family party. Mary behaved much better than Marianne but we all cried a little. It is such an affecting service & was so beautifully read by Mr Somers-Cocks that no one could help it.[63] The bride was attired in white brocaded silk, long blond scarf & bound with a veil & orange flowers. After the ceremony, Charles & Mary set off in a smart new green chariot for Olton, a place near Birmingham belonging to Mary's sister Caroline & Charles writes it is such a picturesque old house with oak panels & wood fires etc, etc that they feel like hero & heroine in an old novel only wanting

---

[62] George Tollet must be acting as Mrs Cunliffe's legal adviser.

[63] There were several clergymen with this name. This one was probably Rev Hon James Somers-Cocks (1790–1856), Canon of Worcester Cathedral.

a hoop & doublet & ruffles.[64] We have had a very gay doings here on occasion of the marriage dinners, bells & music & fireworks & an illumination, dancing, eating, drinking etc, etc & on Saturday when they come home the yeomanry meet them & there is to be a second edition of rejoicing in the village. Yesterday we had the fun of receiving a great part of the bride's trousseau which was sent to us to be unpacked & we were quite astonished at her finery as she is not in general smart but 2 London milliners have rigged her out as if she were a duchess. We counted yesterday 6 different sorts of satin gowns & enough blouses to trim 7 Miss Tollets.

Having now got to the climax for fear of an anti-climax, I will turn to another subject. You have not heard of the my summer trip with William Clive & Marianne to [*gap; stamp removed*] which we went by sea from Liverpool. It is a very lovely place. We met there accid[*entally*] Capt & Mrs Somerville. I must tell the truth [*gap*] we found her grown sadly affected – to my mind [*there*] *is* never still a moment – always wriggling & whatever she is giving to feed her family, I don't know, but she certainly appeared from the constant application of her pocket handkerchief to her mouth, I should imagine she had some very unpleasant sensations, but this is very ill-natured. We shall, I suppose, be rather very different from last year. How one's life is made up of alternate joys & sorrows!

I am going to attend Marianne's lying–in in the middle of December, not an agreeable but a useful office & I don't object to it because I am certain that there is not a happier feeling than that of being useful to others, & I think this great misfortune of single women in general is that they have a great lack of useful employment. However as long as one contributes to the happiness of those one loves, one need not feel quite useless. I wonder what use the poor men think of themselves.

Alas poor Henrietta, we have had some very interesting & affecting letters from her. She seems very humble. God grant her delusion may not be owing to wilful kindness & may not be regarded as such by a merciful judge. Hungerford was here not very long ago. He was very amusing & so

---

[64] This is V's (Caroline Archer Clive) home, where Ellen stays later on her visit to the British Association for the Advancement of Science.

41

fond of talking about proposals, that it is evident he profits by the many novels he reads. He talked a great deal about Miss Cotton & her having refused Lord Pollington & we do suspect he is not without a little sentiment for her. What do you think? Of course, you know of Caroline Brooke's intended marriage. It is a very nice one. Never a very popular marriage. We saw Harriet & Clare at the Egremont [*Hotel*]. I do not think the first so beautiful as at 20 or 17. Marianne, Eliza & Georgy also saw a good deal of the Warburtons & Wilbrahams. They are delighted –both Mrs Wilbrahams – I stayed a few days with M at Welshpool on my way home & we went to christening at Powis Castle. The Duke & Duchess of Montrose were there. She is such a freezing, honoured person that everyone seems to avoid moving within the plane of her orbit as much as possible either in a small or large party, for fear of being congealed by the icy atmosphere which surrounds her.[65] Colder I should think she was, tho' not near as haughty as the Duchess, Countess of Sutherland.[66] Don't you remember your taking her on with your aunt?

A very old friend of ours has been reading a novel *Two Old Men's Tales.*[67] It is very clever but we all think it very improper. I have not read Mr T[*homas Henry*] Lister's[68] *Dacre*[69] but Eliza says it is very stale & sort of *réchauffé*[70] of *Granby, Herbert Lacy* & *Arlington*. Old Mrs Lister & Harriet are coming here in a fortnight. A young lady & neighbour of ours, a Miss Edwards of Trentham, who married Sir John Orde is going to winter at

---

[65] Her daughter Lucy (1793–1875) married the 2nd Earl of Powis in 1818, which explains her presence at Powis Castle.

[66] She also owned Trentham, Dunrobin Castle, Clivedon, Stafford House,…. . In this letter the reader can see how scathing Ellen was about some society ladies.

[67] *Two Old Men's Tales* (1834) by Anne Marsh-Caldwell. It consisted of two stories told by old men reflecting on past events. The Caldwells lived near the Tollets and were family friends, and watched Anne's progress with interest.

[68] Thomas Henry Lister (1800-1842), English novelist. His novels included *Granby* (1826), *Herbert Lacy* (1828) and *Arlington* (1832). *Granby* was an early example of the silver fork novel, that is, a novel about the upper gentry and aristocracy. However, we have not been able to identify the book referred to.

[69] Seems to be some confusion here. The novel *Dacre* (1834) was written by Lady Theresa Lewis.

[70] A dish of warmed-up food left over from a previous meal.

Rome. Mary mentioned her. If you hear of her or meet her she is a very affected friend but is very well-informed & clever. I have not seen her since she married but did not like her at all. Penelope met Mrs ……….. who had seen you at Naples. She says you were liked by every one. I thought as much. How I shall long to see you when once you set foot in England. I must now conclude with affectionate regards from all this house.

Believe me, dearest Annie, your affectionate friend,

Ellen H T

Letter 8 [*cat: 95*]
Annabel staying abroad; Marianne's stillbirth; over-powering women; Mary Wicksted settling into the family; Henrietta's illness & faith; Joseph Sykes; party games; politics; the Egertons in Madeley

Monday, April 27, 1835
Mademoiselle Annabel Crewe, Poste Restante, Rome, Italy

My dearest Annabel,

I will begin by acknowledging the receipt of & thanking you for your last nice letter dated March 4. I must confess that part of its contents disappointed me sadly as I had fully expected it would announce your intended return to old England instead of a protracted stay abroad. I cannot express how glad I shall be when you & your aunt are once more safe on English ground. Anxious, I am sure you are enjoying yourself at Rome & will do so no doubt in Switzerland, and as long as one of you do[*sic*] not forget your native land, not because one of those regular foreignised English who find no pleasure in the old island, of which I never have the least fear of in you. The only regrets arise from selfish causes. Therefore ought all to be smothered by your old John Bull friends.

Thank you, my dear Mrs C, for your condolences on poor dear Marianne's sorrows. She has, I am thankful to say, borne it with the greatest tolerance & is in good health & spirits & able to look with hope to going thro' more tortures some time or other. Mrs Corbett from whom you heard the news is a very near neighbour of hers & she & her daughter are both exceedingly nice people, the latter particularly & I am sorry you have not met them, as I am sure Miss C[orbett] is a girl you would like very much, sensible quite unaffected, with good spirit.

Your account of Miss Doyle & Lord Douglas amused me very much. I do heartily hope she may not succeed but it is surprising how often those designing women do succeed in catching very young men. There is no one character I have a greater contempt for than that which we call a gobbleboy(!). Only think of another foreign prince being taken prisoner by Lady Shrewsbury. Report says the other has lopped thro' the iron grating which I suppose does not matter as the young lady is already dubbed a princess. There is a person from this neighbourhood now at Rome, Lady Orde who is daughter to Mrs [illegible], you may remember. If you have seen her, pray mention her as I should like to know whether her affectation makes as strong an impression on you as it always did on me. I really believe she sleeps & cares affectedly. She has married a man with [a] place in Scotland which she hates & 3 children which she certainly neglects. Her own baby was overlaid by its nurse a year or more ago & this I believe she really did feel. He is, I believe, a clever well-informed, tho' rather coarse, man.

I must tell you the history of our family. Marianne came here a fortnight ago & Charles & Mary left for Worcestershire last week & we were very, very busy for the past week there. We have engaged with our new sister with the greatest affection & harmony. Her society has been peculiarly agreeable with some of the piquancy of a visitor & all the same freedom of a relation. They go to London the end of May & take Carry with them. Eliza is better, tho' not well, but has just lately hit upon a new plan, which I hope provides a more rapid cure. She has no coughing & does not suffer pain in this very cold weather.

You have the advantage of us at Rome, for our Spring & Summer are settling with their usual severity. Yesterday, we had several sharp snow showers, and my fingers are now quite stiff. We had a mild winter & a few hot days in March, but altogether I consider it a very late season. We have been having a good deal of company but now we are going to be very quiet. I think we must devote ourselves to improving our minds.

The Davenports were here a short time ago.[71] He is uglier & as so as ever & will be still more so now that he has lost his law suit, by which his former neighbours, who all hate him, have established a right of road thro' his very garden quite close to his house. This is a real grievance but I believe he has brought on himself by his irritating conduct to them. Mrs D who has a masculine mind with a feminine face has to have a very active part & made his [*illegible*] too conspicuous in court the other day. He is very clever & I think high-minded but so strong as not to be loved, I think & I suspect her temper is not good, tho' of a very different sort from his.

Georgy wrote to Henrietta at Prior Park[72] & asked her to write & I am sorry to say she wrote again a melancholy letter, appearing out of spirits & out of health & speaking of her disinclination to write letters to me or Marianne which leads us to think she means soon to drop our correspondence. But we are determined to continue it as long as we can induce her to do so because, I think, it will be a very bad thing for her to lose all her interests in English people & Protestants, tho' very well understand that to her the remembrances of past days must be rather irksome than agreeable. She complains of weak eyes & says she believes her health would have sunk under a year's noviciate. I should like to know exactly on what grounds her "spirit ancestors" made her give up entering the convent. Poor dear soul, you cannot think how sad my feelings are whenever I think of her. She seems cut off from her family & her nature & friends. Standing alone, it seems mysterious that the act of going to her father, which was one which was mistaken certainly, and must have proceeded from a sense of duty, has been to all appearances the means of leading into this sad apostasy, which I am sure injures very much her earthly happiness. Tho' I am far from thinking that if it is done with sincerity, it will affect her more important & lasting interests.

I hope Hungerford will pay a visit to this country this year & that we shall see him for one of his proper visits & have our usual gossip. We have had a young man named Sykes in the house a month.[73] He was very clever

---

71 The Davenports lived at Capesthorne Hall in Cheshire.

72 Part of the Crewe Estate near Bath.

73 Joseph Sykes, a writer. He figured as a main suitor in Ellen's *Journals*.

& amusing but extremely ugly & unfascinating so not at all dangerous. He had read almost every book that has been published these 10 years.

We used to divert ourselves during his stay with divine games. Our charades were inevitable as far as their ludicrousness was. In one, ingenious Charles & this great 6 foot youth figuring as *The Babes in the Wood*[74] in caps & pinafores & Mary & I as Robin Redbreasts with brown paper beaks & red shawls just before us!![75] Questions & Answers in rhyme were also the fashion & I must repeat to you: you must have that. While at Shrewsbury I was employed by Robert Clive to buy him some checked black & white neckcloths. Well to tease me, Mary wrote the following question:

> There are checks of all sorts in these troublesome times;
> There's a check to the poet who cannot find rhymes;
> There's a check to the house that's in want of a speaker;
> There's a check to the hounds where the scent becomes weaker;
> But what do you think of the checks that were chosen;
> By a maiden so fair for a Nabob half frozen?

Georgina had to answer & did so as follows. Of course, the hero was not present

> These emblems they were of that chequered state;
> To which the young lady was tempting her fate.
> And the next check she gives will
> I guess be <u>check mate</u>.

---

[74]This was the traditional children's tale of two children, who were abandoned for a long time in a wood. They died and were covered with leaves by robins.

[75] In her *Journals* (see references) for this day, Ellen Tollet wrote: "then before dinner we, that is Georgy, Mr Sykes and I had a long poetical conversation. In the evening, we acted a charade fixed on 'courtship' and 'infanticide'. Charles, Mary and Mr S were the actors, etc. The last was 'The Babes in the Wood'. Chas and Mr S were the babes, Papa the cruel uncle, and Mary and I as babes with red hearts and paper beaks".

I was extremely offended at this & made the young lady write one which was less insulting my dignity. So she produced another. They were designed to add to his suit of clothes.

These checks to check his suit she thought,
no doubt, Nabob to perplex.[76]

And if you can't see this you must be behind myself or my friend to marry a very handsome man for I think they are generally too full of themselves to think much of their words. I hope you will deign to laugh at these effusions that I am aware that such wit second hand sometimes fails of producing this desired effect, but I like to tell you everything that enters my head.

Your old friend Emma Biddulph is going to increase her family very soon. I hear she is very happy & comfortable in her Rectory. Oh by the bye, I have always wished much to see her collared. Therefore if Lord Douglas should escape Miss Doyle [to] become your attacker pray don't refuse him & pray let me come & see you. Tho' I must confess if I had a wishing cap I should never wish.

The Leycesters of Toft [Hall] have been here too.[77] Of course, politics are much talked of – much too much. Our family is sadly divided. Mamma was always a Waverer & now a Peelite; Penelope is rattled on account of the Irish Church Bill & Papa & Chas still very staunch. What an awkward thing for the King having to call in again Lord Melbourne whom he described without heart 6 months ago.

We have been much interested in the marriage of our little friend Lady Ribblesdale & Lord John Russell.[78] I hope he will provide worthy successor

---

[76] A Nabob is a governor in India.

[77] Toft Hall was a 17th century country house in Cheshire, the residence of Ralph Leycester (1763-1835), MP for Shrewsbury (1821-1830).

[78] Lord John Russell married Lady Ribblesdale (widow of Thomas Lister) in 1835. Both were small in stature – hence the "horrid caricatures". He was a leading Whig politician in the 1830s to 1850s, and Prime Minister twice, associated with parliamentary, educational and Irish reform. Georgina was referring to the Anglican Church of Ireland being forced to give up its revenues, which threw the

of that excellent Lord Ribblesdale. She has married again sooner than she wishes but she is young & pretty. They say there are horrid caricatures of the B[*ride*] & B[*ride*]groom going about town.

From all accounts Lady J[ohn] Russell is not in this danger. I forgot to tell you that the horrid John Bull's allusion to his littleness calls him the "widow's mite".

Marianne desires me to give a particular message of love to you & her kind friend & be assured that it is with the warmest affection that you & your dear aunt are remembered by the whole family.

I have been a good deal at Madeley lately. I like the Egertons very much. Mary Anne is very kind & active among the poor people. I went with her to see some. They are very grateful & attached to your aunt. I am sure you will be sorry to hear that the church is all but deserted owing to Mr Daltry's very bad reading & preaching.[79] It is a sad pity he seems a nice quiet little man: he has dined here. We went sometime ago to see Crewe the first time. Carry well remembers Annabel & Skipio & often thinks of A as she passes the potato hogs as they are called in Staffordshire. I have [*n*]ever entered the house since your grandfather's death.[80] It was very melancholy. Poor old Pace keeps it very nicely. [81] You really should see her gesticulations when she mentions some of the family affairs. She enquired tenderly after you & Mrs Cunliffe & begged we would let her know if ever you came to Madeley or Betley.

Your truly attached friend,

Ellen H Tollet,

Is this not a long letter?

In her Journals, *on the 22ⁿᵈ May 1835 Ellen wrote, "We [Georgina, Eliza and Ellen] and Emma [Wedgwood] had a very droll talk about marrying Hungerford*

Whigs out of office briefly. Sir Robert Peel's minority government resigned in 1835 and Lord Melbourne was returned as Prime Minister, with Lord John Russell as Leader of the House of Commons.

[79] According to Madeley Church records Rev John Daltry was vicar from 1833 to 1879, followed by his son Thomas who was vicar from 1879 to 1904.

[80] Annabel's father never lived in Crewe Hall after the 1st Baron Crewe died.

[81] A rare reference to a servant.

Crewe. I was very mercenary and said I would rather marry him than a vulgar, though sensible curate. Georgina took the other side. Eliza backed me. Better, say I, to marry for situation or money, than for neither love nor money."

Letter 9 [*cat: 149*]
Family in Malvern; the Bloomfields; Methodism; Hungerford's views on the Tollets and suitors for Annabel; witches in Welshpool; Mrs Turton's baby

Betley, August 14, 1835

To: Annabel Crewe, Campagne Menier, Geneve, Switzerland

My dearest Annabel,

Your last welcome letter reached me at Malvern where we have been spending August. I should have written before, had I not found the dissipation or rather idleness of a watering place rather unfavourable to the composition of a long letter. Never was every thing so delightful as our sojourn there. Glad as I am to come home always, I could not leave that lovely place without deep regret. It is so beautiful, so cheerful & yet not a public dressy place whereas the enchanting walks & rides & drives & more perhaps than all, we had so many nice acquaintances particularly towards the end of our stay, which is always the case, I think.

Col & Mrs Parker of Astle in Cheshire who were natives, heaven knows how, a few years ago are settled there. You seldom see two more agreeable people & at an age when people in general have quite forgotten how to be agreeable in general society. She, as you know, is aunt to your Mr Cholmondeley. I told her that I heard of him from you when we were staying there. Our young friend Hugh Acland & his tutor, the curate of Malvern a most agreeable, excellent manner & the first part of our time was enlivened by Lord & Lady Bloomfield, their single & married daughter Mrs Kingscote & her husband. [*illegible*], another Mrs K & Georgina B[*loomfield*] ran into our room the moment we arrived at our Lodging House, which is sad & dreary & desolate & in which these meetings of affectionate friends are particularly precious. This party contained a most interesting individual, Mr Kingscote. We saw by his first marriage with Lady Somerset a most glorious piece of flesh & blouse. She was beautiful as a sunbeam & as good as a child can be.

The Bloomfields are, what they would call, Methodists & I must say in some respects they go a good deal further than Wesleyite–like. I don't mean to say they are too good, that [I] know well to be impossible, but they (the jests at least) have adopted rather too much the peculiarities of expression etc which belong to a set. This I do object to & it is repugnant to my feelings. They are, however, extremely cheerful – indeed lively, affectionate to a degree & open as the day & it is perhaps that very openness which may lead them sometimes to introduce the subject, which is most interesting to them at times when, those more reserved than themselves or more influenced by the opinions of the world, might wish them to be silent.

While we were at Malvern, Charles & Mary came on their way to Shakenhurst & brought Carry with them for a few days. She was in high glee at the delights of her London campaign. They went out very little but *opera-ised*[?] and French *play-ised* to their hearts content.[82] I think she only went to 3 balls, one at Lady St John's. Miss St John is a beauty at least a very pretty girl whom Lady St J is determined to bring out. Carry had singing lessons of Scappa[83] & is much improved.

I am sure you will be glad to hear that Mary Wicksted holds out distant hopes of son & heir. After our sad disappointment with dear Marianne we dare kindly look forward to this poor baby but still we are very thankful for the hope of one, for it was really of great importance for Charles to have a child not only because he is an only son & it is of consequence in money matters but it will be much more God's blessing such a good thing for his character & besides as none of us are, at present, likely to present grandchildren [to] rejoice that the family is not [to] be quite extinct. The income to his next month [is] for the winter but I believe Mary will make a trip to Ludlow where there is a favourite doctor for her confinement, as we think poor dear Mr Shayle[?] rather too old to trust.

Since I began this letter Hungerford has been & dined with us. He is

----

[82] Unable to make sense of the tentative transcription of two words in this sentence. They seem to have been coined by Ellen to mean the creation of operas and dramas. Perhaps there is an alternative interpretation.

[83] Probably Giuseppe Scappa, a music coach and maestro (I Emerson, *Five Centuries of Women Singers*, Praeger (2005))

wonderfully improved certainly particularly in looks, having grown so much handsome tho' more delicate looking. I talked to him a great deal about you. One job I must tell you, knowing you won't betray me, was enquiring about Lord Etherington about whom he seemed much interested. I said it's a pretty name, *n'est pas*?

"Yes – very" said he, "but don't you think Delamere is very pretty too?"!!!! So you plainly see what his scheme is of writing [*to*] your friend Cholmondeley. My consent gives, if indeed he is not so very conceited as make him, because in that case he perhaps would not deign to speak to me. Hungerford promised to send to us Mr Milnes's verses on Lady G T's marriage[84] & he was surprised & disappointed at our having already read the battles. Indeed he says he is quite surprised at our being so much *au courant du jours*. N B, the book has been out a year & ½. He very kindly offered to bring Mr Pearson to show me & also *Moore's Melodies*.[85] He is the best natured soul in existence and he takes his growth both bodily & mentally so late, but I think by it he will be quite a strong character.[86]

I am rather honoured just now with Fanny Kemble's vulgar part four journal.[87]

I read Lord Brougham's new Theology Book & liked it much. He is certainly a firm believer in Revelation as you & I. The writing is very beautiful, one chapter being interspersed with Latin.

My dear Marianne has had a horrid affair in her little household. Her steady confidential maid named Nancy[?] turned out such a witch, a perfect

---

[84] This is the first reference to the popularity of Monckton Milnes as a poet in the same breath as he was mentioning suitors for Annabel.

[85] *Moore's Melodies* were published between 1808 and 1834, composed by Thomas Moore (1779-1852), an Irish poet, singer and songwriter.

[86] Ellen clearly appreciated Hungerford now that he seemed more mature.

[87] According to Ellen's *Journals* (p. 76), on the 16th October, 1835, "A very nice letter from Annabel. She says she has read Mrs Butler's Journal and thinks of it just as I do. She says she thinks her residence in America will not be very pleasant if it is true, as a Yankee told her, that they cannot realise an actress as being respectable!" The book referred to was *Journal of F A Butler* (1835) by Frances Anne Butler Kemble (1809–1893), the actress of this letter, dated 14th August, 1835.

monster of vice & imputations. Now M is quite upset by it & is still with not one of those necessary witches. How are Price & Thirza?[88]

We hear of somebody always talked of Miss Cotton. Lord Hillsbor', they say, she liked but he is off & Lord Villiers is said to be on. Poor girl, if she has a heart, I dare say she has found that peace & happiness do not always follow in the train of admiration & gaiety, but as I often think it must be a great blessing to girls in that whatever that the nice lover acts upon another as a *chasse amour[euse]*, like a glass of liqueur after coffee. I really don't think I have anything more to tell you that will amuse you or interest you. Oh, by the bye, they say Harriet Brooke is to marry Lord Cole. He is a very excellent man but really such a monster, near Ifad, I think & ugly & odd. I saw him over at Madeley. He is Sir P E's great friend. A poor lady & don't you pity her. They are gone to the [*illegible*]. It really is a dreadful time having a young creature just entering life but she [*is*] very submissive & if he accepts trials as wholesome fatherly connections, they become blessings & privileges. Good to hear that H[*enrietta*] was still at Bath. I wrote to her long time ago at *Bois l'Évêque.*[89]

Well again, my dearest Annabel, how I long to see you. Obviously, this must be your last winter in a foreign country, as God speed you back to old, England! Best love from all to yourself & dear Mrs Cunliffe & believe me,

Your truly affectionate friend,

Ellen H Tollet

PS: Charles says to thank Mrs C for her letter.

PPS: Since this was finished, Hungerford has been again to say that he has got a little box for me & has brought your little note. Pray give my warmest thanks to dear Mrs Cunliffe for her kind & valuable present. I have not yet seen it. I am sure I shall be pleased with [*it*], if the resemblance is ever so slight. H brings it tomorrow with many other persuaded doubts. He begs

---

[88] They were servants, not often referred to. They were with them abroad.

[89] Bois l'Évêque was where her father Lord Crewe lived.

you to write to him soon. He has been at Muxton.[90] Old Offley is still gay[91]
– Oh, that unnatural marriage took place took place a fortnight ago!

I am rearing a little husband for myself – poor Mrs Turton's baby aged now 10 months, only 22 years younger than myself.[92]

On 14th October, 1835, Ellen, in her Journal, *records, "Heard from Hungerford Crewe, who dined here yesterday, that Mrs Cunliffe is coming to winter in Paris.[93] Papa came back from Ingestre. He says Mrs A Talbot talks much of Annabel's charms. ...."*
*The second Lord Crewe, the General, died at Bois l'Évêque in December, 1835. After three weeks his body reached Brussels on its way to England (*The Times, *Dec 25 1835). He was buried at Barthomley.*

It is not unexpected that letters may be missing. In her diary for Saturday 7th November, 1835, Ellen said that she wrote a long letter to Annabel but no letter near that date seems to be in the archive.[94] This was the period when she was looking after the disabled girl Mary Gater (see the preamble to Part II).

Letter 10 [*cat: 102*]
Ellen has not seen Annabel for four years; Annabel's father's death; Hungerford now Lord Crewe; Dorfold house party with Mr Prior

Betley, January 3rd 1836

To: Annabel H Crewe, Poste Restante, Paris

My Dearest Annabel,

You are in general such a dear and regular correspondent that I am a little surprised at not having heard from you lately, but as I have not seen your brother, I cannot ascertain whether you have received some silly drawings I sent by him to you as he intended them going to Paris – a long letter addressed to you Poste Restante I feel more sure of having reached

---

[90] 'Muxton' seems to have been the pronunciation of Mucklestone which was one of the Crewe estates. To add to the confusion there is a village called Muxton in Shropshire.

[91] 'gay' meaning 'happy'.

[92] This Mrs Turton was the first wife of the Betley vicar; she died in childbirth.

[93] The *Morning Post* for 23 Nov 1835 recorded Annabel and Mrs Cunliffe staying in Paris.

[94] *Journals*, p 83.

your hand. My thoughts have been more with you than usual, my dear Annie, in consequence of the late event at Bois l'Évêque, which must have brought many distressing feelings to your dear aunt & yourself. [95] In your sympathy too, for this dreariness of Henrietta's painful situation must have made it a trying time to you both.

I long very much to hear from poor H[*ungerford*]. We wrote to him directly we heard it. I was in before both have seen Hungerford but his stay at Crewe has been so very short that only Papa who called has seen him. You know of course that Edw Hinchliffe has been with him[96] & if you recollect has repaired to Bois l'Évêque almost immediately after your father's death! Perhaps I am ill-natured but I can't help admiring his haste to [*the*] 'Rising Sun'.

Papa called at Crewe yesterday & he said it was really quite affecting of him to see Oakes opening the door just like old times, H[*ungerford*] sitting in your grandfather's room. He was very much pleased by his manner. He seemed very considerate & spoke as much attached to the old place & anxious to have things in the way they were in [*his*] grandfather's time. Indeed I do hope he may show a great deal more judgement than might be expected from him, & if he can but get sensible well disposed people about him. I have quite confidence enough in his kind disposition & gentlemanlike propensity to believe that he will make a very respectable valuable Lord Crewe. Of course I speak to you just as openly as I should to one of my own sisters & you will always I know have discretion enough never to quote my authority for any news, except of course to your Aunt Mary.[97] I told Papa that he believed you would come to England this Spring. Oh how glad I shall be to feel you are once more on British ground & as to a meeting that it too joyous to be thought of!!

Now for our proceedings, we have been almost gay lately. A very large party at Dorfold is one item in our list. The Bros Grosvenors, Dr Delamere & very young men were there. Mr Hopwood ….. was there. He is sharp but

---

[95] Death of her father, 4th Dec 1835.

[96] Edward Hinchliffe is distantly related to Hungerford, and the vicar of Barthomley. We think Hinchliffe was going to the local pub.

[97] Mrs Cunliffe's sister-in-law.

flippant. I don't wonder she refused him. Another friend was meeting at a dull house enough. [*There wa*s] A most agreeable London lawyer named Prior who was a rare specimen in this country, a really clear, sensible & very refined manicured human.[98] He was not the least a flirt & tho' he & I talked incessantly for 3 days & I know we mutually thought each other very pleasant yet not one word of even common place flirtation ever passed. What do you think of this? I shall never see him again but he was a very amusing, pleasant meteor which crossed our path. I must add that Carry was quite as much pleased with him as I was. C and I are going to a gay Chester Ball this week. All the County will be there but I daresay I shan't enjoy it. I never dance at Balls.

We have been reading Sir J Mackendick: *A Life*. It is so interesting particularly to us who know him & all his relations. Pray write soon.
[*Two lines difficult to transcribe*]
 Your affectionate ever,
 Ellen H Tollet

In her Journals, *Ellen reported that she had received a letter from dear Annabel on the 30th January, 1836, seemingly by an indirect route. Presumably this prompted the following reply.*

Letter 11 [*cat: 282*]
Birth of George Wicksted; reading Lamartine; Mr Prior's background; Chester Ball; Mr Wedgwood from Nuneaton; spreading of news
To: The Hon. Annabel Crewe, Hotel Canterbury, Rue de la Pays
Feb 6th 1836
My dearest Annabel,

 Thank you for setting our correspondence straight by writing again. I am most thankful to have very good news to tell you. It is now two days since I have been an aunt to a very nice pretty little boy. We did not obtain him without a serious fright however, both about his life and his mother.[99] For

---

[98] *cf: Journals*, p.105.
[99] More details of the difficult birth of George Wicksted in Betley Hall were given in *Journals*, p 110 (4th Feb) in which Ellen wrote: "[*Mary*] had been suddenly

poor dear Mary had a dangerous time, tho' not a very long one, but she has gone on so well since we really endured six month's anguish. But our state of anxiety was really frightful, and poor Charles was like one distracted, but all's well that ends well tho', as poor Mary was obliged to be bled, I fear she will be very weak when she begins to get about. The boy was baptised directly and in the presence of us all – George, Edward, after Papa & Mary's father [*it*] was an unspeakable comfort to have got their business safely over & we should be ungrateful monsters if our hearts were not filled with thankfulness to the givers of all good.[100]

I think from your account Paris must be rather dull, which one would have thought impossible. However all that depends on circumstances just within our own circle & the general fullness or emptiness of a great city, has but little to do with it. The spread of severe weather in a letter from the Egertons at Naples makes us shiver. A sentinel frozen to death at his post, fountains dressed in icicles, while in England (that climate which M de Lamartine[101] is pleased to describe as "*Les prinas eternals*") are enjoying a very pleasant winter with nothing more than some attempts at frost. By the bye, do pray beg to get a sight of Lamartine.

We are reading his *Voyage en Orient* [*1835*] & are so pleased with it. He is thoroughly French to be sure & very highly [*illegible*] all his disciplines are, but there is sentiment & enthusiasm about it which is charming and that is a handsome portrait of him!

Just as amusing book is old Madam Trollope's *Paris and the Parisians* [*in 1835*] which you must send me this book. I do hate this woman cordially;

---

seized with a frightful convulsive fit. They were obliged to bleed her largely, immediately, and they were going to bring the child into the world artificially. Our agony was intense: Mamma looked like a corpse. Eliza was seized with difficulty in breathing. …. Soon the infinite relief of everyone, the cry of a child was heard …." Both Ellen and Georgina confirmed that Charles was writhing on the stairs. Finally Georgina reported that "…. The darling baby was small but pretty, soon to be baptized". The baptism was performed by Mr Turton on the 5th February. Also according to the *Journals,* Ellen wrote ten letters on this day as well as the *Journal* which indicates the extent of her correspondence.

[100] It was usual to baptize children soon after a difficult birth.

[101] Alphonse de Lamartine (1790-1869), was a French writer, poet and politician.

she is coarse while she apes refinement; vulgar while she worships aristocracy, & full of that extreme violence about politics which, it seems, women cannot avoid if they venture to study or write on the subject. In spite of all this, the book is a very good pastime & I must say has had the very injurious effect on me of making me extremely anxious to take a trip to Paris, in which laudable desire I have at present about as much chance of being gratified, as if I had set my poor heart as visiting Timbuctoo. But who knows but that Jack Neville & I may go out as missionaries to Africa after all!!

I am glad you were charmed with my description of my hero of heroes.[102] My admiration alas has been by no means diminished by his discoursing that [he] was a 3rd Wrangler at Cambridge –that he draws beautifully – added to this the comparatively insignificant circumstances that his mother is very well off. She was a Miss ….. & lives at Hampstead. But my dear child, do not imagine me so green, so youthfully romantic, as I think our ever meeting again within the laws of probabilities or if we did that ….. .

Meanwhile I don't bear the willow.[103] I assure you & am as fat, thriving, jocular, a specimen of a lovelorn damsel as can be seen. It is very well when such things can be laughed at & talked about, is not it?

Your story of the Abel Smiths amused me much. The name is one of annoyance which really I would not endure. I would change tho' the world might laugh at me for it! Oh by the bye, Carry & I went to a Ball at Chester[104] & there we saw Harriet Brooke looking lovely & flirting with Mr Aston, who, everybody now thinks, has the best chance of any of her swains, I am sorry for he is younger than herself & tho', I believe, an amiable youth, it is not exactly the match I should love for her.

And now I must have a laugh against you. Thank you for your kind consideration in asking me whether there is any other preacher I should

---

102 Almost certainly Robert Prior (1812–1889), although listed as *fourth* wrangler (mathematics ranked degree at Cambridge) at Trinity College. He was also referred to in an entry in Ellen's *Journals* for 6th January 1836. He subsequently became a lawyer. (see *Cambridge Alumni, 1261-1900*, Ancestry on-line database.)

103 Meaning she was not in mourning for Mr Prior.

104 See *Journals*, 6th Jan, 1836, p.100.

prefer to Mr Wedgwood.[105] Indeed there is no other preacher I should not prefer to him seeing –that he has never been to parliament this session!! But to report, my dear, I had rather pay for your letters than have any bother of enclosing them to everyone. I think we have all except Marianne's dislike to friends on account of their delays, for we divert one a year direct to Lord Clive,[106] tho' writing to me every week. I or we have one or two friends who amuse us by never sending us a letter that costs anything & who, if the privilege were taken away, would give up our friendship & never write again. Please speed the arrival of letters when you are to turn your heads this way. I have so many letters to write that I must cut this discourse short with united love to Aunt & yourself. I am ever, dearest Annie,

> Your most affectionate,
> Ellen H Tollet

PS: Mrs E Butler told us the other day that there were thoughts of some cousins of hers, the Boileaux, coming to Madeley.

In her Journals *Ellen wrote on the 1st March, 1836:*
> *'Hungerford Crewe told me that Lady Anglesey had said Brooke Greville wished Anne to marry Lord Clarence Paget![107] That would have been a match to be sure! Nothing happened.'*

On the 12th March, 1836 she wrote:
> *'….Lord Crewe called to take leave and frank some letters. I was obliged to assist. This made Mary and Caroline laugh, and I am laughing at Carry about Joe [Sykes] very severely for having stolen him from me in London….'*

---

[105] Probably this was Robert Allen Wedgwood of Nuneaton.

[106] Ellen was referring to the habit of sharing letters with Marianne's brother-in-law, Lord Clive, although this was a difficult paragraph to transcribe and understand.

[107] Became Admiral Lord Sir Clarence Paget (1811–1895), also an MP and obviously in the Royal Navy. He held various Offices of State. He married instead Martha Otway, another Admiral's daughter.

It is obvious that Hungerford had been paying Ellen considerable attention for the past few weeks. She seemed to have changed her mind about him since her discussion with Emma Wedgwood on 22nd May 1835 (Journals and comment after Letter 8).

Here is an interesting statistic from Journals. Between 8th February 1835 and 26th August 1836 when Ellen was keeping a daily journal, Hungerford visited Betley Hall 13 times, frequently staying for dinner. Was he really interested in Ellen?

Letter 12 [*cat: 281*]
Death of Eliza on 3rd May 1836

[*black edged paper*]   8th May 1836

My dearest Annabel,

You will have been surprised at not hearing from me but you have been perhaps by this time seen in the papers the bitter, no, <u>not</u> bitter, but deep

5. Picture of a woman in bed - probably Eliza.

affliction, with which it has pleased God to visit us. We have had long, long preparation or many blessed consolations & yet if you see us sometimes you would almost think we had none. But I honestly pray & trust, that our tender grief is far from being inconsistent with submission & this while we feel as we must being the loss of the most endearing & angelic being that ever as blessed a family circle, we are yet able to rejoice in the confident hope given to us, of the inexpressible happiness of our beloved one.

She had been confined to her room after an attack of increased illness about a month, but tho' we considered the case hopeless as to ultimate recovery, we thought from many circumstances that she might go on for months & so strong was this impression that Marianne, being ill, (in her old way & confined nearly to bed) I made up my mind to go to her for a little while & while I was away the change for the worse came. All was over before I could get home. That I, who with Carry, had been permitted to be her chief attendant for so long should have been denied the satisfaction of spending those last precious, precious days with her has been by far the bitterest part of my trial & often am I tempted to give way to the most poignant regrets & self-reproach. But I know or I try always to remember that as long as we act, as I trust I did, from no bad motive, we are in little as well as great events, over-ruled & guided by an unseen but all powerful Hand. I know I was spared the sight of much bodily suffering & consequently my Trust has not perhaps been greater in quantity, tho' perhaps less nothing in quality than that of my relations. I should fill a volume if I were to tell you all the holy, heavenly patience with which our dearest has supported her long illness, but I must tell you some of our consolations.

You were perhaps too young when you left England truly to appreciate her character,[108] but your dear aunt perhaps knew more & I know loved her. She was indeed highly gifted in mind for she had the clearest memory & the most powerful understanding I ever saw existed to the tenderest heart & the most refined & feminine feelings. Added to these and far, far, above all of them in value was her humble fervent piety, which had, by God's blessing, grown with her growth, strengthened with her strength from her early childhood. The last day of her life was indeed [*illegible*] to all around her. In the midst of a violent attack of difficulty of breathing she kissed her hand to Georgina who happened to be alone with her for a minute & pointing upwards cried, "There," while the most brilliant expression of joy was on her face. She then said, "I shall be with Christ." The attack went off & she was perfectly collected all day & no one thought

---

[108] An indication that Annabel had spent considerable time abroad with her parents..

the end was so very near. Then she gave advice & directions to all. Charles was speaking of something & she said, "Remember, Charles, it must all come to this."

"Yes, Love," he said, "I know it must sooner or later."

"Yes," she said, "you know, but remember it! Remember it!"

One of the last times she spoke it was to tell a kind and faithful servant "not to sit on that hard seat", thus showing the healing care & tenderness of others, strong in death.[109] She was able to the end of the last day hear & attend to such a great deal of reading. Since her death we have found (indeed once she gave me just before I left her) books written by her full of the most beautiful prayers & meditations begun from the early age of 15, or little pieces of poetry which are so beautiful that it is so surprising that she never showed them.

My dearest Annie, may all so follow her good example that we may with her be partakers of that happiness which "Eye hath not seen nor ever heard, nor the heart of man conceived."[110] But we must remember that the path is not an easy one nor even removed from many temptations as she was; we know there was still a blessing with her own natural conception & constant searching after holiness & this not trusting her own merits for acceptance with God, but upon the atoning sacrifice of her Saviour. It is easy for us to remember a thirst for this <u>now</u>, but when our own immediate recollection of this scene is passed, may God, in his mercy, enable us to perfect by it still. Excuse all this. I know you & dear Mrs Cunliffe will feel for us. Mamma is surprising well. Write soon.

Your very affectionate,

Ellen Tollet

P.S: I must add poor Carry's most affectionate love.

---

[109] That was Mary Southwell (see *Journals*, p 131)

[110] A misquotation from Shakespeare's *Midsummer Night's Dream*.

PART II: After Eliza's death, 1836–1841

"Men bear sorrow very differently from women"

"….. now I feel as if I was acting on a stage when I am in society, as if it were no part of my real self that talked & listened & laughed ….."

"…..such as your marrying a prince & I a Welsh curate, a widower with small children"

After the death of Eliza several weeks passed before the family resumed normal activities. Mary Gater, the deaf and dumb girl who had been staying in Betley Hall, was taken to school in Manchester. There was a short holiday in Liverpool and visits to Welshpool and London, where once more Ellen was keeping her pregnant sister company.
Annabel too had been staying in the Crewe's Richmond House with Mrs Cunliffe and Mr & Mrs Morier.
In Journals *(p 174), on the 4th August Ellen wrote in her diary,*

"I had the great delight of seeing my dear, dear friend Annabel Crewe. She is not at all altered in any respect, but grown taller. She is just as simple, pure minded, as sweet tempered as ever and Marianne and I both agreed it was a truly delightful feeling, that of being so completely satisfied with anyone."

Ellen's visit to Hampton Court, and viewing paintings, accompanied by Annabel and Mr Morier, were particularly enjoyable. Later they were taken to the theatre to see 'The Belle's Stratagem' (see also, Journal, *p.178). Mrs Cunliffe escorted Ellen to her family in London the following day. The next light-hearted letter was sent from London.*

Letter 13   *[cat: 37]*
Ellen with William and Marianne in Richmond

17 Grosvr, [London]
1st Sept 1836

To: Annabel, Madeley Manor, Newcastle

My dearest Annabel,

I mean this to greet you on your arrival at Madeley, tho' I am almost afraid you will be rather beforehand with me. I trust it will find you & your dear aunt well after your journey & that the sad tho' poignant recollections which cannot but be raised by her first return, will not have a sad effect on her bodily health. Only think of my – not only my but from all – having been to Richmond since you left.[111]

On Monday we set out for a villa belonging to the father of a clergyman a Mr Selwyn who is Eton Tutor to Lord Clive's boys.[112] It was a great thing having only this bachelor and no family to entertain us. The house was very airy & pleasant, the only fault it was so desperately clean. This demon of cleanliness had eventually taken possession of it; his influence was seen in the white paint, the white papers, white beds, bright grates, fenders on which feet had never warmed & tables on which linen had never lain.[113] However we forgave all this. Mr Selwyn was very cozy, the air was very fresh, the mutton very tender so he did all very charmingly. Marianne was very well, William was very happy and I very agreeable.

One day Mr S(elwyn) & W took me on a delicious row from Kew to Twickenham. We passed under the Carltons' windows. It was a beautiful morning and everything looked its very best.[114] On my return I found a

---

[111] Ellen is referring to Mrs Cunliffe's return to England after her brother's death. The Crewes owned a house called Marsh Gate in Richmond as well as their other London houses.

[112] William and Marianne were staying with their brother Lord Clive, and his sons. They lived in Styche near Market Drayton Rev George Selwyn (1809–1878) became the first Bishop of New Zealand in 1841, and later Bishop of Lichfield. Selwyn College, Cambridge was founded in his honour.

[113] In *Journals* for 12th September on the topic of the 'white house' Ellen wrote: "The only fault we could find was with the over cleanliness and white glare of the house, and our only fear was lest its clean mistress should unexpectedly return and be shocked at us, dirty Londoners."

[114] Also from *Journals* for 12th September Ellen wrote: "In the morning Mr Selwyn and Henry [W?] rowed me from Kew to Twickenham. I never enjoyed anything more in my life. It was a lovely morning and one of those days when there

long letter from home.

They say that the Shrewsburys have given Hungerford a powder charmed by the Pope. He is come back so brightened up & full of Lady Mary Morris[?]. He brought Dr Walsh, their Chaplain, back with him to Crewe & they also say they have no doubt the intention is to marry & convert him or to convert & marry him. I don't think the last way likely at all, but as to the other I really think that it might be, for I fear his principles would not be strong enough to resist long on their wiles & indeed I hope that I am not uncharitable but I do think they are designing & Henrietta's case gives that perhaps the idea.[115] Of course we grow duller every day & the streets have a most dreary appearance. However we do tolerably, what with reading, writing & not arithmetic but use our own lively imaginations.

I hope to be again at home about the 30th of this month. Then I shall amazingly enjoy seeing you & all other enquiring friends. I was very sorry to receive a letter from Mrs Lister the other day giving an account of the death of her mother-in-law at Tunbridge. The whole family were happily with her. Poor dear Harriet's situation is a very sad one but she is most fortunate in having such a kind sister-in-law as Mrs L. Oh dear Annie, I think of Capt Boyle. However he has borne the willow quite as most men do. Mrs Cunlifffe always laughs at the variety of our acquaintances. I am sure she would be amazed if she saw our present visitors – Welsh clergyman & two children – the young fry can hardly speak English at all. They are come up to go to the Clergy School & I have been consoling them with herrings – apple dumplings and peaches.

Marianne is very well and desires her best love to yourself & Mrs Cunliffe. Believe ever, my dearest Annie.

Your very loving friend,
Ellen Tollet

Ellen's daily Journals ended in October 1836.

---

is sort of fine blue, atmospheric look about the distance, and yet no haziness – the river was so bright and clear and the reflections of the fine trees so picturesque".

[115] Would Annabel appreciate this criticism of her family?

Letter 14   [*cat: 101*]
Marianne's stillbirth again; Hungerford's illness; acceptance of misfortune;
little 'O' and their art; Lyell's geology; anti-slavery; feminism and women's
conversation; London house

Betley Hall,
Dec 12, 1836

To: Mademoiselle Annabel Crewe
My dearest Annabel.

Tho' the sad news of our dear Marianne's misfortune had not reached
you when you wrote to me, I feel no doubt but that Georgy has by this
time told you all a bitter bride's trials it is to her[116] & to us all & one which
it requires the full exertion of one's patience & fortitude to be well.
Hitherto she has been wonderfully supported as I really believe is the case.
Her submissions & strength of mind are caused by her heartfelt conviction
that her affliction is appointed for her real benefit by an all wise & merciful
Father. We shall have the happiness of seeing it continue increasing & the
design for which the trial is sent will be answered. It is really quite
wonderful to see the design of providence so clearly as I think we may do
in this case. Never was the heart of this most ambitious man more set upon
self-aggrandisement or that of the vainest worldling upon family than poor
dear Marianne has been on the possession of a child & it is just in this point
she is tried, no doubt, in order to wean her affection from this world – as if
this effort is mercifully produced, her happiness will be increased instead of
diminished by this discipline. She is recovering well, tho' rather slowly.
Only think of that dear little boy the image of William. It is enough to
grieve the hardest heart - to think of those little babies who would have
been so tenderly cherished all lying in their little graves but I really will
dwell no more on this sad subject.

Oh! yes, we heard of the Philippic[117] but as success has crowned our
rashness, Oh dear! a win by mistake.[118] We care not for none of it, tho' I
confess I never was so anxious about Hungerford's health as I was for a
fortnight after. However, so far from the complaint being going off,[119] it
was at its height & lo & behold I bathe it myself a fortnight after & was

---

[116] What were 'bitter bride's trials'? Was this the sad news of Marianne's
stillbirth which took up the rest of the first paragraph?

[117] A tirade or rant.

[118] Who gave the tirade and what was it about?

[119] Seemed to be a quickly spreading illness. What was the epidemic?

very poorly for 5 days, but it is now 3 weeks today since & I am quite recovered. I only saw his Lordship since [*the*] infection was over & then did not shake hands. So he is perfectly safe & I am bound to say no single soul has suffered from us.[120] I forget whether you heard that I let out the fact that very day he received the news with much equanimity.

The portrait of Papa was completed by dear little "O" in a week to our entire satisfaction & his company was most amusing to us all. I flatter myself I could make you laugh with some anecdotes. His conceit is really up at boiling heat.

He told Mr Sneyd who was here one day that Lord C's picture had much of M Angelo's[121] manner & when Papa expressed a wish for me to have instruction, he replied with a grand triteness he has seen me draw! His admiration of Fanny's beauty was enthusiastic; he was dying to make "one of my grand heads in oil" from her. He says Carry & I are neither of us plain but "you have not that beauty you know," but as I am said to draw "fit for the Exhibitions" or to be "at least as clear as Lady Delamere" & Carry's voice "is delicious melody", we are nearly satisfied. We sang glees together and tho' his voice is old, his ear is so perfect we managed very well. You ask me what we have been doing –why really nothing lately, but mourning poor Marianne. We have seen no soul & have read but little.

I am wading thro' 4 vols of Lyell's *Geology,* a science I am seized with a passion for[122], but without practical knowledge, all one can ever gain is just to know what it means, but it is so pleasant to acquire our morsel of new knowledge & so important to those who lead lives of refinement like ours – in addition to my Geology, I have studied Millinery like Miss F Kemble, for our maid is out & I have made a cap & a cape! Pity.

I have also read *Jonathan Jefferson*[123] which is most disgusting in parts but still shews more good feeling, I think, that any of Mrs (Frances) Trollope's former work. I admire her detestation of slavery that she is far too severe against the Americans. There is less of vulgar pretensions in her heroes & heroines. I think this is improved in her own heart, but a coarse mind she

---

[120] Note the real fear of spreading the infection.

[121] Did he mean Michaelangelo?

[122] *Principles of Geology* by the Scottish geologist Charles Lyell (1797–1875). He was working on similar lines to Charles Darwin. As we have seen elsewhere in these letters, Geology was a particular interest of Ellen.

[123] *The Life and Adventures of Jonathan Jefferson Whitlaw* (1836) by Frances Trollope (1779-1863) – an anti-slavery novel written during her stay in America.

must have – Miss Martineau who you know adores the Americans declares that tho' [*the*] slavery's part is not at all overdrawn & [*she*] has brought home some heartrending anecdotes.[124] Her book is not to be in a story which is almost a pity, as she has such time for it.

This brings me to Mrs Marsh.[125] Georgy told me how ungracious she was. What a foolish woman. I am very sorry for she can be most entertaining. She has the greatest horror of being a lion & I suppose that makes her rude to strangers, but it was her own loss for she would have been delighted with Mrs Cunliffe. She has been sadly annoyed by the review of her last book in the *Quarterly*. I agree with it exactly but it showed if had they should have spent all these notices on that, instead of on her first, which was so superior.

I was so glad to hear of your meeting a Frenchman. I wish you would get to know some F[ren]chwomen.[126] I have a great idea of their powers of conversation. I fancy the men & women are much more alike than in England & that the women have not the fear of bluism[127] before their eyes as we have. They have not that awful shocking hang up as a warning & thus the "doll school" of manners has not quite so many followers.[128]

I think you having really found your true beau ideal of a house. We have not begun to hint about Bedford Square at present, but I really have a strong glimmering of hope. Marianne has started the subject several times quite voluntarily & as 6 women are to one man so is our chance of success–

---

[124] Harriet Martineau (1802-1876) was a journalist, social reformer and prolific author. She was also an early feminist and supported the abolition of slavery. In connection with the latter she visited the United States in 1834, where she caused considerable controversy because of her views. It is not possible here to adequately summarise her significant contributions to Victorian Society. The Slavery Abolition Act was passed by Parliament in July 1833 and came into effect the following year.

[125] Anne Marsh-Caldwell, a local novelist. The Caldwells formerly lived in Linley Wood, near Audley, and knew the Tollets well.

[126] This French connection has proved difficult to decipher from the handwriting, but the Crewes spent a great deal of time on the Continent.

[127] This word presented the editors with some difficulty. Bluism is an obsolete word (see OED) meaning the possession of learning in a woman who could also be described as a bluestocking. Was Ellen thinking of herself?

[128] Although not explicitly stated, this paragraph seemed to be comparing French and English women.

this sum in the rule of three I leave to your arithmetic to calculate.[129]

By the bye, I think that is a very good trial of yours about Miss ......
slow talking. If one could induce people to wait for one, it might have a
very good effect & talking very fast is always spoken of with a degree of
contempt – but how difficult it can be to begin checking the torrent – I
have not engineering talent sufficient I am sure – thinking of my tongue
reminds me of my nose.[130]

C[*arry*] & I are going to Liverpool with Papa & I shall speak to
B............ about it, but .... since I ..... to their determination it has been
wonderfully better according to the most approved rule of contrary.

Pray tell me how you like the Christian year – on further acquaintance,
which are your favourite parts? And are you enraged like me at the author
having married only an amiable common place woman?[131] Best love from
all here to yourself & dear Mrs Cunlifffe. Let me hear again before very
long for your letters are wells in the desert to me. Whatever Mrs C[*unliffe*]
may say of your epistolary talents & believe my loss.

Your most affectionate friend,

Ellen H Tollet

PS: Tell Mrs C I hope the flame of her fury against the Manchesterians
has ceased to burn – mine is hotter than ever at their proceedings.[132]

Letter 15   [*cat: 357*]
Hungerford's shock at Lady Combermere's death; Hinchliffe's offensive book; latest reading; the Tollets to take a London house

[*1837*]

The Hon Miss A Crewe,
16 Upper Brook St

---

[129] The rule of three is a literary device in which the reader is more likely to be
engaged in a story with the interaction between three characters rather than any
other number. The sisters are trying to persuade their father or William to move to
Bedford Square.

[130] Was she referring to the speed of her speech?

[131] Difficult to make sense of this paragraph since it proved difficult to
transcribe. Who was the author referred to? Was it a reference to Hinchliffe's
marriage to someone of "lower class"?

[132] Manchesterians belonged to the Manchester School, a body of politicians
meeting in Manchester who advocated the principles of free trade.

My dearest Annabel,

I feel pretty certain that you are this time established in your new house & I take this opportunity of his Lordship's going to London to send you a budget [*to refurbish it*].[133] Your enjoyment at Paris has again been interfered with by melancholy events & I think your recollections of that gay city are doomed to have a hope of *tristesses* upon them there. Poor Lady Combermere: how very sad .... her end was.[134] It seemed to have shocked Hungerford very much as well it might & he was looking poorly & rather low when he came down, but is now quite well again.

I am very anxious to hear how your poor friend bears her trial. Pray write me word about her, for I have particulars only from you. Lord Combermere must, I think, be very sorry for his sister Lady Mainwaring. Sir Harry's affairs are so terribly deranged that they are obliged to leave Peover [*in Cheshire*]. I was so glad to hear of Mrs Greville's legacy to Captain G's children. I only wish he had left something *to* poor Major G's orphans who are in great want of it. I quite forgot in my last letter to write upon a subject which has often been in my mind when I have thought of you & Henrietta.

Have you seen or heard of a book of travels printed & sold at the Tarvin Bazaar this autumn[135] & the author of which is the Rev E Hinchliffe? I have a great wish to send it to you but we did not buy it so the gentleman promised to send me his copy. It has now come but I think your brother must have it. I will ask him. They tell me Mr H is now ashamed but it is too late & I hardly believe it, because he wrote it some years ago. It was revised & printed only so very lately that there must have been a very rapid tropical growth of the plant *repentance* that this exquisite little book is

---

[133] Ellen's description of Hungerford Crewe. He was generous in giving Annabel a larger allowance, when she moved into Upper Brook Street.

[134] Lady Combermere (Caroline Greville) died on 27th January, 1837.

[135] *The Comicalities of Travel* (1836) by E Hinchliffe, the vicar of Barthomley. It was republished in a shortened version and sold in Tarvin with a *nom de plume*. It was about his adventures in Belgium to rescue Miss C from the enemy. Miss C is, of course, Henrietta. This book was difficult to locate because there was no accurate title, but it is still available second-hand and online. See the end of this letter for more details.

unrivalled for its flippancy, its vulgarity & its audacity. His account of going to Bois l'Évêque [*where the 2nd Baron lived*] & his repeated assurances to the

6. Bois l'Évêque near Liege, where Annabel's father lived earlier (from 'The Comicalities of Travel').

reader that whatever might be thought, he was <u>not</u> Miss [*Henrietta*] C[rewe]'s lover - then his description of the contents of her imperial notices of her <u>chemises</u> etc, all this is so unequalled, I think, in the annals of clerical authorship, that we may be forgiven for forgetting his cloth & expecting Henrietta to challenge him to meet her or Hungerford at Chalk Farm.[136] Joking apart, I wonder whether she has read it. As the work is spread over Cheshire anyone may judge for themselves. Therefore don't, I pray, quote my authority against it. My remarks are late now (& a few others) & if it is true that the deluded man repents his audacity we may be so charitable as to extend to him a little mercy. Only one bit more. I know he was light; I knew he was not always too true; I did not know he was vulgar, Did you?

To turn to a widely different subject let me tell you that dear Marianne is going on very well in every respect except one- that is she is stronger & in very fair spirits but the giddy goose has sprained her ankle. However I trust it is nothing of any importance. Georgy came home with her as far as Shrewsbury, where Carry joined them & she will stay with her till just before Easter. We cannot be sufficiently thankful that hitherto she has been

---

[136] On the Crewe estate.

able to bear her sorrow so submissively & Carry describes her as really very cheerful.

My London scheme is still in existence, tho' the only real progress it has made towards perfection is that by repeated judicious hints, allusions etc, Papa is becoming used to the idea & what we say with a smile instead of a groan as heretofore. There is no use looking for a house until within 3 weeks of our journey & then Mamma will write to a certain beloved old retired grocer who does everything for us & everybody. It is to be necessary for some well-educated friend just to look at the object of the grocer's choice before we close the bargain & I daresay Mrs Cunliffe would be kind enough to do this for us.

Have you heard that Miss St John is going to marry Mr McCleod?[137] His residence is where it ought to be on Sky[*e*]. He is good looking, gentlemanlike with about £500 or £600 a year. I don't think it is a grand alliance as Lady St John would have desired, but it seems a very good thing altogether. I think he won't persuade his fine lady to fly with him to Skye - so he must deign to dwell on this nether earth with her.

We have read Mrs Armitage & have been very much pleased with it. There is one scene near the end which is, I think, one of the most striking & at the same time the most true to nature I have read a long time.

I am tremendously busy with my patchwork which, I think you saw. It is very amusing & takes a great deal of taste & consideration & will, I think, be a monument of industry to spread my fame into future generations.

Pray write me - your last was short. Remember - Oh dear! I have never thanked Mrs C[*unliffe*] for her letter about the letters.[138] A calm consciousness of perfect innocence made me feel quite comfortable while I read it. Your brother's directions about the directions were quite clear enough for me, tho' it seems not for himself for he pleads guilty in *propria persona* [*legally — without attorney*].

Will you graciously cause the parcels or rather the gigantic letter to Mr

---

[137] In 1837 Macleod of Macleod married the Hon Louisa St John. (It helps to date the letter.)

[138] Has Mrs Cunliffe commented on the content of Ellen's letters to Annabel, particularly about Marianne's suffering in childbirth?

Allen to be put into the two penny post. N.B. He is a lover of Georgy's, aged 60 but very juvenile- fresh as a rose – only two grown-up sons to mother!

Yours most affectionate,

EHT

From "The Comicalities of Travel" on its content:
>   *"They begin in Madness*
>   *And carried on in Cruelty*
>   *And end in Humbug."*

It was a mischievous piece of writing by a relative of the Crewe family, namely Edward Hinchliffe, the vicar of Barthomley. Ellen complained that it had spread across Cheshire to create scandal for the Crewes, especially Henrietta who was referred to as Miss C. This was a stupid act on Hinchliffe's part because the Crewes had the advowson of his church.

However he went on to produce a second edition under the pen-names Seacombe J, Crane T & Crane William for the Tarvin Bazaar in 1836. The shorter version still referred to Bois l'Évêque, the Château of the second Lord Crewe, and Miss C. In it her father obviously approved when the narrator and Miss C made a wild escape from Belgium.

The narration is light-hearted in its description of travels on the Continent, containing amusing stories of young lovers. There are some pleasant descriptions of the lively towns with their inhabitants. The gallant narrator hears that there are insurgents in Belgium, and he is imprisoned after a skirmish, but escapes with Miss C across the Channel. It is a jolly romp not appreciated by Ellen Tollet but innocuous to a modern reader aware of real events in Belgium in the 1830s.

Letter 16   [*cat: 43*]
House parties at Brand and at Peatswood; Ellen's comments about Mr Allen Baugh's proposal to Georgina; society gossip; first reference to Poor Law Commissioner (Tom Stevens); Ellen to go to London

Betley, Monday 9th [*1838*]

Hon. Annabel Crewe, 16 Upper Brook Street, Grosvenor Square, London[139]

My dearest Anne,

My first impulse in receiving your most entertaining letter was to answer it immediately, which I will put a restraint on myself. I determined to wait until after a visit we were engaged to pay at Peatswood,[140] where we knew there was a probability of our meeting that horrid man who has caused us all so much misery.[141] Georgina thought that seeing him again would do her good. Heaven only knows whether it would or not. However, it was not to be, for the day he & his sister were to come they sent to say they were both so ill with colic they could not stir from home!! Now was not this tantalizing? My first impression was that it was a shirk on his part but afterwards on further consideration I thought not – for he has accepted Mary's invitation to Brand[142] & dined there 2 sisters together tho' he could not be sure she would not be there – besides there were two ways of avoiding going to Peatswood, as he knew.

From the very first G & I were to be there when he came to Brand, Mary Wicksted told me he appeared most miserable. Is not this very odd? But I have now completely given the thing up for I feel as if Providence had ordered that it never should be in marriage & indeed one must ever feel that tho' so very well suited so all other respects & certainly attracted to each other. Yet there must have been a sad deficiency of sympathy between them on other subject[s] upon which of all others it is most important that

---

[139] Upper Brook Street linked Hyde Park to Grosvenor Square (and still does). The houses were built in the C18 as part of the Grosvenor Estate. From 1835, all leases were renewed on condition that there should be no trade in the street – they should be purely residential (*British History Online*: Upper Brook Street,1980).

[140] Peatswood Hall near Market Drayton, home of the Twemlows. They were related to the Twemlows of Betley Court.

[141] The 'horrid man' was Mr Baugh Allen, an unfortunate name for a teacher. He was Head of Dulwich College, and related to the Wedgwoods. He had proposed to Georgina, after Penelope had rejected his offer earlier (see *Journals* p 188).

[142] Charles and Mary Wicksted rented Brand Hall, near Market Drayton from the time their son George was born in 1836. Shortly afterwards they took up residence in Mary's family home at Shakenhurst.

they should agree …. religion. It is or ought to be the thing nearest our hearts as to feel & know that the person you love best can neither understand nor sympathize with you, must be a constant source of uneasiness.

If I could but see my darling Georgy happy again how thankful I should be! I suppose the very romantic people who think people can know only one love in their lives would be quite horrified at one when I say that this affair will make me more anxious for Georgina to marry than I ever was before. Indeed I am sure there is no one to whose character matrimony would be more improving than hers. If it had not been for this affair we should have enjoyed our visit at Peatswood very much.

Mrs Twemlow is always most agreeable & Willoughby Crewe[143] was there. He, as you know, is in the most amicable mood possible, making himself most acceptable to all the ladies being a constant member of all the dinners & parties in the neighbourhood. He is a great deal at the Brand & his house is quite a drive. I have not yet seen it. No doubt he intends to have a wife in it some day. I think he is slowly deliberately …….all the young ladies & turning over in his mind their different advantages. Of course, tho' he conceals it well Georgy & I are among those honoured by a passing consideration & there is great fun to me. I know he in his heart likes G the best but he calculates that I, tho' perhaps a little young, should do more for his money than she.

I am active & equal to a good deal of plain sewing etc, etc so I think my chance is as good or better than G – *entre nous,* however, I must say he really is so dreadfully prosy that after all's said & done, I am afraid no one will marry him except for the sake of the beautiful carpet with flowers on a white ground.

My dear child, what horrid gossip this is now. Take care not to let a word pass your lips even as a joke of this nonsense.

Your account of the Queen is just what I have long fancied was the case *viz* that she was more admirable than lovable.

---

[143] Rector of Mucklestone. Ellen jokes rather sickly that she would be more useful to Willoughby Crewe (1792-1850) than Georgina because with two hands she could sew better!

I see you have been at the drawing room.[144] Pray write & tell me about it & how you are clothed.

Only think of my having proceeded thus far without telling you that there is a great chance of your seeing my sweet face soon for Charles & Mary are going to London & talk of taking me with them but as it is not quite certain I do not build upon this so confidently. How glad I shall be to see you again, my dear soul, tho' in a fortnight's hurry our meetings will not be satisfactory.

While you have been full of Balls and Concerts we have been hearing much [of] Poor Laws. The Commissioner has been here & just you at Madeley & us here into Union. He is a very nice man, the son of a man of fortune, I believe. But he is so fond of the business that he undertakes it for his pastime. He tells wonders of its good effect etc, etc in Berkshire where his house is & he is so human & amiable that I am quite comforted about the new law.[145] Capt Mainwaring is the President of the Guardians[146] & is a most admirable person for the office, active, very sensible & very kind-hearted to the poor so I hope we may have good done tho' the difference in such parishes as ours will be very slight.

Have you seen the *Lady of Lyons?*[147] I hear it is such a pretty play. How do you like *Parsiani?*

This neighbourhood has, of course, been quite exerted by the sad event of Edward Jervis[148] having married the housemaid at Meaford. They are

---

[144] Ellen is referring to the Royal Drawing Room, where Annabel would have been presented to the Queen.

[145] This paragraph refers to Thomas Stevens (1809–1881). He was Assistant Poor Law Officer for North Staffordshire. He was responsible, in the short time he lived there, for the separation of the two Poor Law Unions, the Newcastle Union comprising the borough of Newcastle including Betley, Madeley and Keele from Wolstanton with Burslem and rural areas to the north. Stoke was separate (see *Living the Poor Life* by Paul Anderton, Alun Davies and David Jackson, *Staffordshire Studies*, 19 (2008).

[146] Elected in 1838 in Newcastle-under-Lyme. These elected boards **of** Guardians managed Poor Law Unions. They were established in 1838 (*A Staffordshire Workhouse: Living in the Workhouse of Newcastle under Lyme* by Gladys Dinnacombe).

[147] A romantic melodrama by Edward Bulwer-Lytton.

now in London & I hear she has been seen very smart in Regent Street. They went to Gretna accompanied by her brother, a tailor! We are all truly sorry for poor Lord W who is sadly distressed by this affair. I am glad that you & Harriet Lister get on better. There is a great deal that is very nice about her but she is a very unstable person. Little Lady John [*Russell*] & she are certainly not what 2 only sisters ought to be to each other but it is the world in Lady John's heart that is the cause. Remember long ago hearsay that Lady Ribblesdale did not take Harriet to London with her because she was told people obtained their position in society better without a girl to chaperone. Can one fancy such slavery for the sake of fashion?

I was very sorry to hear of the Duchess of Montrose's ill success …… it is her second failure. I hope Lady Brabazon & she will both be more fortunate. Carry is still at Welshpool. I am so sorry I do not know Hungerford's directions.[149] You should have told me. You see Lord John is married. Poor Sir Alex & poor Sir – for, of course, it is one of your Baronets. When I come to London I shall investigate the matter. Marianne is thinking of London for a very little time. With all our most affectionate loves. I can close a very stupid letter & am ever your most affectionate,

Ellen Tollet

Letter 17   [*cat: 355*]
Railway adventures in 1838; Betley tenants in freezing weather; book society; problems for young women in marriage

Postmark: 26 Feb 1838

The Hon Annabel Crewe, 16 Lower Brook Street, London[150]

My dearest Annie,

I was so very glad to see your handwriting & thought it very good of you to write so soon after your arrival in London. Your history of your railroad adventure was very amusing & as all ended without any accident it can only

---

[148] Edward Jervis, son of Viscount St Vincent of Meaford, married Mary Barker (1819-1884) (presumably the housemaid) on 12th March, 1838. They had 12 children. (From *thepeerage.com*)

[149] Hungerford was notorious for being unable to give accurate directions in space and time (see Letter 68).

[150] Lower Brook Street joins Grosvenor Square to Hanover Square.

afford entertainment now, though I am free to confess, I should never have dared to have cancelled a carriage from the Madeley Station where they are unused to the business, as I should have dreaded it not being properly corded[151] on the truck. When we went, as we sat in our carriage, it was a matter of still greater importance than in your case & I can't tell you how nervous I felt lest, when going at full speed, we should be loosed from our moorings & dashed to pieces.

7. A road carriage being transported by rail.[152]

I suppose you are now like us in great delight at this very decided thaw.[153] Nevertheless we must all agree that it has come in the most disagreeable way possible – a violent east wind & torrents of rain which find their way through every crevice. We hear you have had rain several days this week in London but here today is the first of decided thorough-going thaw. Was there ever anything like the horrors of the end of last week? We were the means of dragging some wretched victims from their homes at that time & we tried their constitution & nicely in our drawing room, which was literally a howling wilderness. Among the sufferers were Mr Clayton & Holmes the artist. Mr C is very gentlemanlike & appears amiable. When we first knew him we thought him extremely quick but now find that he is very talkative.

---

[151] In the early days of the railway in addition to railway carriages passengers could be conveyed in their own complete road carriage which was strapped or corded on to a bogie (see illustration). Presumably this method of travel alarmed Ellen.

[152] *Mike's Railway Hist*ory website (permitted non–commercial use).

[153] There was a severe winter in 1838 which lasted for two months. The lowest recorded temperature was –26C in Kent, and the Thames froze over.

Little 'olmes[154] is as odd as ever & continues to flatter himself & all the rest of the world in the usual style. He gravely assures us that we are the most beautiful, the cleverest & the most amiable family in the world. One of his favourite openings of a sentence is "people of the highest rank & fashion like yourselves". He has made a very pretty picture of Mary Wicksted & her 2 children & certainly excels particularly in children. I have been so bold as to take a likeness of Georgina which he very good-naturedly touched up & made quite pretty & I am now victimising poor Carry who sits glowering in my face 2 or 3 hours a day.

8. Was this the sketch of Carry that Ellen was referring to in Letter 17?

Have you read the 6th vol of Walter Scott?[155] I think it is one of the most interesting things I ever read. I mean his Diary. It appears to be such a faithful record of his feelings as I should think not any people could commit to paper. No wonder Miss Hayman[156] is furious about George 4th

---

[154] Perhaps this was how he pronounced his name.
[155] The journal was written between 1825 and 1832.
[156] Mrs Hayman was one of Princess Charlotte's early governesses.

for I hear the poor dear Princess Charlotte comes off but badly. I hope Lady C B[157] will be ashamed of herself. However, will pay well for everybody will read it. It is already ordered into our Book Society.[158]

Our last account of Marianne was better. She had been amusing herself by sitting in a close carriage (with the horses off) at the edge of a pond in the park watching William teach Lucy & Charlotte their best to skait[159] & what she says was still more amusing - Lady Lucy[160] instructing her two youngest children in the art of sliding. I am sorry poor Lady Hillsbro' suffers so much. I daresay the poor thing is quite steadified & matronized already. There is certainly no state free from care & pains as the single, tho' in almost all cases it is better to compound for more troubles for the sake of more happiness, & matrimony has certainly much the advantage in advanced life. Poor dear good Mrs Hesketh; hers is a happy change I have no doubt, but her children must feel a sad void now she is gone, who must have occupied all their thoughts so much for a long time & whose patience under her sufferings must have endeared her more & more & hence I feel so very sorry for Miss H[esketh] & Mary. That horrid vile woman must be a constant source of annoyance. What does she not know?

What a nice bit of scandal about Lord Melbourne. I can imagine nothing more likely than his being in love but I hope this is not returned. This is a very dull letter but don't punish me by not writing soon. Georgy is pretty well generally but sadly low sometimes.

With best love from all,

your affectionate friend,

EH Tollet

Letter 18 [*cat: 42*]
Lady Hillsborough; shoulder of lamb; deaf and dumb visit; before the Queen's coronation

[*before 28 June, 1838*]

---

[157] Lady Charlotte Bury – lady-in-waiting to Princess Charlotte.

[158] Was this an early record of a public book society?

[159] Archaic spelling of skate.

[160] Lady Lucy was Rev William Clive's sister from Powis Castle.

My dearest Annabel,

Since I parted from you in London I have seen two events in the newspapers which have brought you & dear Mrs Cunliffe much to my remembrance, as I knew they would both be tho' in different degrees, causes of sorrow to you.

Poor Lady Hillsborough's[161] disappointment first & since the death of Mrs Wynn – I remember your telling me a good deal about the illness of the latter when I last saw you, but I think you spoke of her as much better but I suppose some sudden change took place for the worse. It will be a sad, sad loss particularly to her husband & unmarried daughters & I know Mrs Cunliffe will feel much both for them & with them. I shall be quite anxious to hear how poor Lady Hillsb[orough] is going on & whether the premature confinement was brought on by any accident or not. I am sure Lord H will be much annoyed, but if she is well thro' it, he may comfort himself with hopes of better things another time, but it is an unfortunate beginning & I am very sorry for it.

Our journey home per railroad was most prosperous. We left Euston Square at ½ past 9 and arrived at Whitmore at 9. At one of the towns where we changed horses (in the 37 miles gap) we spied a shoulder of lamb going into a farmer's dinner whereupon we jumped out & seized upon it & devoured it much to our satisfaction.[162]

I found all here very flourishing but the weather was so intolerably cold on my first arrival that I really could not find any scope for sentimental ruralities either imagination or action. All I could do was to walk briskly about the grounds in a warm shawl or to sit over the fire relating my

---

[161] Lord Hillsborough married Miss Caroline Stapleton–Cotton on the 23rd August 1837 according to *thepeerage.com*. Miss Cotton, who was related to Lord Crewe through the Grevilles (her mother), was first mentioned in connection with Lord Hillsborough in Letter 9. She had suffered a stillbirth. In the previous letter Ellen noted she was ill.

[162] There was a gap in the line of the London and Birmingham Railway which was covered by passengers using stage coaches. The problem on the line was the delay in the construction of the Kilsby tunnel near Rugby which was finally completed in 1838. At the time it was the longest railway tunnel in the world at 2432 yards.

London adventures. This has now given place to running between the showers for it is now very warm tho' very rainy. This place looks lovely when the sun shines as the rhododendrons, azaleas & thorn trees are in beautiful bloom.

It has been a sad thing the death of poor Henry Tomkinson of Rease Heath who has left 5 children. The other Henry & Julia are much the same I believe. What an afflicted family they are! Mary Anne Egerton is coming here next week & she came by railroad to her brother's at Hodnet. They were steaming on happily at a slow pace [*when*] the engine broke down & they were jolted, she with her face against the window & was a good deal cut; tho' nothing of any serious consequence. This is a reverse to my picture of railway travelling; certainly our luck was great for 2 more charming journies [*sic*] no one could have.

We are going to have great festivities at the "Crownation" as the people here call it. We feast the school children, sing 'God save the Q[*ueen*]' & dance (weather permitting) on the lawn.[163]

Papa, Penelope & Georgina have been on an expedition to Manchester to see after our deaf & dumb child[164] & to see the manufactories & Miss Georgy is returned wonderfully au fait about all the wheels & axles & levers etc, etc, etc. - an excellent thing that she has these interests to occupy her mind. She is really much better. Farewell, dearest Annie,
with best love from all here,

ever your affectionate,

E H Tollet

Letter 19   [*cat: 44*]
Travel arrangements by coach and train; Roman Catholicism; Tom; visit to Olton

Betley Hall, Feb 25, 1839

Hon. Annabel Crewe, 16 Upper Brook Street,

---

[163] There was a document of detailed arrangements for the celebration in the BLHS archives (see Appendix 4).

[164] Mary Gater, whom the Tollets sponsored at the Special School.

Grosvenor Square, London

Dearest Annabel,

As you desire me to write, I can do no less than obey but really I hope to see you soon, that I cannot feel as if I had a great deal to say. My present intention is to leave home this day week & spend a few days with Miss Wigley at Olton[165] & proceed to London about Thursday. I shall travel on the mail with a maid & as Caroline W's carriage will meet me at Bir[mingham] & William [*Clive*] will be at Euston Sqr[166] to receive me. I think I shall do very well – as by staying at Olton my journey will all be performed in broad daylight. What a horrid collision was that in the tunnel.

9. The Hon Mrs Cunliffe-Offley of Madeley Manor, aunt of Henrietta, Hungerford and Annabel.

I saw Mr Blackburne the other day whose sisters were in the train. How wonderful it is the knack the railway accidents have of killing nobody outright.

---

[165] This was the home of Caroline Wigley (Mrs Archer Clive). She was a novelist and poet, known as V, and sister of Mary Wicksted.

[166] The line from Birmingham to Euston was officially fully opened on 17th September 1838. Trains took about 5 hours to cover the 112 mile journey.

Did you read an article in the last *Quarterly* but one called *Railroad in Ireland?* It was by Sir Frank Head & was one of the most entertaining things I ever read. I am quite glad to hear from everyone how nicely arrived is H[*enrietta*] in her [*London*] house.

Well I think I had rather be anywhere than in that melancholy house in Grosvenor Square & how indeed a melancholy house to us since the dear Mrs Allington, who once made it cheerful, is gone. I am surprised however that she was smart, as she said she meant to have her best gowns here. She says Mrs Cunliffe has heard of Tom [*Stevens*]'s popery from somebody. Don't be alarmed, my dear friends, I feel confident he has too much good sense & right feeling to move into any extremes & Carry & I believe myself too, have influence [to] be "different" .... so both will use it to persuade & modify him. I think he has something against the Romanists as .... there than we are – that is the only reason I see at present for fearing he may become one [*transcription problems with this paragraph*].

I know you read Newman's *Sermons* & therefore are not afraid of your fancying any one very popish for admiring them & confessing they have derived more benefit from them than from any other uninspired writings – so far I am compelled to confess myself. I speak of the 1st & 3rd volumes with the 4th. I don't recommend it as there are several very startling things in them & I have sad misgivings that the Oxford party are going on & on into extremes. I do think Newman believes in transcendentalism as much as an educated Roman C. does. I suppose M. told you of the books Henrietta sent to Georgy. She & the B(isho)p have evidently hopes of her & she wants her to visit her without me – so I am thought both hopeless myself & likely to hold G. back from the truth!! Now for curacies - Newton has no salary only the house & it is a disagreeable parish. He [*Tom*] is thinking of another & we shall perhaps hear today I will keep my letter open. The post is come but no letter so you must wait to hear till I come.

How wretchedly anxious I shall grow when I have been in Town a few days. The horrid event [*the birth of Marianne's baby*] may happen any day after my arrival tho' I don't really expect it till near the 20th. Georgy & Carry are going tomorrow to a gay party at Peatswood & I go for a farewell visit to

Brand.[167] I have tried the eyewaters for which many thanks but I think it was rather strong – I shall try it weaker but my eyes, I know, are very unmanageable. I am very well now but horribly thin. I shall feel very anxious to see poor dear Harriet Lister. G has had lately a very interesting letter from her. She gives a most delightful account of Lord John [*Russell*]. I have never said how glad we all were that your aunt was so much better.

Goodbye dearest Annabel, ever your most affectionate,

E H Tollet

Tom Stevens had now given up his role as Assistant Poor Law Commissioner to enter the Church, and also to marry the youngest daughter of the Tolletts, Caroline. The marriage ceremony on the 8th June 1839 was conducted by her brother-in-law Rev William Clive. As the curate at Keele, Tom and his new wife lived in the vicarage where they were both very popular.

Much later Tom returned to Bradfield, his family home in Berkshire, where he eventually succeeded to his father's living as rector. There he rebuilt the church and designed the famous Bradfield Church of England School, employing the architect Sir G G Scott. He had first made his acquaintance in Lichfield when he was discussing the plans for workhouses in the 1830s.

Letter 20   [*cat: 275*]
British Association and Science; Olton House; Archer Clives; Mary Wicksted's stillbirth; Carry at Keele; Marianne's next pregnancy.

Postmark: London, 2 Sep 1839

Betley, Aug 31 1839

My dearest Annabel,

In obedience to you, Carry and I sat down to write to you tho' I am surely afraid that this precious document may be doomed to make a tour to the Brunnens[168] & finally to be consigned to an ignominious fate. I think you will have left Ems [?] almost by this time & your movements after that must be a little uncertain. *The Morning Post* 9 days ago announced your

---

[167] Charles and Mary were moving to Shakenhurst, their permanent home and the seat of the Meysey-Wigleys.

[168] A resort on Lake Lucerne, Switzerland.

84

departure for Madeley Manor! Well you will expect a scientific discussion from my pen when I tell you I have been at the meeting of the savants at Birmingham[169] all the week.

On Monday Penelope & I set off for railway to Olton, 6 miles from Birmingham where dwells Miss Wigley, Mary's sister.[170] It is an old house beautifully fitted with quantities of curved oak & all done in most excellent taste. She is very clever & agreeable & knows many nice people so it is always pleasant there. Her party consisted of Mr & Mrs Scudamore (Herefordshire) Sir Wil[*liam*] Broughton, Mr Archer Clive, Chevalier Neukomm[171] & visitors[?], besides Lady Sykes (one day who, by the bye, was a failure, being a very tiresome woman tho' very good natured with the exception), all were clever & agreeable.

Mr Scudamore was especial good company – a talkative, lively, nice dear man, a little dandified in appearance. He came with Caroline's carriage to Birmingham to meet us, so he was our first acquaintance. I found that he was married & expected to find such a lovely elegant creature – his wife – I was very surprised to see the most ordinary woman with regularly kitchen-maid features & figure like her planks! She is Sir Harford-Jones Bridge's daughter & had a fortune – his marrying bad is the deepest problem to me. She is sensible & energetic but uninteresting.

Chevalier Neukomm is the most unpretending musical genius I ever saw. However, I don't admire his playing so very intensely tho' we heard him on that fine organ as well as on the pianoforte every evening.

We went to the Geological Section & heard some very entertaining speeches from Dr Buckland yesterday.[172] We steamed home – & positively

---

[169] The 9th British Association for the Advancement of Science met in Birmingham, August 1839 (see Appendix 3).

[170] *Bradshaw's Railway Companion* was first published in 1839 giving timetables and fares. Ellen and Penelope could have boarded the 2-50pm train from their usual station at Whitmore. This was a first class limited stop to Birmingham, arriving at 4-45pm, at a cost of 9 shillings each.

[171] Sigismond Neukomm (1778-1858) was an Austrian composer and pianist. He studied under Haydn and wrote 'over 1,000 works, all now forgotten' (*Concise Oxford Dictionary of Music* (1980), M Kennedy, OUP).

[172] Rev W Buckland FRS was President for Geology at BAAS meeting (see Appendix 3). At the time he was Canon of Christ Church Cathedral, Oxford. An

I am going off by the same conveyance on Monday to Shakenhurst with the Hammonds for events.

You will be sorry to hear that about 3 weeks ago. Mary [Wicksted] was prematurely confined of a little girl still born. It was a great disappointment to us all but she is prodigiously well as you may know by her having company so soon. I shall have a very dull visit except the pleasure of Charles, Mary & the children for, you know, the Hammonds are not charming.

I am disappointed by the Worcester music meeting. We have seen his Lordship often. He is grown much more lively, I think. He told me about the Shelleys & their money troubles but did not mention the H Grevilles. Just lately he has been away so I have not seen him. Only think of Henrietta writing to G & saying she hoped we should all visit Mrs E Hinchcliffe!!![173] It is doubtful what to do when a man only marries a low woman but, when he does it after completely compromising her character, it appears to me that there can be but one opinion of the subject with those who consider morality of huge importance & the desecration of the clerical office as a sin deserving most punishment.

I have been a week at Keel.[174] Carry has really made her wee tiny drawing room as pretty as possible altogether there is a great deal of comfort & pleasingness in the little abode. I long to go with you there some day. Your inkstand seated on a rug of my work forms decidedly the most beautiful object in the room.

Georgy is returned from Welshpool bringing very good accounts of Marianne who is fat & well tho' not strong. The birthday of Lord Clive is to be kept with a grand dinner & a ball.[175] I shall be there. Goodbye, my

---

eccentric clergyman, he claimed he wished to eat examples of every animal in the world. These included mice on toast for breakfast, moles, crocodiles, and various droppings [*The Field Guide to the English Clergy*, by Rev Fergus Butler-Gallie, Oneworld (2018)].

[173] Henrietta hoped Mr Hinchliffe would be forgiven after his scandalous book.

[174] Keele Vicarage where Carry and Tom lived.

[175] This was the 21st birthday of the heir of Powis Castle. His father had commemorated this coming of age by building a new church in Welshpool.

dearest Annie. I do hope you will come back strong & healthy as dear Mrs Cunliffe is. We have nothing but rains. The corn is in a very dreadful state.

Your most affectionate,

EHT

Letter 21 [*cat: 45*]

Carry's report about Annabel's carriage; new church at Powis; Worcester Music Meeting; joke about the Queen; future visit of Ellen to Powis

Welshpool, October 18, 1839

To: M. Crewe, Poste Restante, Bruxelles

My dearest Annie,

In obedience to your honoured commands I begin this letter but must forewarn you that it will be an exceedingly dull affair, but as we shall not, I fear, meet just at present, I will tell you all I can. A report had spread raised certainly by Offley Crewe that you were coming home the 1st of October & Carry fancied she saw your carriage coming down Keel Hill so I wrote you a note to Madeley & was going to call but happily before I mounted the hill I expired & found you were not come, only expected that day.

Your brother seems to have fallen into the same error about your plans, for Georgy who forwarded your last letter to me here said the mystery, which he, as well as to historians, was now cleared up. He left 10 days ago with his Dr Sharp, is returned from Scotland & Chatsworth. Georgy says [*he*] has seemed very gay when he sneaked at dusk into the breakfast room all fresh from his travels.

I am so glad to hear such good accounts of you. I hope your Schlangenbad beauty will not go off before we meet. [176]

The gaieties here don't happen till the week beginning the 4th but very soon after that, I shall come home. There are to be grand doings [*at Powis Castle*]. The silly people wished to build a column, but as a church is sadly wanted, William persuaded them to build that instead & they have already got £3000. Lord Powis guarantees it with £100 a year. There will be a Ball at the Castle, which I suppose will be very grand, as there is an enormous ballroom but whether they will be able to fill it or not is a question, I think.

---

[176] Schlangenbad is a spa town in Germany, noted for its thermal springs.

To tell you the truth I daresay it will be all very well as a sight but I guess it will be dull in any other way.

I am happy to say Marianne is very tolerably well in much better spirits than one would expect after all. Mary was well enough to go for one day to

10. Vicarage at Welshpool

the Worcester Music Meeting - very pleasant it was. Clara Neville is come and a very fine singer, wonderfully improved in style & her voice is most splendid. Everyone says it is Mrs Sclinon over again. There is something disagreeable looking in her countenance & manner which prevents her singing touching me but in songs like *From mighty kings* or *Let the bright Seraph*, this is not felt so much. I heard *Palestine* for the first time rather a great deal of good & friendly music in it but a chorus of Haydn's which came just after, forced upon in a comparison from which Dr Crotch could not help suffering.[177] I have heard a good deal of the people you mention. Lady Pomfret & Dr Thorpe. I am sorry to say nothing very favourable of the latter which is, I fear, one of those most melancholy instances of a person whose practice is far below his profession. I am sure I could not endure to hear his high Calvinistic sermons, often objectionable enough in themselves, I have no doubt. His marriage was highly discreditable to him,

---

[177] William Crotch (1775-1847), composer and organist.

as I have heard from very good authority worse charges against him. Don't I sound rather like Mrs Candour or Lady Teazle?[178]

You ask me about the Queen. I had a letter from her the other day in which *she* mentioned having quarrelled again with her mother who had gone off in a huff to London but came back by the D(uke) of Wellington's advice. Victoria did not mention (any clue of his) her determination with regard to Prince Albert, but I do think that after all [*the*] divided reports as in the newspapers, this would not have had him so soon at Windsor if she were quite innocent of any intentions of marrying him. Joking apart, this is all I hear or fancy but M Sismondi knows some relations of P Albert very intimately[179] & she says her impression always is that he is a tendresse[?]. It is odd that since he has come to England the newspapers are all quite silent. The *Globe* treats the reports with great scorn. [180] I was very sorry to see in the paper Lady Hillsbor's 2nd misfortune & really she is much ...... but I hope her own health will not materially suffer.

Mary was well again directly. How delighted I will be to have you at Madeley again. I expect this winter rather dreary but the Wicksteds will enliven us the first part of it. You have perhaps heard of the son & heir at Barthomley.[181]

The Willoughby Crewes & Offleys were two days with us a little time ago. We were all much pleased with the latter. He is very silent and unassuming but when you talk to him, he has plenty to say & very sensible manner & he seems thoroughly well-disposed to us & very quiet here.

Tomorrow we arrive at the Powis Castle to meet the old Miss Walpoles – it will not be very entertaining but comfortable. I daresay Tom & Carry were here a week which they enjoyed much. They have very hard work but are doing a great deal of good, I hope. There is a sad fever in the parish [*of Keele*].

Goodbye, dear Annie. This is a very dull letter for you to pay postage for, but you must forgive me. With our best love to Mrs C & you,

---

178 Characters from Sheridan's *School for Scandal*.
179 Swiss husband of Josiah Wedgwood's daughter.
180 The *Globe* was a newspaper.
181 The birth of Edward Hinchliffe's son.

Your Most Affectionate,
EHT

PS: Don't make yourself ill with raisins.

Letter 22 *[cat: 356]*
Hungerford interested no longer in Sophy; packing for travel; the Queen's marriage

Post marked: Chester
Feb 16, 1840

Miss Annabel Crewe, Madeley Manor, Newcastle, Staffordshire
Dearest Annabel,

I am prompted by the workings of true French curiosity to write you a few lines. Henrietta has written a long letter to G full of Lady Arundel & a little popery but at the end she says, "Have you heard that all is over between Hungerford & Sophy? I must confess I am glad." You see I am dying to know whether she means that, as is so often the case, there has been another *éclaircissement* *[clarification]* or that it has died a natural death for this season by the Greville's leaving Rome. In short with the ruling passion of my sex in great activity, I want you to tell me all about it – only I am sadly afraid "the mountain etc, etc " as is so often the case. Lady Arundel seems to be H's ruling passion just now & I do not think it is not only a very pleasant, but a very advantageous, thing for her having another lady in circumstances similar to her own.

We hear from the Bloomfields that the Queen is really already thinking of a Prince of Wales. Tell me what you hear. H Lister says she has seen you several times looking very well & p----y *[Ellen's deletion]*. Poor Carry is no better at present but we live in hopes. They say the Q suffers but as she goes about, it can't be much. It is very early days for it to be known after being almost in June we have been pushed back to January.[182]

It is horribly cold with north wind. Knowing how much packing & unpacking always occupies the time of my respected friends at Madeley Manor, I can hardly repeat that if they only come down for a short time at

---

[182] The Queen married on 10th February 1840.

Easter that they can be sufficiently recovered from the arrival before preparations for departure commencing, to enable me to have an opportunity of seeing them being grown fresh. I conclude, your affectionate,

EHT

P.S.: I am happy to tell you we have excellent accounts from Marianne. She is much better & not in any <u>situation</u> at all.[183] Goodbye, dear Annie. This is a very dull letter for you to pay postage for, but you must forgive me. With our best love to Mrs C & you. Your most affectionate,

EHT

P.S: Don't make yourself ill with raisins.

Letter 23 *[cat: 118]*
Hugh Acland & Ellen; gossip & diamond tiara; Carry's difficult pregnancy; society gossip; Hungerford as Lord of the Bedchamber
28 March 1840
To : Hon Annabel Crewe, 16 Upper Brook Street, London

My Dearest Annabel,

I hasten to thank you for the [*news* of] young couples with whom you are very much delighted. You can't think how useful they have been this week in helping to entertain some visitors & one picture actually suggested the idea for a charade which was performed last night with great success. A clever, naughty boy by name Hugh Acland is a very capital performer & tho' I feel rather too old for this part, yet I could not help giving a helping hand. The word was "nursery", acted *"nurse area"* (that is) *"airy"*.[184] Rather a free translation but the acting was so good that the spelling was forgiven.

I have now to turn to a subject remotely connected certainly with the word "nursery" but still of a very different nature than our charade, being very sad & dismal. Poor dear Carry has been suffering in the most horrid way from a removal of hopes - at present there is certainly nothing of the brightness of hope about the affairs, but that I hope will come in time. She

---

[183] Marianne was not pregnant.
[184] Concerned with the pronunciation of the word "nursery".

has been confined to her room & even to her bed but I shall not tell you how bad she has been for I am sure Mrs Cunliffe would accuse me of a vile intent to scare you away from the shores of matrimony, tho' to be sure if you regarded such warnings as little as most people do but I should not have many to answer. For everyone of the experienced people try to cheer Carry, by telling her that she will soon be better indeed - quite well & I trust it will prove so. I don't think there is any fear of another mishap & this is a great blessing & heaven grant she may be rewarded in October with a live child.

What an entertaining letter you sent me with the history of your Covent Garden observations.

There is no end to the ridiculous stories about the Queen & PA. Even in this remote region nobody can ever enter the house without bringing some new nonsense which they have had from the highest authority. I am all anxiety to see this handsome Prince[185] but I fear I have no chance this year for tho' I think Charles & Mary will go to London and it will be for a very short time & to an hotel & as I think they are rather poor for this year. I think they would take me, which indeed I ought not to expect, for they are always very kind & pleasant.

I have had some more particulars about Miss Jervis & Mr Said Dyce Sombre wh(ich) is his name.[186] I have seen a friend of hers who she says she has strongly remonstrated with her on the impropriety of receiving such presents from him. She has refused a tiara of diamonds but has accepted all sorts of other jewels – a string of pearls – a diamond & emerald brooch   etc, etc, etc. They say he is evidently in love with her. However he is for the present gone off to St Petersburg whether to fetch some sables or not, I don't know. I don't believe it possible she will marry him but some people think she will. I think I told you that he is the son of

---

[185] Was she referring to Prince Albert and the marriage of Queen Victoria on 10th February 1840?

[186] David Dyce Sombre (1808–1851) was the first person of Indian descent to become a Member of Parliament. He was elected for the constituency of Sudbury but only lasted for about six months.

the husband of Begum Sombre[187] & his mother, exciting the jealousy of the Begum, she caused her to be buried alive under her throne – but adopted the child! Miss Jervis met him first at Lady Cork's & afterwards her father was of service to him about his affairs – so gratitude to Lord J may assist his generosity to his daughters.

We have not had Lord Dudley's letters but mean if we can to read them. Only think of Hungerford's chance of being a Lord of the Bedchamber. I am sure he would detest the thing & to a shy person like him I can't imagine a greater nuisance. Lord R Grosvenor seems highly delighted with Albert. I do hope you will come down at Easter if this is only for a few days. I should like just to have a peep at you & at that time we may hope for a little fine weather. It is horridly cold now with NE wind.

I am quite glad to hear so good a report of Davis. Will you give her the little note; it is about a kitchen maid. I am sorry to hear that Mrs Morier is still so poorly. This is a very dull letter; pray forgive it. Carry has been so little used to illness that she is a good deal cast down by it, but it is very good discipline which we are all obliged to have sometimes in our lives. I am better.

Your most affectionate,

EHT

On 14th May 1840 Carry died in child birth. There is a description of her death in Ellen's Journals, p. 191. Ellen was writing to Emma Darwin saying, "Tom was reading the Communion Service and she had my head and kept stroking it," before she died.

Letter 24   [cat: 318]
Soon after Carry's death; Tom Stevens' bereavement; visit to the New Forest
3 June 1840

---

187 Begum Samru (or Sumru) (1753–1836), a Catholic convert in India. She became Joanna Nobilis Sombre by marriage to European Walter Sombre. She led a colourful life.

To: Hon Annabel Crewe, 16 Upper Brook St, London

My own dearest Annabel,

I never can thank you enough for your two dear letters, such tender, affectionate sympathy as yours is indeed, a drop of sweetness in our bitter cup. I never can be grateful enough to God for having given me a place in such a heart as yours & the remembrance that it was shared with my lost darling, Carry, will make it invaluable indeed. Do you remember the last time we three were together at Betley & the evening that was spent on the library sofa? I, sitting between you, is impressed in my memory as one of particular happiness. I can recall the very sensation of my head on her shoulder & my hand holding yours. I can see her & hear her voice & remember the very words she said. At such moments of vivid recollection all that has passed since seems a dream & vision & it is hardly possible to believe the reality of the desolation. The agony & excitement of the first grief are now past but each day makes the future appear more cheerless. I can from today, but I think from tomorrow – like a coward.

We are going from home next week. We are going (Tom, Georgy and I) by railway to Southampton & from thence the New Forest to a sea place called Bourne, recommended by H Lister, who was there last Autumn.[188] She says it is perfectly quiet & pretty. The impropriety of employment at home makes me glad to go. Besides, we all require sea for our health & one does not wish to bring more trouble & anxiety by being ill. Dearest Tom looks wretchedly.

Men bear sorrow very differently from women. They are much more capable of exertion but it breaks them down in health quite as much. I think he is much more oppressed with his misery now than he was a fortnight ago, but he is really so heavenly minded that he can deal with actual pleasure or the thought of her happy end & her present peace & safety. She is now present with him in his imagination- but still, in spite of all his nature, will seek & (I believe he constantly most heartily) wishes to follow her. When I remember how intensely he enjoyed his happiness with her, with what rapture he thought of the possibility of being a father, I

---

[188] The London (Nine Elms) to Southampton railway opened on 11th May 1840, so Ellen and her party must have been among the first passengers.

really consider his nature under the blow as a most wonderful instance of the power of divine grace. The way he clings to Georgy & me is very touching. His affection is something she has bequeathed to us.

He was very much touched the other day by learning that the inhabitants of Keel & the farmers & poor people are determined to put up a tablet to her memory in the church. She had been here for only so short a time that it was wonderful how she had won their affection. Many have been the tears shed over her by the poor both here & at Keel. You remember Newman's *Sermon on the Intermediate State?* I think it is the most satisfactory and comfortable view of the, I believe possible, popish - that it is peaceful & a state of improvement not of the full fruition of joy that we know cannot be until the body is [*blot obscures writing*] with the spirit. I remember being much harassed with uncertainty about this when Eliza died but I think I am quite satisfied now & also I fear much less dread of death, since I have seen one so timid pass through its dark valley without a fear - thank God, who in his mercy, has appointed for his children that whatever darkens earth does brightens heaven. I mean that such a trial as this of ours does not make unseen things more real, more near to us. I found a mark 'AC' in her Bible. It was put to a poem you especially admired, I suppose, as a great favourite of Tom's was marked, 'T S'.

Dearest Annie, I must conclude – will you write to me & [*William*] Clive when you receive this & mention the name of your lapidary, as least if you recommend him as a jeweller also. Did he make your bracelet of your aunt's heir? We are going to have some stones & think we should like to employ him if you advise us. I will let you know when, dearest, to [*illegible cross-writing*]. With best love to our dear Mrs Cunliffe.

Your most affectionate,

EHT

[*Added are words indicating she would like to see Annabel when they had left Tom at his parents' home in Bradfield on their way back to Betley.*]

The death of Carry was particularly upsetting for Ellen. Henrietta wrote to Annabel a letter [cat: 270] from Prior Park, Bath; an excerpt is shown below:

"Ellen's suffering, I am very sure, will be tremendous – greater, I should think, than any of the others, from the extreme fondness for Caroline, which made even the idea of her marriage quite a source of misery to her – poor, poor thing – I am heartily sorry for them all, but find it almost difficult in spite of his good nursing and in spite of what, of course, his sorrow must <u>now</u> be, to feel quite in charity with Mr Stevens ...."

Letter 25   *[cat: 320]*
A break for Tom after Carry's death; rail journey in 1840 to south coast

Bourne, June 18, 1840
To: The Hon Annabel Crewe, 16 Upper Brook Street, London

My Dearest Annabel,
    I must fulfil my promise of writing from here. We arrived here on Monday. We came through London to Winchester the whole way by rail road. We stayed in London & most wretched we were, both in mind & body. At Winchester we stayed Saturday & Sunday & went to the Cathedral to see a very curious & beautiful church & remains of a charitable institution called St Cross,[189] a mile from the town. Then to Southampton by railway & from there to this place in a very nice & easy carriage. We hired them through the New Forest – a most beautiful drive & I could not help wishing I had seen it when I was young & happy. This is a very nice, very quiet place. In short it would be an extremely dull place if it were not for the most magnificent sea view. I mean a grand open sea with a steep shore so that it never recedes far. The country around is hilly & healthy, particularly bracing air.
    The hotel very comfortable but, Dear, now I must tell you that since we have been here, Tom's spirits have been 20 times worse than ever & since we got here he has been wretched. He does not like the place & we are

---

[189] The Hospital of St Cross. Also the Almshouses of Noble Poverty were medieval almshouses in Winchester founded between 1132 and 1136.

determined to leave on Monday to Muddiford,[190] then to Christchurch about 7 miles off where there is some fishing which, I hope, he will be amused with watching. Of course, it has been dreadful that seeing him so bad, but I think in time his health will really be benefited by the change when his spirits will improve.

My own health is better. I am much less weak & I am quiet in body but I feel a sort of confused apathy of mind which is only varied by occasional sensations of bitter anguish but I believe this dead, cold, dull state is just what it was after violent mental suffering to allow the bodily frame to revive.

11. Fanny, an older sister of Ellen.

Thank you for recommending Mr Sheppard who seems likely to do something very nicely for us. I long to know what your plans are.

We shall stay at Muddiford a fortnight there, then go to Bradfield when ready & then we think of proceeding to Shakenhurst where my father, mother & Penelope will very soon be. Fanny is gone to Marianne.

Do write to me, my darling Annabel, & tell me all about yourself.

We have been much interested about the sad fright to the poor dear little Queen. What a horrid feeling it must be to fear for the first time that any human being could wish to kill her! She seems to have the nerves of a man, indeed much more.[191]

---

[190] Assume she meant what is now called Mudeford: Muddiford is some distance away in Devon.

[191] An attempt by Edward Oxford to assassinate Queen Victoria occurred on 10 June 1840.

We saw your brother before we left home. Pray say how Henrietta is & my dear love, forward this stamped letter & direct to me – Hotel Muddiford, Christchurch, Hants. Georgy is pretty well & getting good from this beautiful air. I daresay you are talking of heat in London, but here there is such a brisk breeze we are obliged to wrap up quite warm. We have very good accounts from Betley but I shall be glad when they are at Shakenhurst. It will be good for Papa & Mamma.

Your ever most affectionate,

EHT

Letter 26   [*cat: 322*]
Discussion on letter writing; philosophising about marriage; danger in sea journeys; Tom; Ellen glad that Annabel is still single; Ellen's thoughts on pre-destination; (incomplete letter)

[*probably 1840*]

My dearest Annabel,

You see I am a very good correspondent & answer your dear letter in a twinkling. It is such a pleasure to talk to you & hear from you that I can't deny it myself tho' really the speciality of writing I have is extraordinary & I think I shall turn out a job of letter-writing old maid. It really is an important thing for I am sure that my postage increases it so much that it forms a great item in the list of one's employments.

Georgy writes every alternate day & of course, I ditto. She goes on very well & says the kindness of the D[*avenports*] to her is unbounded so she is now rather in doubt about her return home as they are very anxious to keep her to meet the Dods of Edge. A Signor Felice Fortunato - someone else – Randi - is there now who is said to be very charming & the Spanish Ambassador Alaan was prevented by illness. They have been in a great fuss about Mr Tuffnell who was between L[iver]pool & Dublin on Saturday night in that bad storm & his wife was terribly anxious. However, he got safe after a horrid passage of 22 hours. I am very glad of this visit. For anything is better for her than always resting at home.

I am glad dear Mrs C likes Mary Wicksted. She is a very popular person indeed. How much of both pain & pleasure you gave me by what you said of my dear Tom.[192] Pleasure to think that you felt to know him & like him & a pang of suffering to think how much pleasure your doing so would have given to one who is far beyond the reach of all this now. It makes me very sad when I think that these are the last days of that. Then follows living amongst us. What wretched days they must be to him & when I return I shall find it all swept & cleared & the objects of my hopes & interests are gone. How many good people there are who never have loved or can love intensely anything but husband or children. I feel that such can as little understand us, as if we were of different natures but you can, dearest Nancy.

I am so glad you have not a husband & children at present; all in good time you know. It is the proper & happy thing for some body at last to have them but only I am in no hurry for you. Happily I believe quite to superstition in a sort of fatality or rather the immediate superintendence of providence in such matters. And for myself should hardly dare to hold up my fingers to bring about anything for myself. Of course, we are free agents as to refusing or accepting, but before it comes to that I think it is all ordered for us. This, I hope, would always keep one very easy about all distant matters – when they come very near, poor human nature will worry itself.

How I long for you to come here & surely we may see something of each other in spite of your being in your vortex. I think we might take healthy walks in a morning together.
[*Unusually an unsigned letter; could be pages missing*]

Letter 27   [*cat: 315*]
Hungerford at Holkham; (partial letter)

[*London*], 16 Jan 1841
To: The Hon Annabel Crewe, Madeley Manor, Newcastle, Staffordshire

[*A section had been cut out to remove the stamp.*]

From the single incomplete side, it can be deduced that Annabel's brother [Hungerford]

---

[192] After Carry's death in 1840 (date check for the letter).

has gone to Holkham Hall in cold weather.[193] Ellen invited Annabel to go to Betley at the beginning of February. She wrote, "I like the old nurse's appearance but to see her turning over the baby's clothes makes me sick." *Is Ellen referring to the baby clothes of Carry? The letter ended,*

I am your most affectionate friend

EHT

Letter 28   *[cat: 313]*
The superficial life of society; looking forward to a real talk; (partial letter)
(From the postmark) 26 Jan 1841
To: Hon Annabel Crewe, Madeley Manor, Newcastle, Staffordshire

…… sat a good while chatting when the door opened & Mr Lockhart was announced. Mrs W did not want to speak to him so she hurried off & I gave a glance at him & his little daughter who has, they say, just the *[gap]* …… - I should have felt amused & *[gap]* with the visit in times past when I was happy, but now I feel as if I was acting on a stage when I am in society, as if it were no part of my real self that talked & listened & laughed – the under–current of heart happiness which gave all the real charm to the superficial pleasures is all gone.

I am reading with great admiration Gladstone's new book[194] & I have been to see Brocky's[195] drawings. He boasts of your hair.[196]

How glad I shall be to see thee – pretty dear Annie & then for our talk about reading. I have such deficiency to accuse you of & even dear Mrs C too if I dared, which I don't. Your loving friend,

EHT

---

[193] Holkham Hall in Norfolk was renowned as the centre of the Agrarian Revolution, of which George Tollet was an advocate.   Hungerford could be seeking agricultural advice for his many farms.

[194] The likely book is: *The State in Its Relations with the Church* (1841) by W E Gladstone.

[195] Charles Brocky (1807-1855), artist. He was commissioned by Queen Victoria to do portraits of herself and Prince Albert.

[196] Annabel is in royal company! There is an implication that Brocky might have painted Annabel but no record of a portrait has been found.

On the envelope:
Pray tell me when you come & don't spend 3 days in unpacking.

PART III: The infancy of Marianne's daughter, 1841-1845

"…never fix your heart on other people's children"

"Friendship is out and lovers is in for 1844"

A new era began for Ellen with the birth of baby Marianne (Minny). The third journal of Ellen Tollet dealt solely with Minny's upbringing. It was no longer a day-by-day diary covering the period 1841–1846, but a series of observations at irregular intervals, Annabel was not mentioned (see Journals*).*

Also in her diary for April 4th 1835 she wrote:

'How I would adore a nice child that loved me, for which reason I suppose I am never to be an aunt, and the trouble of being a mother is too great for one to desire it very vehemently, I think.'

What she wished for six years before is now about to become true.

Letter 29   *[cat: 272]*
Minny born Tuesday Feb 9, 1841; red mark on baby; Dr Locock

                           Friday Morning, 12th February, 1841

Dearest Annie,

    I have behaved very ill to you but I knew you would love good news. Nothing indeed can do better. They are both very well & M[*arianne*] is already making an excellent nurse which is a great wonder. The baby improves already & will be a beauty if a red mark on her forehead will go off, which we hope it will. Her health is perfect & she is very lively looking. I am in love with Locock[197] tho' he has no credit in this case except that of the dearest, pleasantest man on earth. He is so kind to me without one

---

[197] Sir Charles Locock was the Queen's obstetrician.

atom of humbug & so free from presumption or anything wrong. Bless him! As to the nurse she is a tiger but a civil one now but she was impertinence itself to me beforehand & I complained to Locock who hates her & begged me to ride the high horse & stand no nonsense!

I do wish you would come to London. It is warm enough now; do make haste if dear Mrs C. is well again which I hope. Of course I daren't recommend a book. Oh! No! But I like *Night & Morning*[198] rather, but have only read half.

Hungerford Lord Crewe of Crewe has been very rude & never called upon us. He must be either in love or grows very fine! I hope the first which will answer much the best. You can't think how strange I feel with such a cause as I have for joy & gratitude & yet not feeling that I can be happy, I almost seem to lose my identity. My own dearest Nancy, farewell.

Your most affectionate,

EHT

P.S.: 100 loves to Aunty & beg her to get very well & come here.

Marianne died a few days afterwards and her body was taken back to Welshpool, where she was buried and deeply mourned by the parishioners (see Journals. *p 194). Now the Tollet family had lost two daughters in child birth in two years. They helped William in Welshpool to care for his baby daughter, Minny, by taking part in her upbringing. Ellen seemed to be the mother figure, helped by Georgina who was limited by only having one hand. For her first month, Minny was taken by Ellen to Betley by train.*

Letter 30 [*cat: 317*]
Black edged letter; after Marianne's death; Minny in Betley; German card case; child rearing; Brocky
[*There was a problem with the page sequence which might have affected the continuity, and also a stamp has been removed.*]

Betley

March 15, 1841

To: The Hon Annabel Crewe, 16 Upper Brook Street, London

---

[198] A novel (1841) by Edward Bulwer Lytton.

Dearest Annie,

You would have heard from Hungerford that he had seen the baby who has quite recovered from her journey & has grown immensely since she came here. Sweet child, I wish you could see her round, fat little face & see her smiling so knowingly – but there is much anxiety in such a little treasure. All babies face little indigestions & as she is sadly greedy, she has them sometimes & the fuss she makes is quite dreadful. Then one cannot think it of any consequence, as long as she thrives so beautifully as all important internal arrangements seem to go on quite right.

A mother's care without a mother's rights, my dear, are most bitter partings in those for us, though for the present we are thankful that William likes us to have her here. He is gone home alone at his own desire & returns in a month & fetches Georgy.

My dear old soul, it is said that you have in possession a German card case of mine, given to you at Betley when you called, so keep it or send by my Lord of C[*rewe*] the next time he flies across the earth. I am not quite so well as I have been – for one thing London naturally agrees with me, for another one perhaps feels such trials as I have had more when the strong motion for exertion is over. I mean bodily.

I have an interest & occupation in this baby but I feel more than ever how very insufficient as any child could ever be in making up for the loss of a much loved grown up person! A kindred soul that has felt with you for your 20 years, whose love has grown with your growth & strengthened with your strength & in whom one saw the fruition of hope, not merely its germ. These are the thoughts I am filled with when I compare my present state with my former & which are brought to my mind by returning to this place which is always full of Carry.

You ask about Brocky.[199] I get to like it better every day & all here think just as you do - not a strong likeness but a pretty picture. It is only the mouth that fails. By the bye, my dear girl, I could not find a time for a bit

---

[199] Charles Brocky (already cited) came to London from Hungary in 1838 and was soon gaining commissions from influential patrons. His chalk portraits were widely admired. In 1841, the Queen saw his portrait of the Hon. Georgiana Liddell, one of her Maids of Honour, and commissioned an elegant portrait and its companion of the Prince.

of sly gossip but it was so odd that Brocky said Mr Veevean had said something about your picture & the blue walls – so he has been to see you. I am certain he is going to propose I believe [*postage stamp removed*] whatever you may think & I pray tell me about the mistresses[?] unknown.[200]. I will be secret as the Grand Inquisitor.

The weather is beyond description. Mr EHC Sheppard[?] has made me the most beautiful hood (a gift of W Clive) I ever saw. I am sure it [*illegible two lines*] grateful little being in the world. It is in my very best taste tho' I left it almost entirely to him. Fare thee well, write soon. Only think how melancholy it has been raking up from Welshpool all the baby's clothes, prepared 8 years ago & never used till now.

All her industrious preparations & now previous yellows & old fashioned for her first living child is to wear & that child motherless! Once more Goodbye,

    Ever Your most loving friend,
    Ellen Tollet.

The following letter is very long-winded but explains Ellen's guilt in feeling the happiness of looking after Minny. She would always remember with sorrow her two sisters' deaths. She moralised about her present state of mind and added that there are different kinds of family love. However, she did not reject the idea of having a husband herself though - even at her age of 28+! Had Ellen been expressing her views about marriage and childbirth too forcefully, so that Mrs Cunliffe would complain that she was turning Annabel against marriage?

Letter 31   [*cat: 319*]
Black edged letter; card case resolved; Ellen's comments on Annabel's suitors; Ellen's thoughts on her own future happiness; snub from Mrs Lister
                                   Mar[?] 29, 1841 [*from date stamp*]
To: Hon Annabel Crewe, 16 Upper Brook Street, London

Dearest Annabel,

---

[200] Intriguing.

I was so glad to get your letter for I thought it rather long in coming & I raised up a vision of influenza, etc, which was happily dissipated. I am very good writing so soon, but I happen to be in a chattery mood. First the card case is safe. Mamma had puzzled herself about it but had laid it safely in a drawer of mine.

Next I will tell you that our baby is as fat & lovely of these(? as possible. What would dear Mrs Cunliffe say if she saw her now laughing till all toothless gums are seen & making such a noise, but she is not so precocious for her age as she was at 3 weeks. One day she was very ill with a little internal disorder & we were wretched, but caster oil wrought a cure & she has improved hourly since. She now sleeps almost all night - no more of this - but don't fancy us completely absorbed in this child. Oh, no! She does not love me yet & like them [*the nurses*]; I shall not give her my heart entirely. Indeed truth to say her nurses are her great favourites.

I am sorry you thought our dear Tom (Stevens) looking ill. I fear Tom is but low & feels the separation from us most heartily. It is very flattering that it is so, but I can truly say I wish it were otherwise for his dear sake. He says he lives in a scramble at Bradfield. I am so glad you liked the drawing. He seems very much pleased himself & I long for us to serve poor Mr Vivian, I think! He has burnt his wings in the candle. Georgina rejoices in your snubbing for she conceived a great dislike to him, but pray don't let that prevent you relenting if you feel so disposed. I hope you give me credit for my sharpness about the matter.

I fear from your account that neither the ……. Lady Fanny nor Miss Ellison has made any good choices at last & so beware that you do the same. Not but what I am quite delighted that you are not married & must haste [to] hope that you may not find any one to suit you for several years. Did I tell you of the intense happiness of Miss Egerton who has received an old lover back from India twice after 12 years absence! It is a most curious affair & I believe her to be the happiest of women at the moment in spite of her many afflictions. She is very elastic in nature & it is indeed a rare piece of happiness that has befallen her.

You have heard it perhaps from Lady Hillsborough as the lover is Charles Cotton. They are to live with Lady Egerton. I liked reading your novel *Inflections* of all things, dearest A. It has been your blessed lot to desire all the benefit from the trials & experience of those around you which more thoughtless people are obliged to wail for, from their own afflictions & more heartily do, I hope, that you may pass through life with as few [*problems*] as possible.

What you say of the influence past trials have on the capability of happiness [*is*] what I feel more sharply than I can tell you. For myself I have nothing could bring back the feelings of my youth, but reason tells me that at my age some new or absent affection might do it – but I can heartily say that I am convinced that any very truly intense happiness would only bring me more suffering – that it would, as it were, disturb me & put me in a state of tumult & anxiety, that I can honestly say I do not deserve it. I don't mean to say that I always wish to be lonely as unhappy. Quite the contrary, I hope it will please God always to give me some object of interest & occupation through life, & whether they are <u>nice</u> brothers & sisters or husband & children, I am content to leave entirely in His Hands, but all I mean is that I really don't fail to wish for that state of ecstatic happiness which I was so capable of in my youth. I am so much better in spirits I can't complain. It seems extraordinary but it is in God's mercy & I am most thankful for it & not ashamed to own it. I am much better than before dear Marianne's confinement. That sad scene seemed to divert my mind from those most painful recollections, with which I was before perpetually haunted. It covers the sense of loss like seen in Carry which has changed all the current of my mind, as all my hopes & views of life cannot be said to have been lessened. But I no longer am hourly haunted by all kinds of harrowing scenes, vivid, terrible remembrances that have .... present to my niece when I lay down & when I rise up. I felt it all over as a thing some times past, a great event which had befallen me & changed me, but now is all that minute away.

Well I have proved myself the greatest of egotists but I love you to be an egotist too. G[*eorgina*] [*stamp removed*] never talks too much of Annabel Crewe to Ellen Tollet.

To change the subject to a much less interesting person than either of us, have you seen H(arriet) Lister? She has behaved so strangely. Before we went to town before Xmas, I [*wrote*] by poor M's desire to her, inviting her if she were in town to come & spend a week in Qⁿ A S^t [*Queen Anne Street*].

I received a most affectionate reply saying she could not be in town but would write to me the moment she came. Since that moment, I have never (nor Georgy) had one line from her. I found out accidentally that she was in London before Marianne was confined, but of course, would not call but we did call on Lady Theresa who returned it! So we are cut by the family, H certainly has quite done for herself with me & unless she can explain it by the treachery of the post. I will never have any dealings with her again & G[*eorgina*] is karate also. In all family events, Mr Lister has always written & he may have written now to Charles, without my knowing. He did so last Spring. It was odd that Lady T………did not return our call nor ever enquired but that is nothing to Harriet's conduct. Do tell me what you think.

Will you ask Hungerford whether there is any chance of his going to see Henrietta before he comes down here because if so I have a wicked book which I want her to lend me & be so kind as to bring it. How I wish you were coming for Easter & such a beautiful season as it is, Georgina is very well & has benefited, I am sure, by Dr Holland's advice, also for having had her mind comforted as to her complaints. However she is as well as possible, thank God, in all respects & goes on.

Your most loving friend,
Ellen Tollet

Have the problems been solved between Ellen and Annabel? The tone of the following letters has changed enormously.

Letter 32 [*cat: 296*]
Ellen fully occupied with Minny; music at Chester; Powis; Henrietta's views on miracles

Welshpool
Dec 3 1841

The Hon Annabel Crewe, Madeley Manor, Newcastle, Staffordshire
My dearest Annabel,

What with nursing & writing letters about nurses' characters, my time has been as   much occupied as if I were a married woman with 10 children or with <u>one</u> which after all is, I believe, often made quite as much a cause of occupation as the 10 according to that wise proverb which saith, "as busy as a hen with one chick." Of course, my chick is not at all pretty. Oh! dear! no! but she is very clever & has cut another tooth. She also knows where her shoes are & how to pull her own hair (& mine) & she kisses & hugs her friends & scolds strangers & is altogether a marvellous infant & more grown & improved since you saw her (Oh, friendship you came thro' the rain) than you would believe & now wishing you a happy release, I will close the subject only adding that after much turmoil we have a prospect of Mrs Buller's nurse after all, Mrs R Cavendish having released her – Amen.

Perhaps you may have seen Mamma & heard of my safe arrival in Chester where to my dismay I found myself engaged to a grand citizen party at Dean Anson's.[201] I was very much pleased with his daughter but the music was rather wearisome, indifferently sung glees which I hate particularly: "Frisky, Frisky, Listen, Listen". If you don't know it Mrs Cunliffe does.[202]

But the next evening I had real delight in having the Cathedral organist, who is a great genius & quite a gentleman, play Mozart & Beethoven's symphonies on a very fine P[*iano*] Forte at Mr Humberstone's.[203] He is to my taste one of the best players I have heard. Of course I almost lived in the Cathedral tho' I was unlucky in the anthems & altogether the singing is not yet first rate, but promises to be in time, tho' I don't fancy the Dean's taste is very high tho' he takes great delight in it.

Coming out of the Cathedral I saw the Grevilles but not to speak to. By that light I thought Emma much the handsomest. Surely they will commit suicide if allowed to remain in Chester. I can't fancy anything so dull.

I found Georgy rather low just as parting with poor Rome,[204] but she is now very well indeed & studying ferns & working hard at the Penny Club.[205] Lady Lucy is coming to help today by way of a trial for her as the good little thing likes to be useful to Cousin Clive.[206]

---

[201] Frederick Anson (1779 – 1867) was Dean of Chester Cathedral from (1839) until his death.

[202] Mrs Cunliffe was famed for her good singing voice.

[203] Probably Philip Humberstone's (1812-1891) (or his father's) house. He was a Conservative politician who was elected MP for Chester in 1859.

[204] Parting from the Catholic Church not the city.

[205] Possibly a penny-a-week for medical treatment, or a Penny Bank.

[206] Lady Lucy, in her teens, was from Walcot Hall in Shropshire, and acting as a nanny/governess. (See *Journals*.)

I skilfully escaped a mortal dull dinner at the Castle. Lady Powis & Charlotte were out but there was horrid Lady Caroline & a rather silly Miss Cornwallis & I had said all I could think of to the latter in 2 morning visits. It was thing to beware of, was it not?

Have you read Miss Sedgwick's *Letters from Abroad?*[207] I think they are very amusing.

We had such an odd dinner the other day about 12 clergy (a clerical meeting) all talking Welshy but happily. One out of the set was very clever, original, amusing man so I made him talk & that did for the whole twelve. No doubt he thought all his listeners very agreeable people.

I have been vaccinated as the small pox is about very much. I don't know yet when it will take effect.

A Miss Mytton has been staying here 2 days. She is not very young but still good looking – to be sure she lives by herself & may happily be called an old maid. I hope her separation will not suffer. You see I can't forget her moral lessons I have received. It is a great blessing to have such a correct friend as I have being myself only a prude in one particular line!

Your most amusing letter is just arrived & I shall keep this till tomorrow that I may add our safe remarks on Henrietta – "Tollet on Crewe on miracles." What she says of there being as much evidence to prove the facts as is considered enough to prove things in general is the very answer that I made for her in arguing over with myself. But if you observe she only dwells on 2 points: the existence of those <u>appearances</u> & the question of supernatural or not, which she professes to think an <u>open</u> question. The idea of <u>imposture</u> she evidently can't for one moment entertain & this seems to be the chief difference between her & ourselves for I am sure I believe Lord Shrewsbury did <u>see</u> all the sights he describes – but only doubt whether there were not some subtle impostors.

What she says about all miracles is at first startlingly Protestant "not obliged to believe any but those recorded in scripture." But dare a Catholic believe that there is pretence or imposture in the liquefying of St Januarius' blood[208] or any other of their miracles? I should think that would be heterodox. As long as the Church permits the public exhibition of such

---

[207] *Letters from Abroad to Kindred at Home* by Catharine Sedgwick (1812–1891).

[208] St Januarius was famous for the supposed annual liquefaction of his blood, which was kept in an ampoule in Naples Cathedral. The blood was supposed to liquefy three times a year.

miracles, she must believe in their authenticity & begging his pardon I rather doubt whether the presumption to believe in none but scripture miracles would be so easily granted at Rome, as perhaps it may be at Prior Park! The question of natural causes for miracles strikes me at the very root because the <u>natural</u> cause is known by the priest & concealed from the people; it immediately becomes imposture.

You can't think how amusing your letter was. I saw the little Queen with a face flushed blue scratching at the names after that horrid piece, impertinence.

It is Sunday morning & I must conclude. I am not at all affronted at H[*enrietta*]'s criticisms. I am aware of the danger & trust providence will preserve the little brain but as you know the nature of the child was shown at a fortnight old. I am convinced it would be perfectly possible to prevent her being so very lively – I think walking out for hours every day alone with her nurse is a good remedy. Her passion for me is quite ludicrous & without my speaking to her she screams & laughs at me & even will talk to my legs under the table when she can't see my face. But I try to sit very loose to her & often try to fancy her ill & lying dead. But I pray God to preserve her if only for her father's sake. The girls at the castle doat[209] upon her & she is very fond of them. Our best love to you both, dearest A.

Your most affectionate,
EHT

The tension between the friends has changed; Ellen was more relaxed.

Letter 33 [*cat: 294*]
A humorous letter about Minny; London with the Clives; painting; V's poetry; fashion

[*from Welshpool?*]
Jan 1842

Most dear & excellent Annabel,

What a capital correspondent you have been, sending me that nice long budget from Brighton. I cannot be ungrateful & indeed it is a treat to chatter to you & here I am in solitude for an hour or two while the child is out of doors & asleep.

---

[209] Obsolete spelling of dote.

What shall I begin with – historical recollections I think & then proceed to Literary Notices "the Arts" & "Births, Deaths & Marriages.[210] Well, I came here nearly a fortnight ago to finish the weaning & I expected the baby would hardly know me. Instead of which she showed the most rapturous joy at seeing me, hugged me, kissed me, screamed, & kicked & showed me to her nurses, smacking her lips to show how she kissed me & for the first 2 or 3 days could hardly be made to leave me. She is now settled down into a state of calm admiration. I never was so adored before & it made me feel very sad to feel the love which could have been hers [*Marianne's*], to whom it would have given such perfect happiness was lavished. Oh me, who can only desire a very mixed enjoyment from it! However I am truly thankful to see the child looking so robust, such a colour & so strong & well & the weaning is over & she is so amusing & clever to a ridiculous degree. Of course she is not pretty – no really not a regular beauty but so bright & intelligent & such an exquisite figure that she passes for a striking looking child & she has a power of fascinating people quite wonderfully. The shyness is gone.

Well, we go to Betley next week & stay there till May when I propose going on my travels. I think your hit at me & my set was a very fine retort after my skit at you & yours – but, my dear child, I can never be in any set that will console me not seeing you, the friend of my heart, so meet we must, & only you know I can't come rattling in a green fly to Brook St, & have "Not at home" pronounced by the long Footman's that's all, & I shan't expect you to come rolling in your coach to Gower St to call & have " not at home" squeaked in your ears by the maid (footman being out) but we must write notes & understand each other. I call on my "*Voyage en Orient*" & perhaps I shall publish "*Oriental Tales*" in the style of *The Mirza* [*1841*].[211]

---

[210] Ellen was probably referring to *The Times* to which they almost certainly subscribed.

[211] Refers to a three-volume work by James Justinian Morier (1780–1849), who was a diplomat and novelist. He married Harriet Greville (1789–1858), and they had a son Greville Morier (1831–1867). The name Morier occurs frequently in these letters. After his death, his wife Harriet with her son lived with Henrietta Crewe (see Census Return, Appendix 2).

12. *Archdeacon William Clive,
father of Minny.*

W Clive is going to London for a short time to Berkeley Square, & I shall make him useful tho' he is not so "knock–aboutable" [*sic*] a man as Tom, but I think I shall get him to come too, to his friend David Watts Russell's [*1812–1879*] who has invited him & then I shall do well! Well now, dearest, I want to know whether you are going to have any lessons from Dewint[212] because I have a wish that way myself & I think I could manage to go to him if he will take new pupils. Perhaps if he requires pressing, I could get him pressed by Powys people who are great allies of his. Doesn't he live 'en orient'? If you don't mean to have him, is there anyone else you have a fancy for that would do me any good, but there are few masters worth much? I am certain I want to draw from nature a good deal this summer & should like some help. Please to answer this when you write. Georgina wrote to enquire after Mr Lister (a short note) & there came a very long affectionate answer from Henrietta [*Annabel's sister*]. The account she gave did not dissuade me and to us seem quite satisfactory - so very slow & recovering from a complaint on the lungs would …….. him, but I trust he

---

[212] An English landscape artist (1784–1849).

is going on better now. How much affliction that family have had yet mingled with so much prosperity!

Oh! I think we agree wonderfully in our thoughts on V.[213]

By the bye, does not the title strike you as very bad & likely to be parodied into "I watched the H C"?[214] I have written her a long letter full of our criticisms & hope for an answer which I will send you & told her that Mrs C[*unliffe*] would not commit herself. I have read Mrs Sedgwick & was very much amused. The Wedgwoods say that she has behaved very ill in quite endangering some of those political men in Italy by what she has published & of course they laugh very much at her anecdotes of Sismondi & *"je te remercie, ma chere."*

I was amused at Lady Powys liking it so much. I should have thought it much too free & easy for her. Have you read the book of books Stephen's *Central America [1842]*? I have seen it & think it really is the most wonderful & interesting & curious book of travel that I can remember.

I forgot to say a propos to V that I never read Dante & don't think that I ever shall, but Georgina does not think there is any plagiarism & that the subject is treated as differently as it can be, but I quite agree with you that it was very amusing to choose such a subject.

Buzz[215] has been dining at Betley & they thought him not as lively as usual, but Georgina says she is sure that in spite of any sentimentality he may have, he is in reality looking out for a little money as he seemed quite curious when she told him there is a Mr Marsh [*Caldwell?*] whom he knows a little, was going to marry Miss Edwards with some hundreds[216] & now a few more to come & wish you were present.

---

[213] Mary Wicksted's sister, Mrs Archer Clive.

[214] The title was "I watched the heavens" by V. Under the title *IX Poems* it was published in 1840. It was much discussed, and even compared with Dante's masterpiece.

[215] The similar sobriquet *Boz* was used for Charles Dickens (1812–1870), whose father spent his childhood in Crewe Hall. His grandfather William Dickens (?–1785) was the butler to the first Baron Crewe, and his grandmother, Elizabeth (?–1824), was the housekeeper. On becoming widowed she remained there as housekeeper (see Gladden (2011), p.30).

[216] Was G going to publish in *Household Words*?

My compliments to Mrs White & ask her to be so good as to send me the pattern of a fashionable long sleeve. I want a silk gown done up by Morton [*servant*] before I leave home. I shall bring my pink beauty to be done in London. I don't object to light sleeves if they are really worn, but I think they require a nice epaulette. What beautiful weather. I fear they will not be so fine.

A friend of mine writes the word that nothing was ever so pretty as *Thoughts on Past Years* by Williams [*1838*], the Oxford man. She says it is like Wordsworth & Keble which certainly survived & is very fine. Of course it must be very Puseyistic,[217] but she does not say anything about that. She is Miss Bagot, one of those people who enjoy reading never more than it is possible to describe & who, living alone, with a very old but clever mother, finds it her great amusement & solace. She is very nice indeed & so fond of me but very assured & stiff in her nature - so many years older, that I can't really intimate – she writes folios.

Farewell, dearest A.

[*PS*]   Penelope is gone into Hampshire.[218] Having a baby at Betley is as great a pleasure as my present state of existence is capable of affording & I must try to make the most of it. It will be pleasant to see my mother's surprise & delight in her little tom fool of a grandchild & I expect G papa's room will be the Great Gentry Tour, I hope even my poor dear, darling, melancholy Georgy will be stunned by the baby's smiles.[219] Augusta Vaughan is coming to join us.

Best love to Aunt. Your most affectionate,

EHT

Letter 34   [*cat: 297*]
Gift of a dress; French revolution; date check from Marianne's funeral
Feb 1842

To: Hon Annabel Crewe, 16 Upper Brook St, Grosvenor Square, London

---

[217] A derogatory term for the Oxford Movement.
[218] To see Florence Nightingale.
[219] Was Georgy still depressed?

My Dearest Annabel

I must thank you for the beautiful gown I received yesterday. It is really a most beautiful pink, the first blush of Aurora or something of that kind. I shall wear it & value it & love it for your dear sake, but I must have my laugh, in spite of my gratitude at your recommending 7 widths. I have always 7 of silk & one gown with 8 & thanks to your noble number of yards, I shall have 8 in my sweet pink & with my crinoline beneath it. Who shall say that I am not 1/2 a mile round - my slender waist will look quite dangerous. I think & I fear I shall be accused of tight lacing! Well dearest, your letter was so pleasant & the little soirées & matinees sounded so pleasant that I was very near wishing myself a London lady like you, but on reflection remembered that I should have most likely gone very chatteracious[*sic*] & frivolous or then very cross & disappointed not having half the natural sobriety that you have. Talking of sobriety reminds me of Sidney.

Thank you for the very good account of the VR affair. It is wonderful how people can go on being so merry & dressing up year after year! The most odd coincidence is that I feel sure we know about the Mr & Mrs Hampton you met at the Grevilles. His father & mother were vulgar people who once lived near my father & mother in Gloucestershire & afterwards he met them all one year at Beaumaris where they have a place. This, I think, is the eldest son, a dark moustached youth, who was then in the army, afterwards married. I do think they are the same. Your description was excellent. Your news of the Dyce Sombre was really horrid.[220] Was there ever such a marriage as that? Mr Wicksted is returned & left Mrs V [*his sister-in-law*] very well & nursing little & very industriously – moreover she has produced a twin - at least in the Press – a poem *a L'inferno* at least I suppose from Mary's account. I am sorry for I doubt whether it will add to the fame attained by the *9 Poems*, at least it is a risk of perhaps improving it, which seems a pity. It has been written a long time ago.

The children were quite well before their mother returned. I suppose they will all move off next week. Penelope is going on her tour or circuit the week after Easter & I shall still talk of mine for May but it is very

---

[220] See Letter 23 for reference to Dyce Sombre.

uncertain indeed. We have wholesale invitations from the Nightingales. P will be a few days in London at the Wedgwoods but you will not see her – she is determined to be incognito & to call on no-one. She then goes to Lady Bloomfield's at Woolwich[221] & then into Hants, not to the Nightingales but to the Haygarths. I hope she will enjoy herself but she misses the baby here, which I wonder she can do. We have had a great many books lately & I have read the 3rd vol. of *Patchwork*[222] which I really like in spite of hating Capt Hall, but the most interesting is Smyth's *Lectures on the French Revolution*.[223]

I believe an old thing but new to me. Have you an insatiable interest in the Fr Rev? There are 2 or 3 subjects that I profess myself tired of, yet never could help reading anything I see about them & that is one. I shall always be able to spare a tear for Marie Antoinette if I live to be a 100. I have also begun a very readable novel – *Susan Hopley*.[224]

I hardly dare tell you what Spring weather we have. It is really indescribable – wind SSW, sun brilliant. Still a walk in Hyde Park is very pleasant & I dare say it has done very well for you this morning.

I wonder you thought of us on Ash Wednesday. It was the 9th & our baby's birthday & also Ash Wednesday last year was the day of her mother's funeral. It brought indeed sad recollections to us but so does every day. From this time till the middle of May is filled with sad anniversaries in our family history -but I dare not think of the past; I can only say "Lead kindly light; lead thou me on."

I have been poorly & made it an opportunity of some dosing which has done me great good & I am now better than usual & building myself strong again with some bitters.[225] How are the headaches? We see in the papers

---

[221] Lady Bloomfield was a family friend, as mentioned when they were in Malvern.

[222] *Patchwork* (1841) by Basil Hall.

[223] William Smyth (1765-1849) was a poet and historian: he was Regius Professor at Cambridge.

[224] *Susan Hopley*, or *The Adventures of a Maid-Servant* (1841) by Catherine Crowe (1803–1876).

[225] Herbal remedies.

Lord & Lady Crewe for Brighton!![226] I hope there is no scandal![227] Did you see an account of Miss Rathbone at Bath being poisoned? She was Tom's cousin & and only daughter, only 24!! Darling Georgy is looking so well & lovely. I rejoice to say a little more cheery, than she has been. Our best love to dear Mrs Aunt & believe me, your most loving & grateful friend,

E H Tollet

Letter 35 *[cat: 295]*
Letter writing; Hungerford's unusual mind; analysis of V's poem; Buzz visits Betley; future visit to the Darwins; gossip

Betley Hall,
Monday before Easter March 21st 1842

To: Hon Annabel Crewe, 16 Upper Brook St, London

Dearest Annabel,

Your last letter deserves best thanks. It was a great treat & it had, what I consider, the greatest perfection a letter can possess - that of giving one the idea that it was a pleasure to the writer to write it as well as the reader to read it. Don't you know what I mean? I have a very quiet time today for trying to pay you in kind, for a little dose has made Church impossible to me & all the rest are there, it being Monday in Passion Week as I suppose you know!

I have many sad reasons for sad thoughts at this season & am never likely to forget to mourn during Lent even without the assistance of Henrietta's sackcloth & ashes.[228] Well, how are you both? You give a famous account of yourself, but Hungerford mentioned Mrs C being rather poorly - but I hope it was only a passing ail that she was a little weary. But really he was so brilliant yesterday when he dined here that you would have been quite edified. We all agreed we never saw him at all equal to it & he

---

[226] There is not a Lady Crewe; so who is Hungerford's companion? More likely to have been a newspaper error.

[227] The newspaper must be referring mischievously to Hungerford and one of his sisters.

[228] This seemed to be an unkind reference again to the Roman Catholicism of Annabel's sister.

looked so happy. I really thought he must be going to be married. He was very full of the Queens of England & is so knowing about the dates, so it

13. Lord Hungerford Crewe, with Crewe Hall in the background.

brought out so many bits of knowledge that we were quite awe-struck at his learning! It is really perfectly ridiculous the way he varies, for the other day when he called he went meandering on about a doctor in such a way Mamma & I thought he was odder than ever.

Well I have 2 letters from V & she has sent *"I watched the Heavens"* as a present to us & we have read it.[229] It is a bold thing to criticise before one has heard a single soul speak of it. I don't think it will injure her fame, tho'

---

[229] See Letter 33.

it is open to more criticism than *9 Poems*. There are beautiful bits in it, but I hate horrors & always think it is a way to be clever very cheaply, & disagreeable to describe them. The opening I admire much. The description

---

I Watch'd the Heavens, a poem by V

Stanza I

I watch'd the heav'ns above me, and a star
Appear'd before my meditative eyes;
I mark'd the solitary beam afar
Pursue its journey in th' eternal skies.
Calm from its distant glory, came the rays
Through all of space between us, on my gaze;
No other signs of those who dwelt therein
Fell on my sense, except that beam serene;
And fancy, soothed beneath the streaming light,
Pursued the orb along its high career,

And deem'd it some new world, all fresh and bright
With its ten thousand hopes, and not one fear.

From the first lines the reader can see that V's attempts to write an epic poem were doomed to failure and ridicule. She was not a second Dante.

---

of the lovers it, I think, borders on the ridiculous, but I can't help thinking the idea of them all playing as being dead rather fine. Mamma is so amusing about it. She can't view it merely as a fancy, but thinks there is an intended moral in it to show that many people besides the very wicked will go to a bad place. The stanza about the sucking child must have been tacked on, since V commenced maternity herself – it is so very graphic, quite coarsely so I think; now all this is merely to make you send me (& soon too, or we shall forget & not care) your Mrs C's criticisms on the said poem. She

(Caroline) sends good accounts of the son and heir[230] & Mary & Charles have been helping to christen him.

Poor dear 'Buzz'. I weep for his saviour & I am so unlucky he is coming they say next week.

I am going on Monday to Welshpool for a fortnight & bring the duck (Minny) here to stay till May. I will now tell you a piece of news which I can't answer for the rejoicing so very much –which is that I have had a most kind invitation from dear Emma Darwin, to visit her.[231] I intend to go if possible with W Clive up to London in May & go with him to Bradfield[232] & visit Emma [*Darwin*]. But you know it is the oriental region of Bedford Square & therefore if you do call upon me, I shall consider it an act of heroism. [*Following comment added by Ellen*] I think a Buzzian friend in Gower[233] – that will be a capital bow to a fine lady friendship.

I hope she [*Emma Darwin*] will be well enough to enjoy me, but I don't care for her & her husband, being both rather sickly, we shall be quiet & comfortable & intellectual, if the 2 children don't prevent it. My Nightingale scheme is uncertain as they seem to think they may not go into the country at Whitsuntide.[234]

Rev Justin Edwards is going to be married to Miss Heathcote, rather a wild mannered young lady and daughter of Mr Heathcote & poor Lady Elizabeth – He is the very bad character & married since a housemaid with whom he had laid for years. It is something of a case like you & Mrs Vivian. Georgina is almost angry with me because I am not the least vexed. If I had the least wished to marry him myself, I should not have been vexed very, but as I never did, I don't feel anything, except how much suited he is

---

[230] Caroline [*Wigley*] (1801-1872) was in her late 30s when she married the Rev Archer Clive. It seemed unusual then to have a child at that age.

[231] Emma Darwin (1808–1896) from Maer Hall, a daughter of Josiah Wedgwood, was a close friend of Ellen (see *Journals*). She married Charles Darwin in 1839. Surprisingly, this is the first reference to Emma (in 1842) in these letters. Shortly afterwards they moved to Down House where they raised 10 children, which probably accounts for them being 'sickly'.

[232] To see Tom Stevens, his brother-in-law.

[233] Part of London?

[234] Ellen stayed with Florence Nightingale in 1842 when she was ill. (Claydon House Archive, bundle 369, letter from Georgina)

to Miss H's taste than to mine. All the world here think it is a most strange marriage on account of his being such a very strict clergyman, but I see it all in a different way.

Poor Mr Lister – I hope he is really getting well. I think G must enquire after him.

Thanks for the notes which we thought not worth returning. There is not a word of truth about A L & Mr Rich, for Miss Philips asked her poor dear Desdemona – she will certainly never escape from Othello's rage if she stays with him. You say you have lost your heart to Milman.[235] I remember being struck with his appearance at Babbage's but I don' think I could very much like him - I dislike his German-ish theology so much & his histories, tho' so clear are so irreverent in their style. His wife is very pretty. At least I have seen a very pretty Mrs Milman. You say 'like man is not the Mirza – very dull.' I say, could you suppose me, dear, and support me as to read it? I just opened it & thought that if it were written by my dear husband I could not have read it, so horribly childish & stupid.

Who was the very agreeable neighbour at Montefiore's? I demand his name. Have you read Miss Martineau's "*Playfellow*"?[236] *The Feats on the Fiord* is very pretty & I have the Crofton boys highly praised by all the wise people. Have you read *Proverbial Philosophy* by Martin Farquhar Tupper?[237] Mrs Davenport gave it to G & we are very fond of it. Tell Mrs C with my love that our singing goes so well & we have attempted a chant with good success; I have some difficulties with pronunciation. To is always Tu & Through – Threw.

Tell her also that I suppose Tom is bribing her with Apples, not to accuse him of Heresy. I think she must have thought it an inconsistency in him providing her with a feast for Lent.

I have not much good material for letters as you have, so you must excuse my infirmity. Papa is quite well again, I am thankful to say. Farewell with abundance of love from all, believe me, Dearest A,

---

[235] Henry Hart Milman (1791-1868) was an historian and ecclesiastic.

[236] As an addition to a previous reference to Harriet Martineau, she also wrote the *Playfellow* Series (1841) and *The Feats on the Fiord* for children.

[237] Martin Tupper (1810-1889) was an English writer, and poet, and the author of *Proverbial Philosophy*.

your faithful & affectionate,
    Ellen Tollet

Letter 36   [*cat: 314*]
Hungerford going abroad after renovating Crewe Hall; looking after
children; Tom Stevens and William Clive as brothers-in-law; comment about
politics

Shakenhurst
July 22nd   1842
To: Hon Annabel Crewe, 16 Upper Brook St, Grosvenor Square

Dearest dear Annabel,
    Before I begin upon other subjects I must thank you for your letter &
say how truly glad we were of your informed accounts. I feel very sanguine

14. Shakenhurst, the home of Charles and Mary Wicksted.

as to the good that Brighton will do & also the German tour if you really
find a desirable companion. The scheme of wintering abroad surprises us,
as it does not appear that there is any complaint to render a warm climate
necessary. On the contrary bracing seems required.[238] It appears so bad I

---

[238] It did not seem tactful to try to influence the Crewe family's plans.

think for mind & consequently for body in the end to fly from house & home duties & it seems such a July that after all the expense & trouble at Crewe that he should not live there & enjoy it,[239] & enjoy it one should think he would, with you & the Cunliffe's news to enliven his solitude. Indeed now the house is inhabitable it need not be solitude, if he liked to have people. But perhaps he wishes much to winter abroad. Does he seem to have anything particular on his mind or is it only general depression from languor etc? Poor dear Henrietta, I can imagine his distress & anxiety but I can readily understand there being objections to her being with Hungerford. I must now tell you of us & our affairs.

I have nothing very bright to write about. I don't know that I ever felt more low without any actual cause for particular anxiety about any one of our family, who are all well at this moment, but I suppose the loss of the employment, to kind thoughts & affection & which has been affecting them for 5 months by our own sweet baby is natural cause to account for the difficulty I feel in keeping up my spirits to a proper pitch. Indeed I do make valiant exertions & you may believe they are necessary.

When I tell you we have had 9 children in this house for the last week & often all together in one room & sometimes when my heart has been sinking, wicked me, I have had to rouse & join in some game or play our piano for the first time for a year & for these young creatures to dance!! To explain this extraordinary influx of young things, I must tell you this. Mary has kindly [brought] before July on these poor unfortunate children of our old dear friend Mr Allington. The widower has just now remarried disgracefully, as she sent for 4 of them (besides 2 nephews of her own) & the 2 girls stay some time longer & then come to Betley. They are very good & one of them charming but backward in education & I have actually begun to correct [with] exercises & to make crooked drawings straight & what is much worse try to make wrong notes right. Their mother was the best & dearest of women & I can never forget her love for our dear Eliza nor her kindness to her when we visited her in Grosvenor St, so I am determined to do what I can - but the eldest girl is rather fat & dull & with my irritability permanent, I am sure I shall sometimes feel disposed to box

---

[239] Hungerford employed the architect Edward Blore to refurbish the Hall.

her ears when she plays 6 semiquavers, each in different times. I suppose they will in time be here & at 5yr 2 months or more.

Well dearest, you ask about our parting, [*with Minny*] you may think we baptised her with tears, precious pet. There never was anything like her intellect. She is the most 'spirituable' baby. There is a sentiment in her large blue eyes quite indescribable; she is as much a companion as many at 2 years old, & oh alas! Her father begins to seem restive about leaving her a month with us this autumn & this is a deep well. In short, my dear A, never fix your heart on other people's children if you can help it. One's feelings are so much more like a mother's than one's position can ever be.

The boys here are very nice & the baby magnificent, George [*Wicksted*] is amusing. Yesterday he said he should like joining the Allingtons at Betley. "It will be better than their staying on here. You know they'll be so fresh," What a blasé youth!

I think it is a very bad thing all these beaten Whigs flying abroad[240] – it looks like shame or even an attempt to punish the Country!

You must write me a little bit just to say how Brighton answers & then I hope soon after that we shall meet & talk - of everything, every one of my few pleasures in this life. I think your favourite Charley [*Wicksted*] is a degree less ugly than he used to be, but still very plain.

You ask after dear Tom [*Stevens*]. Alas I sadly fear we may not see him this autumn. He is so occupied; his father is much the same but the apoplexy seems as if it might return at any moment. Tom always asks after you & Mrs Cunliffe & I think I told you that Charles & William went to visit him & they were both quite delighted with Bradfield. Charles of course declared that no one had ever told him how it was pretty but that was, only because he had [*hole caused by stamp removal*]. Tom had tried to drown care by being very busy in farming & I am thankful he has any reserves to cheer his sad, sad life. I always thought that W Clive would have been as much to be pitied as Tom but it is not the case. I am [*hole*] to be sure he is so much

---

240 'Whigs flying abroad' The government was seemingly unaware of the poverty and widespread hardship of the population caused by high food prices. Ellen, a Whig, was aware that nothing was being done, and politicians were being irresponsible.

more assured that one knows less of his sufferings, but I am sure also that they have not been nearly so acute. I hope I may in time see poor Tom married again which after all is with young people the only way through which happiness can return. Few people have ever lost such an angel as he did but I know he feels he had rather have had the blessing & lose it, than not have had it. Farewell, dearest.

We go home on Friday 30th.

Your most affectionate,

EHTollet

Letter 37   [*cat: 298*]

Problem in the friendship? perhaps Mrs Cunliffe feels Ellen is being too critical; dancing on carpets; Castle in Scotland; Wedgwoods; reading; Picturesque movement; visiting Down

Saturday, May 20, 1843

The Hon Annabel Crewe, 16 Upper Brook Street, London

My dearest Annabel,

You ask for an immediate answer & I am quite willing to give you one for I feel quite eager to talk to you again. Your letter makes me fancy you very pleasant with health to bear in your London life and be delightful as long as you keep from very hot dances on carpets & indeed for my taste, all Balls might be omitted but seeing all your acquaintances & getting pleasant talks as you seem to do would be a very amusing way of spending our <u>small</u> portion of this life.

How inadvertently I have flattered the Squire of Keel by leading you to call him the <u>He</u> of Staffordshire, I think the highest compliment one can pay a man is to call him "He"& I am sure your friendship to him is as normal as mine was unintentional. I am charmed to hear that your aunts are both so well & blooming.

We are all prospering. Charles & Mary are gone for a fortnight to look at the Aberdeenshire Castle & we fully expect to hear of their having been moved up, such bitter cold weather have we had in this south country. William & his child have been a week at Styche but come here again today. Rob[ert] C[live] went with the Wicksteds & the Archer[Clive]s were to be

found at Abergeldie.[241] Fancy her impudence being in an interesting state &
having fears of mischance. But she knows she can do whatever she likes in
this world & if I were she & had compassed marrying Archer, I dare say, I
should think the same. As it is, I swear I have none of that comfortable
confidence, have you?

This leads me very much to doubt if I shall be able to accomplish my
southern expedition & truth to say I should not break my heart if I did not.
Emma Darwin wants me to come as soon as I can & I am looking out for
an escort for the very first days of June in time to go straight to Down near
Bromley only sleeping one night in London. On my return I shall probably
stay a little while with one or two friends who will have me but all this is
very uncertain for Mr Wedgwood of Maer's state is such that his increased
illness or death may put an end to the plan at any moment. [242]

Wm Clive & the child stay here till quite the end of the month & I will
not miss a day of them if I can help it. What a crowd of rejected lovers
greeted your arrival! And I can see you are now getting quite spiteful against
Mr Crockery.[243] I think Sir F Doyle seems rather up in the world.[244] Mr
Joseph Ridgeway's marriage I saw in the paper. It sounds rather <u>cottony</u>
[*soft*], but it is much better than being gloomy like Mrs Wynn's. My dear,
what a very singular circumstance that you should ask me whether I had
read Price on *The Picturesque*.[245] It was perpetually talked about &
recommended to us by our friends, Mr Winder & Mr Lyon & it was the
very book that the latter offered to send me & never did (to my unutterable

---

[241] They stayed in Abergeldie Castle on the River Dee near Balmoral in
Scotland. The visit was also referred to by Caroline Clive [Clive 1948, p 163]. The
Wicksteds and Clives had rented the castle for a year at a cost of 500 guineas. From
May 10th, 1842, the Clives took a week to reach Abergeldie, spent 9 days there and
spent a week returning. They sailed from Liverpool to Inverary and travelled by
coach from there (over 130 miles). They returned by ship from Aberdeen to
Edinburgh. The castle was seriously affected by recent flooding of the River Dee.

[242] Mr J Wedgwood II died in 1843.

[243] Ellen's humorous nickname for Mr Wedgwood.

[244] Sir Francis Hastings Charles Doyle, 2nd Baronet (1810 – 1888) was an
English poet.

[245] Sir Uvedale Price (1747–1829) was the author of an *Essay on the Picturesque*
(1794 and 1842).

disgust). Well when we come home the first book we got accidentally from our Society, was the new edition by Sir Tho Dick Lander[246] (having as it proves the old edition in our own Library!) Of course we set to read it & were exceedingly amused. The vignettes are so pretty & tho' he must have been quite an oddity; his taste is delightful. Did not you think Sir TDL's additions very troubling? Of course you have had Payne Knight on *Taste*.[247] I don't care for many of Price's dissertations on the beautiful & the picturesque but I like his practical landscape gardening so very much- I have been very deep in the *Last of the Barons*[248] & it is very interesting, tho' there are disappointing bits in it, as Bulwer always contrives to have.

I am glad to hear of Caroline Cunliffe's engagement she must be quite delighted at your Aunt's kindness.[249] I think when I am once there, I shall enjoy the Darwins' society extremely. It will be perfectly quiet but a new county & pleasant friends will be quite enough for me, but I feel rather lazy about setting out on my own if I can't persuade G to go too. Perhaps it is better she should not as she will be company for Mamma & Penelope. She is, thank God, in very good spirits tho' I hope & trust not too much so. How I feel that you understand & enter into every feeling of my heart on this subject. My dear, dear friend & indeed now I think you & I have hardly any friends from each other & as regards this of G's, I am sure dear Mrs Cunliffe is as mindful as you are. All I can hope and pray is that she may be preserved from suffering even if she is not to be made happy. Farewell with best of love,
your most affectionate,

Ellen Tollet

Letter 38   [*cat: 280*]
Ellen unwell; whooping cough; promotion to Archdeacon of William Clive; illness of Betley children

---

[246] Author of *Landscape Design*.
[247] Richard Payne Knight (1751-1824) connoisseur of taste, archaeologist and Member of Parliament.
[248] *The Last of the Barons* (1843), a historical novel by Edward Bulwer-Lytton.
[249] A niece of Annabel's aunt, Mrs Cunliffe.

19th Feb, 1844

To: The Hon. Annabel Crewe, 16 Upper Brook Street, Grosvenor Square, London

My dearest Annabel,

I willingly obey your commands of writing to you soon & comfort myself for having but few materials by the reflection that sometimes letters all about nothing are just as satisfactory to one's friends as any others. You are entered upon your gay season. Friendship is out and lovers is in for 1844.

Your letter was really a very naughty one with so many coarse allusions & as to your fancies about my postscript note truly only shows how far a wild imagination will lead people far, far away from all probabilities indeed. You said this was a shade of gloom over my last letter. I can most honestly say it was caused certainly by my not feeling well – indeed I was much the worse of will & now I am grown old that is the difference I find in my spirits; they never need to be cast down by poorliness, tho' I used to have far more of that than I have now – but now I feel low & sad – it is very humbling to feel virtue like cheerfulness dependent on a mere physical cause! But all that is past & I am quite well.

These were the best reasons for my saying nothing of those people you enquire about [*whom*] we had not met. We have now heaven & everything is just as it was in the Autumn but it is nothing but friendship I suppose. How amused & yet amazed you would have been at the Fete yesterday. At breakfast came notes of invites from a Mrs Fiedler to dine there on Wednesday next. To dinner came Mr Clive & when Mr Winder began: "I want to persuade you & your sister & Clive to dine with us," I trusted it would be on Wednesday & so it proved!

Today William has received notice from the B(ishop?) that he is to be appointed Archdeacon of Montgomery immediately.[250] It will be good for him to have a cannonry of St Asaph attached to it, which will entail a residence of 2 or 3 months at St A. It will be 300 a year[251] & some more

---

[250] William was made Archdeacon in 1844.
[251] Assume this means £300 pa.

work but not perhaps a great deal as he has always been Rural Dean. Must be droll to hear him called Mr Archdeacon – but he will look beautiful in a shovel hat.[252] The clergy are delighted at the appointment, we are told. I send you a note I had the other day f(rom) V.[253]

I wish you had enough of her former charade & antipathies for your folly to relish the account of the baby - I am glad to hear of Jessie Greville's marriage which I have done f(rom) all quarters. I hope it will really come to pass. I suppose you have heard nothing more of Crockery since the last frump.[254]

I must tell you of Minny's first speech to me this morning & said, "Aunty Nelly. I've got a birthday & I have had some toast & I am a big girl." It is indeed the darling's birthday, a solemn day of reflection to us & still more to her father but he said to G this morning, if we make such an idol of that child what would she [*Marianne*] have done! It is indeed a sweet thing. The first day the snow fell she ran to the window & said, "Oh Papa, I am afraid the snow will put out all of the pretty flowers." Was it not practical the idea of the snow extinguishing the flowers?

We have good accounts for Betley tho' they have a had disappointment in Mary & her children having been prevented coming by colds & return of (w)hooping cough but I hope they will yet come during our absence as it will amuse my mother so much to have them.

Georgina is, you will be glad to hear, looking uncommonly well & in surprisingly good spirits, considering that she has been so completely laid low after being taken up, but he does look so old & is, I am sure, such a confirmed old bachelor that it consoles us. I shan't care a bit when I flopped down which is to be expected shortly. I will not fail to let you know directly. Today we met another set of people to eat up the remains of

---

[252] A broad-brimmed hat worn by clergymen as befits an Archdeacon.

[253] There is a current link with St Margaret's Betley. Barry Wilson who was Vicar at Madeley and Betley churches, subsequently Rector at St Mary's Nantwich and Vice-Dean of Chester Cathedral, has recently been appointed Archdeacon of Montgomery in the Diocese of St Asaph, the same post as that occupied by William Clive.

[254] Mr Wedgwood!

yesterday's feast. I release your injunction and write soon[255] & with our best love to you both – am your most affectionate friend,   Ellen Tollet

Letter 39   [*cat: 301*]
Religion; health; Henrietta's Roman Catholicism & the Bishop's death; Mr Milnes; Queen's minuets; child rearing

Welshpool
June 10, 1844

To: The Hon Annabel Crewe, Upper Brook St, Grosvenor Square, London

Shall I return Henrietta's letter - I have got it safe? [*Crossed out*]
My dearest Annabel,
    Your last few lines enclosing poor H's letter reached me just as we were moving from Betley. We were indeed truly grieved to hear of this bad affliction having befallen her. It is such a melancholy addition to the great loss she had in the Bishop.[256] It really seems as if she were to be quite rooted up & left alone as far as her Catholic friends are concerned & of course, we know that to her they must be a value which even her oldest Protestant ever cannot supply the loss of. I am sure I feel as if I could have almost entire sympathy with a good Roman Catholic, because a person believing rather more than you do is no great annoyance, but in the second case it is quite different as I confess I feel most painfully with my Unitarian friends,[257] whom I love so much & who love me so warmly & yet there is a gulph [*obsolete spelling*)] between us & my feelings are doubly wounded & my mind disturbed & harassed by their doubts & infidelities. It seems hard to us that the RC's should feel this with regard to us, who so entirely believe those grand doctrines, but so it is at least with Henrietta, I am sure. And all this makes us nervous for her most heartily, but I feel she has really a spirit of submission to the Divine Will & this must comfort her. Georgy wrote a

---

[255] The two friends must have agreed to write at certain intervals.
[256] Bishop Peter Baines b 1787, d 4 July, 1843, was of the Benedictine Order at Prior Park. He had established a Roman Catholic College there, supported financially to a large degree by Henrietta, who lived for some time at Prior Park.
[257] The Wedgwoods.

few lines to her immediately but we can't expect her to write yet so we must depend on you for further intelligence.

Now let me thank you for your most entertaining amusing letter. I feel so incapable of answering it, leading as I do a life which allows no materials for making itself amusing, tho' one very suited to my strength of body & mind. This leads me to tell you that I am wonderfully improved. I have done with Locock's pills having taken 120 or 30.[258] I believe they agreed very well but I think the return to cold bathing has done more for me.[259] Soda I have quite excluded. I am certainly fatter and tho' my back is far from well but it is better & I can walk better so I am very well satisfied & hope for still further progress.

You will perceive by our being actually here that we have determined to spend August at Betley. This will make our visit here profoundly quiet as all the neighbours are in London,[260] but I am sure we shall enjoy our August – of all things & now I do make a bargain that you are to come & spend some days at Betley. Some of our views are really very pretty & you have never done them. We have had a great pleasure in Philip the Artist having been at Betley painting the little Wicksteds. I think he has done it very successfully. The boys are at an ugly age but he has managed them well & the girl makes a pretty picture with her auburn hair. I am glad you liked our Minny, tho' she was not so smart as she ought to have been. Philip's admiration of her is very great. He thinks her face the most expressive he has seen.

You did indeed win her heart. I never saw anyone who had so pleasant a manner with children as you have - you speak sensibly to them which so few people do. It is a 1000 pities you should not have some more exercise for your talents in this line. It is very odd that I should have mine called forth in this way, albeit as an old maid. There is no danger of precocity in

---

[258] The Queen's physician was obviously running profitable business besides his royal attendance.

[259] Cold water treatment was fashionable in the C19th as a cure for many ailments. Charles Darwin and Florence Nightingale tried the waters at Malvern. There were many forms of hydrotherapy.

[260] The neighbours from Betley Court and the vicarage.

one way for Miss Mary is grown so idle she will hardly look in a book.[261] We enjoyed the Wicksteds' visit much. I never saw anything so kind as Charles was to Minny & one day when his wife was not present, he showed such strong feeling as perfectly to astonish us all. He & Mary promise to come here in July which will be very pleasant. She is very cheerful & agreeable & I hope they will bring their girl. She is a most dear child & the friendship between her & Minny is very warm tho' sometimes the Miss Clive was rather too *vive* for Miss Wicksted yet the latter who is very shy & reserved generally was so fond of being with her cousin that she could never be kept in her own nursery. When in the drawing room, I always attended to them myself & the fatigue was passing description, but was rewarded by great love from them both & wonderful to tell by some expressions of gratitude for Mary [*Wicksted*]! when they went away.

Your account of the Queen's Ball was so amusing & that bit of spice about Disraeli too. Don't you think Sir R[obert] Peel must have been very

15. A watercolour by Ellen or Georgina.

angry at her so distinguishing his mortal enemy? I have heard thro' the Duchess of Roxburgh [*Annabel's relation*] that the Prince of Wales is really very dull indeed. How ridiculous that all were practising minuets with the Queen. What a bore to the men! & hardly less so to the women. I think the

---

[261] Mary Wicksted, (or Mab) was the third child of Charles and Mary. She became a nun in a high Anglican Order.

Duke must have been very handsome & the sight a very beautiful one. You will have many entertaining bits to tell me, I know.

Yesterday we made such a beautiful expedition – how you would have enjoyed for one hour or two to have been in the picture of the spot where we made tolerable drawings but it is the worst of all moments just now – so thoroughly green. It is impossible to do anything well but buildings.

We are at a great loss for books just now. I have read nothing since the *Rose of Tistelon*.[262] We are expecting Lord Powis so we shall hear some news tomorrow. I want to read Mr Milnes very much.[263] Farewell dearest A. With my best love to Mrs C.

Ever your most affectionate,
Ellen Tollet

Letter 40   [*cat: 305*]
Ellen deciding to stay in Betley; Harriet Lister's engagement; Archer Clives; gossip; Minny
Postmarked Newcastle-under-Lyme 4 June 1844

To: The Hon Annabel Crewe, 16 Upper Brook Street, Grosvenor Square, London

My dearest Annabel,

I waited to hear from you for Mrs Cunliffe said in her letter to Mamma, "Annabel will write from London", but I did feel when I see your nice long entertaining letter, 'Now I must write to Annabel instantly,' but then what a week of hard work followed. The Archer Clives, Mr W^y[*Willoughby*] Crewe, Robert Clive, August Vaughan, Emma Darwin, etc, etc & I have been really worked to death. Then on Saturday I said, 'Now for my letter to A' when in comes the Post bringing me a most kind, pressing invitation to London from Mrs Marsh.[264] This threw me into consternation for tho' I had fully made up my mind to stay at home this spring. It was rather a temptation to

---

[262] *The Rose of Tistelon* by Emilie Carlen.
[263] *Palm Leaves*, a book of poetry was written by Richard Monckton-Milnes in 1844.
[264] The novelist.

fly up with W Clive who goes to Berkeley Square tomorrow. All Saturday I was in indecision but at last made up my mind to stay where I am & as I am i.e. very happy & comfortable & being of some use in my generation. They would none of them advise me but I was pleased to see how glad Mamma was when I said should stay. She says I manage for Minny & take all trouble & anxiety off her mind so I rejoice I was not over tempted.

I have written my warmest gratitude to my hospitable friend & her husband & feel no regrets, tho' of course I have missed some pleasant hours. Where shall I begin? Firstly with <u>the</u> marriage. Very romantic, poetical & poor. I can fancy how interested you & Mrs C are in it all. What a year it is in this way! H[*arried*] Lister wrote a very nice letter to G announcing hers. I think Lady J L is rather a gay widow & I am sure she is spoiling her boy. The taste for acting is not good for children. From poor Mrs Tuffnell's account he is far too full of imagination & too wanting in truth.

We have had a very pleasant week with A[*rcher*] Clives. She is really the high priest person that can be & she seems quite at ease & not tormented with jealously & does not watch him as she did before marriage. He was in a pleasant mood & seemed to enjoy his visit. They staid 4 days & poor Charles is still suffering from his arm which is quite useless.[265] He is going to London. I trust Brodin[?] may find something to do him good. He bears it very patiently, <u>too</u> patiently I think.

I have been harrowing up our hearts by reading *Ellen Middleton [A Tale]*.[266] It is without exception the most miserable book I ever read but it is very clever. I certainly was disappointed for I cannot think that a novel at all answers the proper end when it makes you wretched, but many people admire it excessively.

The negotiation with Mrs Boots[?] has come to a happy termination & her nephew, a very nice looking youth is established here. It was dull enough that we found he was a protégé of people we knew - the Kingscotes & had left. Sir J Kennaway (who married one of them) to better

---

[265] Mary Clive writing in her biography of the Archer Clives [Clive (1948), p185] stated that, "His left arm at the shoulder joint is quite useless owing to the effects of an effort he made in flinging a stick at a cow in the winter."

[266] A novel by Lady Georgina Fullerton (1812–1885). It was an early example of a thriller but not to Ellen's taste.

himself.[267] I am glad <u>John</u> is so personable & shall be quite interested in seeing him in his high estate. I hear that Lord C Wellesley is to marry a girl we once met at Powis Castle – Miss Pierrepont, not pretty nor clever but unaffected & nice. It is an amazing marriage for her, tho' I believe she has a good fortune.[268] I mean amazing on account of Lord Douro having no children.[269] Georgy has had a long letter from Henrietta saying just what you know about her movements.

The Wilbrahams of Rode were here the other day & told us how wonderfully well poor Mrs W was bearing her affliction but as you say; it is most likely a life–long sorrow. They think her boy delicate!

What sad weather this is - very soon we shall have terrible distress. Many farmers have turned their cows into their mowing grass.

We are, as you say, revelling in Minny. She is admired by every one, her grace & innocent beauty are now quite admired – never saw a child improve so much but I don't think her nearly as clever as she was. She is only very lively & quick not at all <u>profound</u>. Mamma sends her best love to your aunt & will write to her very soon but she has been busy.

Can't you fancy how matter of fact, if coy, Willoughby was about Sir J Doyle?

William is gone to London & Bradfield.[270] He returns to Welshpool: we join him with Minny the end of this month. You are such a good creature about writing that I know I need not say let me hear; before I go your accounts of Mrs C are very comfortable. Mamma will tell her what Mr Twemlow's answer to our question was.

Farewell, your affectionate friend,
Ellen Tollet

Letter 41   *[cat: 306]*
Ellen ill in Welshpool; philosophising about the future and her love for Minny; society gossip; plans to see the Darwins

Welshpool

---

[267] Sir John Kennaway (1797–1873), 2nd Baronet, married Emily Frances Kingscote (1805–1858) on 28 April 1831.

[268] Lord Charles Wellesley (1808–1858), second son of the Duke of Wellington was married to Miss Augusta Pierrepont (1820-1893).

[269] The Duke of Wellington also had the title the Marquess of Duoro. What does the sentence mean?

[270] To see his brother-in-law, Tom.

Thursday Jan 16, 1845
Postmarked, 19th Jan, Newcastle under Lyme
To: The Hon Annabel, Madeley Manor, Newcastle, Staffordshire

Dearest A,

Penelope will have told you how ill I have been or I would not been so long silent. The very moment I wrote to you last, I was taken ill & it is now nearly 5 weeks that I have been confined. Just another violent cold & then a relapse. I have suffered much more than my illness warranted. I mean I have been more bad than dangerous! Latterly a mysterious pain in the head has made me utterly prostrate for hours in the day, but thank God it is better & my very first letter is to you. It has been a sore trial to be in the

16. Madeley Manor

house with my darling & yet not to bear to play with her or hear her lessons but her love has stood the test wonderfully.[271] At one time my cough was so very obstinate I felt so unnaturally ill all over, that I could not help having some solemn thoughts as to what it might be the beginning of.

---

[271] It was the custom to repeat what had been taught the day before. Ellen comments about this illness in *Journals*, p 225.

The thought of leaving Minny so unfinished was the pain that struck me most. Never had she appeared to me so enchanting as just before when I fell ill. A child is a future to one who has no other. I mean of course in this world's future. All one's other dear friends do not afford this. Our dear parents are our past & present – but no future, alas! in them & for those older than myself who are near & dear to me, the future can bring nothing to which I can look with pleasure – but in a child it is all bright. I love to think I shall be allowed to attend her path & endeavour to remove each snare & smooth the rough for her.

Thanks for a delightful letter & the news you sent through Mamma that your investigation was so satisfactory. What you say of Mrs W N is so true I have long known that freedom from prejudice is the crossing place that education gives. I don't mean that all educated people have it – but very few uneducated ones possess it.

I heard a most amusing contrast to your account of Sir F Doyle from Mrs Griffiths Parry who was at the wedding & who said, "His face looked white & his lips black," & "I am sure he was very ill, Miss Tollet." The pun was lost on lost on "The Attorney".

I have discovered the article in the Quarterly. Poor dear Milnes, what a cutting satire it is! [272]   I feel good to detect the writer & think it may be Lockhart, but I thought Haywood. As to P's guess of Smythe it is a very bad one – it is wholly unlike his character. However, it is amusing in the highest degree. The writer has no love of domestic life, I am sure, but is much given to society & would like his wife to shine & dine out with him. I

---

[272] In the *Quarterly Review*, Vol CXLIX (1844) p 94, there is a vicious attack on *Palm Leaves*, a book of poetry, by 'dear Milnes', much of the poems based on his travels in the Levant and Egypt. The anonymous reviewer is particularly concerned as to how the author gained access to an eastern harem to write about unfortunate women. The rights of women and feminism by three further female authors are also reviewed, the most important being by Anna Bronwell Jameson. Ellen was trying to guess who the author was. She must have realised Annabel's continued interest in RMM and made a shrewd observation about his character.

Physical and Moral Blindness

The hab'ts here alluded to are familiar to every traveller in those parts of
the East where a large portion of the population are subject to ophthalmia and
other diseases of the eyes, brought on by dirt and carelessness. In Egypt the
number is much increased by those who have blinded themselves, or been
blinded by their parents, to avoid conscription.

The child whose eyes were never blest
With heavenly light, or lost it soon,
About another's neck will rest
Its arm, and walk like you at noon;
The blind old man will place his palm
Upon a child's fresh-blooming head,
And follow through the croud (*sic*) on calm
That infantine and trusty tread.

We, too, that in our spirits dark
Traverse a wild and weary way,
May in these sweet resources mark
A lesson, and be safe as they:
Resting, when young, in happy faith
On fair affection's daily bond,
And afterwards resigned to death,
Feeling the childly life beyond.

*The poem quoted is short example of Monckton Milnes' style. Notice the
strong moral theme, the use of regular rhyme and the conventional
alliterations – 'trusty tread' and 'wild and weary way'. His poetry was very
popular in Victorian England, but is now largely forgotten.*

have often felt that what he says that it was no use making a remark that
really had been original when it already appeared in the newspaper & where
you [were] excited about Mrs Tyrrwhitt, I was furious.

Have you read the letters from Mr Greenhow's account of Miss
Martineau's case? It entirely destroys all the wonder of it & is to my mind

quite conclusive. I have got *The Atheneum* with all her letters, as I wanted to study the subject.[273]

This neighbourhood has been very gay with balls & theatricals & I have never even been to P(owis) Castle. I hear that you are very gay with Grevilles & Shelleys, & Mrs Cholmondley. G(eorgina) has had a long letter from Henrietta. I fear she is poorly – she complains of much attacks of languor but the Devonshire climate may perhaps be the cause.

The Wicksteds are coming to us in February & they say again in May. If I dare look forward, I have many pleasures in store. My dear friend, Mrs C Darwin is counting upon my going to her in April & she makes me so proud by saying her husband is quite as anxious to see me as she is!. She made it a stipulation before they married that he should begin to love us immediately & he has been so obliging as to consent. Then Mary will bring William & Minny to Betley & summer will come & drive off coughs & colds & miseries.

Mrs H Wedgwood told me about *Vestiges of Creation*.[274] She had heard Mr Lyell discussing it. He said he fancied it was by Sir R Vyvyan. He got W Clive to order it, but from Penelope's account I fear it is a sad presumptuous book which neither lights the Mosaic History.

If I can get a little stronger I am going to try to copy Minny's picture in water colours, It is a very pretty thing & has only one fault, but that fault is, alas, one in the drawing. Lady Powys & I are the only two people who are annoyed by it. Henrietta Clive who is a good judge pronounces it the prettiest picture she has seen in a long time. Don't you wish to know who wrote *Eothen?*[275] It must be a very clever book.

---

[273] Miss Martineau's case mentioned in *The Athenium* about her belief in Mesmerism to cure illnesses. Mesmerism is the act of hypnotising or putting a person to sleep so that a person's thoughts can be manipulated. (see later Letter 46 on this topic).

[274] *Vestiges of the Natural History of Creation* (1844) (published anonymously originally) was written by Robert Chambers not Vyvyan.

[275] Written by Alexander William Kinglake (1809-1891) in 1844 on *Eastern Travel*.

Farewell dearest A. This has been 2 days in hand. When are you off to London? Ever with love from G to you both. Your most loving friend,

Ellen Tollet

Letter 42 [*cat: 302*]
What happens at a dull house party at Dudmaston; chess; visiting the school
Shakenhurst, Cleobury Mortimer
Nov 22, 1845

To: The Hon Annabel Crewe, Madeley Manor, Newcastle, Staffs
My Dearest A,

Mamma enclosed this morning a little note for Mrs Cunliffe which showed me that you have really been quite poorly ever since I saw you – so provoking that we should not have Sense <u>or</u> Sensibility enough to possess Miss Austen's works. I am reconciled as to fancy perhaps that by writing rather than I intended, I may amuse you for 5 minutes with an account of our visitings & by way of being very historical I will begin with our journey.

A very civil nice woman with an aristocratic countenance offered us *Punch*[276] as soon as we got into the railway. She had an ugly husband & 2 pleasing daughters. At Stafford we spied Lord Talbot [*of Sandon*] who came up & hailed us all & we found our companions were Mr Wortley & Lady Georgina going to London. When we arrived at Dudmaston, we were very hungry, having had no luncheon & that [*a*] bedroom fire would not be lit because we could see it was a very nice large handsome square house full of large high rooms with big doors & big windows all uninteresting but convenient. Mr W(hitmore)'s sister, Mrs Isaac, received us – a good natured, insipid woman. At 7 o'clock down we came to dinner & were assembled in a little square ante room with no furniture while we were presented to 6 of the dullest women I ever saw. Lady Ryan (another sister) Mrs R her daughter-in-law, a Calcutta beauty & vulgar 2 Miss Ryans & a Miss Laing. Fancy this round talk at dinner with them – 8 ladies, Mr W[277]

---

[276] First published in 1841.
[277] Almost certainly William Wolryche–Whitmore (1787-1858), the owner of Dudmaston at the time. In 1810 he married Lady Lucy Bridgeman, the daughter of

forming the apex. W certainly did his best but the ladies all spoke in undertones to each other & looked at us as if we were 2 tigers as if they thought us 'very clever'.

Our host accompanied us into the drawing room, being aware that his ladies would not entertain us – but the next morning he took us by ourselves a long drive to see his school & farming, one which we enjoyed much & at dinner then arrived Mr & Mrs Henry Burton & Mr & Mrs Dayrah, the latter was an old friend, but the great blessing to us was Miss Barrington, Lord B's sister - very handsome & really a most attractive woman who at 42 took up with a hideous Mr Burton, who had been refused by many girls in Shropshire. She seems to conform to her fate wonderfully, but by his constant attention to her horrid husband, betrays her anxiety to prove to you that she is much delighted with him. She is very open & a good talker so we did capitally & I had some chess & beat everybody. There the walks are very pretty & our host so very [cultivated] that we got on well & defied the 8 dull women who retired to their rooms & left us in possession of the fields. Mr Whitmore is a very well cultivated man so that he is good company. I think he must marry again for his health is restored & I cannot think he can allow his guests to be dullified for ever by those women of his. The best joke was he begged & prayed us to come again next week! Fancy!

We are going to have people here next week - Lord & Lady Gifford, the Blounts & the week after we move on to Welshpool, we have got Thiers[278] & plenty of other books to amuse us. My dearest child, I hope this will find you getting quite well. I long to hear how you are, yet commend you not to write till you can really like to do it. Farewell dear old friend. Our best love to Mrs C who is, I fear, not quite herself yet. I am sure you have both done something imprudent & foolish.

Your most affectionate,

EHT

---

the Earl of Bradford, with, interestingly, a link to the person whom Minny eventually married. Later he became MP for Bridgnorth. Dudmaston, nearby is now a National Trust property.

[278] Adolphe Thiers was a French statesman and historian.

Letter 43   [*cat: 304*]
Thanking Annabel for a pleasant evening; playing chess
Betley
19 Sept 1845
To: The Hon Annabel Crewe, Madeley Manor
Dear A,

Your note this morning was so very pleasant an event & quite brightened up my breakfast. I think this last visit of yours was imperfect in one point only; we had no walk together & I think there is something in a walking talk different if not superior to a sitting talk, but it is ungrateful to acknowledge even one imperfection in what was so happy. Augusta says Dr Howe wrote a letter to her sister not long ago speaking of himself as likely to die so that was the reason she was so incredulous about his marriage.

As to the other I know not what to think, only that I saw a parallel case of a person who had 2 strings to his bow & pulled one string just as every one thought he was going to pull the other one.

It would indeed not do to seem anxious to meet the J A Smiths. You will do what you feel to be right & then whether it pleases him or not won't really signify, but I do think you will find he likes it.

I am really affronted at your old maidishness about the penny.[279] I beat Augusta at chess last night. She is tougher than you rather. I begin to fancy myself fit for the Club & want taking down sadly. [280]

Ever dearest kindest A, your attached friend,
EHT

Letter 44   [*cat: 303*]
Powis people; Ellen's religious beliefs; gift of a pomegranate; amusing gossip and politics; corn laws; lease of Abergeldie Castle; Minny's education; interest in RMM; dancing with father; gossip
Welshpool
Dec 16th 1845

---

[279] Was Annabel not prepared to bet one penny on a game of chess?
[280] It seems that there was a local Chess Club, but where? What was the Penny Club?

143

The Hon Annabel Crewe, Madeley Manor, Newcastle, Staffordshire
My dearest A,

I really will not delay writing another day, in the vain hope of growing more amusing, but trust to your charity to receive again a dull letter with satisfaction. First let me thank you for your prompt & comfortable answer to my enquiries after your health. I gather from your not mentioning yourself to Minny that you got well in the regular course of things.

Where are you now, I wonder? I expect to be astonished by some grand flight to London or elsewhere. A Tomlinson thanks you for your spoiling of our child. Her letter to you was all her own, but I assure you her scribble, "Thank you for your present", was a very inadequate representation of her feelings towards the pomegranate which has afforded endless delight & is exhibited 3 or 4 times every day & strange to say is yet uninjured. I could not help contrasting a child's way or a grown person's. We should have expressed more thanks, & not felt for the pleasure.

The latter part of our visit to Shakenhurst was very pleasant. We had Lord & Lady Gifford [*of Chillington*], a very nice, merry young couple just married & both very open & did I tell you of a pretty young widow in black velvet, a bouquet & long ringlets who asked G at dinner what she thought of praying for the dead? And afterwards treated us all to a constant mention of her poor dear husband, till we all were obliged to wish her another! When the people were gone, which was no bad thing (for often the dinners were deadly dull) we enjoyed the children's company. The eldest boy [*George Wicksted*] is most promising. Our reception here was most cheering & our child looking like Aurora - but I have not been thoroughly well- light colds - just enough to make me feel languid & to prevent going much into the air & I really have felt considerable temptation to lowness.

G has been remarkably well. We have seen no one hardly except in evening visits. The Castle's people have been out this week. I am going to the grand doings at Oakley Park. All the world is going down. Charles & Mary now have had some pleasant little gossips with Lucy Herbert, tho' her account of Lady Adela quite takes away all surprise at her want of propriety.[281] She seems to have had no sense of that. Lucy said she had

---

[281] Lady Adela Villiers & Capt C P Ibbotson married in 1845.

seen her call to a young man to come to speak to her at the rails when she was walking in the square! But still they thought she had plenty of worldly wisdom to keep her from marrying a poor man. They speak of her great extravagance so alas! Poor Ibbotson!

Of course I have been driven to reading by way of solace. *The Athenian* for October is a particularly good monthly part. Pray read it. We have read Sewell's *Sermons: The Place of Conscience.* There are very excellent passages in it but I can't think that it makes that most difficult of all subjects much easier. There was one passage in your letter which quite astonished me & that was your saying that I must not expect you to listen to any defence of Newman! G and I both really laughed at that idea of MY defending him, but I think I shall remember saying to you that I did not believe that either he or Pusey (both such ascetics) were influenced by any interested motives in leaving or sticking to our Church.[282]

This is all the defence I should ever be inclined to make & depend upon it, we High Church people who feel that our right cause has been destroyed [*are*] in more temptation to be angry with Newman than those to whom his fall only appears a triumph. I have been studying Manning's *Sermons.*[283] They are more powerful than Wilberforce's but not so practical. At least they are more high strained & you might admire them more. You would not agree with him so well.

Do pray read *Gertrude.* I have such admiration of it from such varieties of people that it must be clever. It is a sort of half child's book by the author of *Amy Herbert,*[284] which is quite a child's book but I think capital.

What wondrous news this is of the Ministry. The Tory papers are raving mad; their vulgarity in their rage is beyond description. For myself I am sorry in this first place; society is pleasanter when the Tories are in tolerable humour & moreover I do not think that if the Corn Laws are to go, Sir R Peel had better have the job. He has a stronger head for a financial matter & broader shoulders to bear the blame if it don't answer. This affair took

---

[282] Reference to the Oxford Movement, which divided the Church of England.

[283] *Sermons* (1842) by H E Manning, Archdeacon of Chichester.

[284] By Elizabeth Missing Sewell (1815–1906).

Lord Powys quite by surprise. Well it is all their own quarrel among themselves. Even my mother can't say the Whigs have driven them out by factious Opposition. I suppose the Mil(nes) must wait to see you till February. Will he get anything in the scramble?[285]

My mother seems to have been highly pleased with Mrs Morier's call & pleasant chat. From what she says I suppose you are still at Madeley. They have had the Wicksteds for a few days. My mother is dismayed at their having recently taken that place in Aberdeenshire for 3 years with the A(rcher) Clives![286] It does seem foolish to take that capacious place for 3 years, but as no one would blame them if they went to London every year, I don't see why they should not spend money in what is quite or almost as rational a way. '*Chacun a son goût.*'

I have not told you much of our child's doings. Education is really beginning by small degrees each step shows how easy the next will be. Her clearness is really striking, both as to reflection & handiness - but I suppose you only spend 1/2 an hour in lessons- all the rest in play & exercise. Her dancing is beautiful. I wish you could see her graceful steps & her fits of laughing at her Papa's dancing which she says is really a very vulgar way, tho' he boasts he was much admired at school.

Do not keep me waiting for news of you. Pray give our best love to Mrs Cunliffe. I am just going to be so good to copy a sketch of Hoylake to be sold for the benefit of a stone pulpit in Chester Cathedral. If it gets 5/- all's well - if anyone likes to give it. Farewell dearest old A. Miss Hesketh, the least admired of Henrietta, marries Mr Long, heir to £20,000 a year & of a good steady family - Wiltshire - a most capital marriage. Miss Edwards really refused Lord W. Graham, Mr Corbet & Mr Cholmondley & they say Mr Long looked at her first. Your most lovingest,

EHT.

Inside flap of envelope:
My love to Mrs Crewe & my love to you.

---

[285] A position in Government presumably. Note the continued interest in Monckton Milnes.

[286] Abergeldie Castle previously described: apparently the lease was for 3 years not one year.

Letter 45 *[cat: 216]*

News about Annabel's and Mrs Tollet's illnesses; Georgina in Capesthorne; Buzz; politics – fear that Sir Robert Peel would resign; Constable; Minny

[1846]

My Dearest A,

Not one word had I heard of your illness till Mrs C[*unliffe*]'s letter to P[enelope] arrived & then she said you were writing to me, so I waited till I got your delightful letter today, but I should have written to console & pity you long before if I had known.

Poor dear child, how awkward a beginning of your London campaign it appears & yet all may be (nay must be) for the best & I do hope a thorough strengthening at B[*righton?*] will prepare both body & mind for all exertions that may be required in the coming season. I cannot delay an hour writing to you but you must not think I am by putting you in my debt again so soon that I mean to make you write again sooner than you feel quite inclined.

I feel that my last letter was written when I was feeling worried & uncomfortable as if I had written directly on my return home. It would have been still more so for this slack?? I have never for a moment ceased to rejoice that I came. It was most dismal at first returning alone to this once brightish of houses & finding it all so sad & dark.

My mother's time of illness is one that no-one can understand or describe but which is the most difficult to bear for the patient to be here & to be only bearable from the absence of society as to its affecting life. About 4 or 5 days after my return a blessed change took place entirely- I believe in consequence of a stronger opiate being given <u>without</u> her knowledge which has done wonders for her sleep & now things are all bright in comparison & I feel sure her improvement will go on. I have had the unexpressible comfort of feeling that I have been of use & comfort even to her. I have had experience in illness & she thinks me an authority in matters of medicine & I have been able to appear quite cheerful all the time & to feel to do a great part of it. When dear G came home she was agreeably surprised at my mother but I fear we all seemed rather empty after her intellectual treats at Capesthorne.

Having no events of my own to tell you besides driving with Mamma in the close carriage & trying to read her to sleep, I must give you a history of G's adventures instead. You made a good hit about hoping she had met something charming but I shall begin regularly. When she got to C[apesthorne], she found a large party, some strangers & several old acquaintances, but the pleasantest man was old Young, the actor, who (*sic*) she likes extremely. Of course, you know him, as he is a friend of the Moriers. You know, I suppose, how ill Mr W Bromley has been ever since his accident & even today the account from Mrs D[avenport?] is rather unsatisfactory. She has nursed him most carefully & his father & sisters came while G[eorgina] was there. Mrs D gave her a warm reception & seems to have taken a fancy to us when she next meets us at the Bullers[?]. She & G got quite intimate. She seems to be full of faults & extravagances …. a very interesting character. Lady ……..'s death seems to have made a great impression upon her.

In the autumn G had met these Misses Tufnells & Tremenheere[287] & had liked them very little. She saw of the latter very much. Well, they came again. Mr E T in his new character of a fiancé so brushed up & happy & full of his situation & the others everything that was most agreeable & delightful. Instead of giving all his talk to Mrs D[*avenport*] as most men do, in that house he gave G this benefit & very much it seems to have been appreciated. Do you know him? I wish you could contrive to see him & tell me what you think of him. Mrs D forwarded to G a letter she has had from him since he went, alluding to a little transaction with which I shall amuse you when ever we meet but which I cannot possibly contrive to put in a letter.

Your news about Buzz was quite new, not that about Harper which it seems has been a well-known for some time here, as also the employment of Mr Martin, who seems a master of congratulations[288] – everybody has a good opinion of him & I have long learnt to think that what everybody says

---

[287] Miss Tremenheere's father was a barrister, schools' inspector and Poor Law officer.

[288] Mr Martin was Hungerford's highly efficient agent. Harper was in dispute with Mrs Cunliffe for a long period about outstanding debts: see Letter 55.

has generally some <u>foundation</u> in truth. I only hope this is not so with regard to everybody saying Sir R[*obert*] P[*eel*] will resign.[289] I firmly believe we shall all be ruined if he does, but as as long as he is alive he would surely reign the reins again if he saw the coach was going to be upset. The notion of the Duke of Richmond as Premier! However when the Corn Laws are repealed I don't see what he would have to do. I think it would be quite wrong in Sir R to retire till he had just got us through the crisis safely. Even the most sanguine think there may be some disarrangements in consequence of these changes & as he has given the nation a strong dose he ought to watch its effect.

I send you an extract of a letter Papa had from a man who studies public affairs much. I think it is clever. I feel doubtful whether you go the full length of Peel's proposed measures. He certainly comments as a thorough

17. A sample envelope postmarked Welshpool.

Free Trader & with more talent than consistency. To those who have steadily held Free Trade Doctrines for years past, the moral triumph of so 'illustrious' a convert is great & he ought not to carp at his change for what is all argument but an appeal to others for a change of their opinion.

---

[289] Peel did resign in June 1846 which probably helps to date this letter earlier in 1846 before May.

I must recommend you to read *Life of Constable* by Leslie by some dullness at first[290] & the stupidest love letters, but got him once married & launched in his first passion & I was delighted. The friendship between him & Archbishop Fisher is quite charming[291] & the letters are so brimfull[292] of drawings that they will I hope quite improve one's sketches. His own mind seems to have been like his pictures full of freshness & health. Do you know his pictures well? I feel, to know them from engravings, but they can give but little idea. Yes, our darling child is left without an aunt. They have been at Walcot,[293] where she has been happy beyond telling & as usual excessively made of. But her simplicity will not, I hope, be lost now she seems to have no tendency to grow affected & as it is not in either family, I hope she will always keep free. The day we went she cried & said, "I shall have no more happiness all day now my Aunties are gone." I was so unfeeling as not to ask about Ney & so you don't mention him in your letter - you are always so interested always about Minny that I take shame for neglecting your son & heir.

Is there any hope of your coming down in May? It would delight me so to show my darling to you again after your appreciation last year.

The Duchess d'Abrantes[294] is most amusing tho' one can't believe her - & her making out that Napoleon was in love with her is so excellent! I have read some rather later & very entertaining memories of N & I forgot the man's name but they coarsened the hero sadly. He seems to have had such meannesses. Your M history was very amusing.[295]

Dearest A, how I hope that this will find you & Mrs C both improving. P[enelope] did not think her looking well when she saw her last but that

---

[290] *Memoirs of the Life of John Constable* (1843) London, by C R Leslie.

[291] John Fisher (1748-1825) finally Bishop of Salisbury. He was noted for his friendship with John Constable, and his commission of the well-known painting of Salisbury by Constable.

[292] Obsolete spelling.

[293] Walcot Hall, near Bishops Castle, 5 miles south-east of Welshpool, the home of Edward Clive, the first Earl of Powis, and Henrietta Clive.

[294] Laure Junot, Duchess of Abrantes, French writer.

[295] Who is this? Could it be Richard Monckton Milnes?

might be owing to her business papers. How I do hope she may in future have more of the comfort & satisfaction in Madeley that her kindness & generosity to the people so entirely deserved & not be fatigued & worried like she is glad to get away from them. This living of Nantwich will bother her a little, I fear. I really must wind up my lengthy discourse with G's best loves & mine.[296]

Your Most Affectionate,

Ellen Tollet

It is unclear how often the two friends have seen each other because they meet in different social groups.

18. St Mary's Church, Welshpool seen from Broad Road

---

[296] She had the advowson of the Madeley Parish. Did she also have the advowson of Nantwich, or was she advising Hungerford?

PART IV: The end of an era at Madeley Manor, 1846-1851

*"Mr Darwin said Sumner's Lectures were more than he could understand but he
delighted in listening to them, as he would to good music"*

"Active usefulness is the only remedy for desolation"

"Our dear parents are our past & present – but no future, alas!"

Letter 46   [*cat: 220*]
**A short letter on Mesmerism; continued concern for mother; Miss
Martineau travelling to Egypt**

[*Welshpool? 1845-6*]

To: Annabel Crewe, Madeley Manor

Dearest A,

I return you your *Good Little Man's Book*. His nervous anxiety to prove
that the New Testament miracles were something more than Mesmerism is
very amiable tho' to me very necessary.[297] He is also evidently uneasy about
the Old Testament prophets, but his agreement in their favour is miserably
weak that he will do their cause no good. I mean his saying that it is much
easier to foretell what will happen in a week or a month than in 100 years. I
fear this logic, p 224, will hardly do for those who believe in the fact of
Mesmeric Prophecies. As to there being something in it good for some
diseases & some people, I don't doubt & I should be rather inclined to get
my mother "mesmering", but sleep, if we had a performer in this country
for you. So you see I am not <u>very</u> prejudiced. I send you a little more of
Miss Martineau. Her chances of accident to her arm will be increased by

---

[297] Mesmerism was becoming increasingly important in Victorian medicine.

152

going to Egypt. Of course she is going not to see the pyramids but the magicians.

The letter is from Mrs Darwin. Were you not rejoiced to hear of our treat in Minny's coming? We don't tell Mamma till just the day before to prevent her worrying herself, which she did most thoroughly about the Wicksteds. After all, their visit did her not the slightest harm. Mary was particularly agreeable & cheered us up very much.

Dear Georgina is very well & good & very much occupied with the cows & reading Thomas à Kempis in Latin. P[*enolope*] is just returned from Crewe.[298] The party was a small one but did very well. I hope you will enjoy yours on Monday. Pray let me have some signs of your existence before long & believe I am, your most loving of friends,

EHT

P.S: I have 1000 things to tell you.

Letter 47   [*cat: 217*]
The Blackburnes; Mrs Hesketh; Royal Academy; books; Minny
[Probably after May 1846]

My Dearest Annabel,

If you will send me such glorious books & still more charming letters, you must submit to a speedy reply - will be glad to hear that the beautiful binding was not injured in the journey. It is perfect inside & out, & will be a lasting & precious keepsake. Your letter waited 3 days for me here. G & I had gone in broiling heat to perform a great act of duty by going to visit a very old friend near Liverpool & taking Minny with us. [299] The heat was unsupportable. I never felt anything like this oppression of body [&] mind that it caused for a day or two, but now it is rather better. However even the evenings are scarcely cool, tho' late yesterday we took Minny to gather yellow irises by the water-side, which she enjoyed wonderfully.

My Lord drank tea here & received our congrats upon his feat of generosity with great modesty assuring us it "originated with Mr

---

[298] Thomas à Kempis (c1380 – 1471) was a German-Dutch writer, best known for Christian books on devotion.

[299] Jane Lawrence was Ellen's school friend.

Hinchliffe". I told him it was very easy to suggest such things so I did not give Mr H so much credit!

At the railway station we had met Mr T Blackburne, who told us all the sad news.[300] He seemed to think all hope was over & described the dropsy as having reached a terrible height & so suddenly. He said he had he had never seen his wife so completely overwhelmed. He was carrying forced raspberries from Lord Wilton's garden.[301] I am so grieved for all her friends, tho' for herself one can have no regrets. A solitary life & a suffering one will be exchanged for the Communion of Saints & the Life Everlasting – he may & ought to think that to all poor children to die is gain, but I can't say how differently I feel about those who have to leave, as it were, their work unperformed, when Life has been unfinished who are taken away in the midst, as it were, but this is because we see through "a glass darkly" – we see the loss, the failure, the destruction of so much happiness & usefulness, but we don't see far enough & it is a great trial of faith.

I thought dear Miss Hesketh looking so very ill when she was at Madeley & the moment Mrs B told me, I said it is liver, I suppose. He said the liver was entirely useless, but, of course, you have had many more particulars. Did you hear that she sent him home for some great school meeting at Prestwick, thinking of it herself in the night?

Dear Mrs Cunliffe, how you will feel this, but I hope you are better now that you have left Tunbridge, which was perhaps too exciting an air for you. As for you, Miss A, you give a very fine account, but I beg to say I hope you will play no tricks.

This season might be devoted to gaining strength, not knowledge, nor even amusement except as a secondary consideration. My mother is decidedly better but her nights still vary. She is able to be a great deal out of doors which is the best thing for her nerves. So to my London campaign - it ended quickly enough as it began. I saw a few Lions at Mrs Bull's. Miss Rigby was one. What a very clever woman! Did you read her "*German Painting*" in *The Quarterly*?[302] I do long to hear what you say of [*illegible*] this

---

[300] Presumably this was Rev Thomas Blackburne, wife of Emma.
[301] Was Ellen referring to the garden of the Summer House at Wrinehill?
[302] *The Quarterly Review*, Vol 77, p 332..

year especially the Thames one. What bliss it would be to have him down here! But I fear his visit to Italy will spoil him. I also must hear your critique on that delightful R[oyal] Academy, which we may glory in this year. For the first time I admire Etty,[303] tho' one ought not to confess it but the *Circe* is a most *particao*[304] lovely picture I think. Landseer's *Great Stag*[305] I don't care for but his smaller ones are charming. I like the 2 Danbys very much & the Stanfields are beautiful summer landscapes of Lee, above all portraits that delightful one of Miss Digby so superior even to Grant's who has made a vulgar Queen with Albert, I think. No more twaddle of mine about art.

Now for *Emilia*.[306] I have read it & was much fascinated & could not lay it down after the first volume, which I most truly object very much to the bad taste of making Mr Danby say such brutal things about her father to Emilia. He might have been just as awkward, but not so brutal. I think the account of her behaviour & feelings after she had engaged herself at the marriage, the most striking, touching, true & affecting picture possible & I felt my eyes very twinkling. I object violently to her making 5 years of misery after the marriage. It should have been one. His mother's influence & his own ignorance might have made him coop her up & be disagreeable for the first year but if it had gone on for [*long*], she would not have been so easily converted by Susan, besides Susan would naturally have spoken sooner. I have just been talking it over with Mrs Marsh's sister & she agrees with me exactly about the 5 years. I heard of Syke's death ['*Oliver Twist' in instalments*] from some of our villagers, who had heard it from Mrs Boots & was sorry the poor dear dog should have suffered so long, after all the pain of loving him.

I know how I should feel if I indulged myself in a pet, but I really should be too sure of its fate. "I never missed a dear Gazelle" & I think Minny would have felt low if it had been Lassie. I wish you had heard her improvising just now with a book before her. Minny began "The Duke of

---

[303] William Etty (1787-1849), an English painter of the nude.

[304] Means *separate* in Portuguese.

[305] *The Great Stag at Bay* by Sir Edwin Landseer (1802–1873), first exhibited in 1846.

[306] *Emilia Wyndham* (1846) by Anne Marsh-Caldwell.

Kent was a very great man & fidgetty & the Princess Royal & Governess came to London but the Lady did not, for she was poorly & they thought another air would be better," Then she went on about "The Duke of Hellington pleased Albert better than any of them & Sir John Parker went to Aberystwyth to mind his duty of picking up stones etc, etc". Was it not droll for a country child? An old friend, who saw her here the other day, thinks her so like our darling Carry & I quite see it in the figure & complexion, but her eyes are so much lighter.

I forgot to say how much I like the part of *Emilia* where she feels when she sees Lenox again, that she prefers poor old Danby! I hope I am not prosy - rather, I suspect your Bromley History is very amusing. I had not heard of Mrs Tufnell's illness. I do think tho' the poor woman may be a loss that Miss Horton will be the very best person for Teresa to be with & perhaps Providence intends that.   C says there will be a 3rd Mrs T.

You will be very sorry to hear that our beautiful cows are dying of distemper but Papa bears it like a philosopher.

After all my apologies for a speedy reply, I have kept my letter in one portfolio till it is quite stale. I cannot describe to you the pleasure & the bother[307] of Minny, I have no time for anything. Thank goodness the dreadful heat is passed tho' we have yet no rain.

Ever thine, my dear love,
EHT

Letter 48   [*cat: 221*]
Georgina & Ellen away for Christmas; education of Minny; Powis hopes for the future

[*Welshpool*]
[*likely 1846, from date-check in this letter*]

My Dearest Annabel,

I need not wait for something to say for I don't expect much in the way fresh materials & I know your obliging partiality will lead you to be interested in our annals, however, jog trot[308] our life may be. Before we left

---

[307] An unusual word to describe the feelings of Ellen about her niece.
[308] An uneventful, humdrum way of living.

home we received Henrietta's promised letter & a number of an Irish periodical containing a Xmas story translated from the German of Canon Schmidt. This was for Minny & as any nice innocent story it is & does very

19. A modern photograph of Powis Castle.

well for her tho' I see there is a marriage at the end - a finale this much of which I am sure she will not appreciate. H[*enrietta*]'s account of herself was not brilliant, poor dear soul.

We slept at the Potts at Chester. Miss P. was schoolfellow of G's & is a niceish person – a great geologist & botanist. One of the daughters[*?*] was intimate with poor Sophy Greville when they lived at Chester & heard from her such horror of her own history as makes one's blood run cold. A life of such admiration in society & of such misery at home - so brilliant externally & so wretched internally one has seldom known of & it offers I think one of the most melancholy pictures of this world that it is possible to contemplate. She should think nemesis must be the bitterest part of his mother's grief if she has either heart or a conscience.

We arrived here on Tuesday evening & had a warm reception. To console me for a terrible headache which has lasted almost ever since but I hope it is going off. Minny is really very charming & tho' I don't think the first delight of meeting after absence is so good as it was when we had to see the fresh beauties of mind & body opening upon us. I do not find my interests in her really diminished nor my mind less cheered by her society. It is true that at present her teeth are all quite firm & as she never had long curly hair there is no change in her being cropped! So perfect I can't judge but I think this little tendering of affectation which peeps out sometimes & which we make earnest attempts to snip in the bud, warns us of a much greater danger to her attractiveness. Nothing would seem very plain to her so much as her losing her simplicity but I fully believe by care she will be preserved from it. Education is quite a pleasure about an hour ½ in the day, is most happily spent in reading, writing, arithmetic & French.

We have already dined ourselves at the Castle & seen Mr Montgomery. He is the picture of a good tempered, not over wise youth & Lady C Cooper very happy & unaffected & nice. She has brought little sketches for the windows of her new home & I only hope she will settle well down there & amuse herself with doing good. If it was Lucy who had married Mr Montgomery she would, I am sure, find her happiness in looking after the poor Paddies[309] in the village close by but Charlotte has not quite the same tastes. You never in your life, I know, had so dull a dinner & evening as we had there. It is impossible to tell why but so it is & I believe if Lady Morley & all the wits in London were there it would be exactly the same!

On Monday is the Children's Ball. We actually begin dining there at 5 o'clock & are to be merry or wise for that time like 2 in the morning! The only possible pleasure I can think of is seeing Minny in a beautiful new sash! We have heard from Betley of Mrs Turton having the biggest boy ever seen & our poor old servant Pollard is dead. Mr C. Wynn j(*unio*)r was at P[*owis*]. Castle but I never was near him. We have plenty of books to read & am very quiet & comfortable feeling of use to Minny & I confess I rather enjoy a holiday from all the schooling & parish business at Betley,[310] which Xmas times had made so very great. Poor Fanny was very sorry to part with

---

[309] Reference to the Irish? From 1840 many Irish emigrated to Wales as a result of the potato famine in Ireland.

[310] Ellen was involved with the school and Betley administration.

us. Penelope will make up to Mamma for our loss but not to F. Thank you dearest for the nice little note I got just as I left home. We have had very happy meetings indeed & our enjoyment of each other's society is a pleasure which years can only I hope increase – at best as long as no circumstances of a dividing tendency happen to us, such as your marrying a prince & I a Welsh curate, a widower with small children!

As to 1847, I only hope it will be no more sorrowful than 1846 - [311] i.e. that an additional year's improvement & experience may make up for the necessary worsening which each year must bring in outward affairs even if they are allowed to stay as they are. Don't think me gloomy I assure you I am not a bit. But I don't build up a false cheerfulness by anticipating all sorts of fine things to come as one perhaps used to do. There are plenty of bright, bright hopes for us if we will only look far enough - & many, many comforts & pleasures for the present moment too.

I am sure, dearest A, you have this true philosophy of enjoying what you have & I think I have it too, tho' I think we owe this power more to natural temperament than we perhaps like to own which ought to make so very lenient to those who have it in less degree. This reminds me to say that dear G is pretty. Will she [be] martyred at the Castle on Thursday but declined at the Ball!!

Heaven bless thee, ever thine,

EHT

Letter 49 [cat: 300]
Painting; Mr Cholmondeley's visit; matchmaking for Annabel and Georgina; Mrs Cunliffe's opinion

Welshpool

Aug 15/16 [1847?]

To: The Hon Annabel Crewe, Madeley Manor, Newcastle, Staffordshire

Dearest Annabel,

I am going to write you a long letter which is not to be despatched till tomorrow when I shall have some particulars to add which will be

---

[311] Indicates the letter was written in 1846.

interesting. First I must console with you on your illness, tho' I hope it is now completely past. Mamma mentions strange flying visits from My Lord & has heard of your being poorly but I hope mine is the latest intelligence. My heart did not reprove me for I had only rather expected a letter for some days here but I will be glad to get out of London now it is so hot. It is not good weather for this country, it being so very hazy that the hills are almost hid. I have only done one drawing but that one, I think, is my best.

20. Painting of Crewe Hall(?) by Ellen or Georgina.

However it is only a house & some trees, which might be anywhere, as well as in this lovely country, but I find so many more difficulties in my apparatus etc about here than at Betley, that I feel I don't make the most of my time, but I adore drawing more than ever.

I regret not seeing Callow again[312] & I should be curious to see whether he would at all approve of anything I have done, but Crockery's opinion [*Wedgwood*] would be worth 100 Callow's & to have him suddenly reduced

---

[312] William Callow (1812–1908), was an English landscape painter. He was the artist of Madeley Manor reproduced in this book.

by an earthquake swallowing up Badger [*Annabel's suitor?*] getting his bread as an artist would be perfection!

I must tell you that just as I was reading your nice chatty letter, the door flew open & Mr Cholmondeley was announced. He entered the room as if he meant to enchain us (only G and me), but we made low curtsies & gave him a chair saying Mr Clive was out. It was, of course, a Member of Parliament visit & I felt more inclined to laugh at him than I can tell you, but he was so good natured & so innocently, openly conceited that I soon fell to laughing with him & it would have amused you to see & hear, as I know. The child came running in, so I attacked him and said of course in his capacity of a popular Member he was prepared to advise her so then he was very lively on that subject only saying in a parenthesis: "but joking apart that is an uncommonly pretty creature"!!! Then I began about you & told him all the news out of your letter & we talked of *Moonshine*[313] & the 'Young England',[314] ......[?] which I thought sounded personal & such a pace as we went on till in came in Miss Clive & put him to flight when he shook hands & thanked me for my news & such. I can't help liking him, though I don't think him quite fit to be Mr Annabel, but he would be a better friend to me than Crockery or many others. His temper is good, I am sure & that is a great thing. How I long for Crockeriana. Keep it all safe till we meet.

Now I know you will expect to hear of G. She behaved beautifully but things have not pleased her at all. No calling, no invite to stay there, but only a dinner there today! H[315] met William more than a week ago & asked us. You see there can be nothing serious in it, only no one can tell what every meeting may bring forth when there is a penchant which there undoubtedly is - tho' no intentions, but surely I can tell more after this evening & you shall hear. Will you like to hear of my lover? – with light hair & blue eyes & fair complexion & rather short, but so lively, so affectionate

---

[313] *Moonshine*, a comedy by Emmeline Charlotte Wortley (1806–1855).

[314] 'Young England' was a Victorian political group; it is possible that Richard Monckton Milnes suggested this name. It was a group, headed by Disraeli, which broke away from the Tory party supporting more liberal policies.

[315] Is this Hungerford? He has been interested in finding Annabel a suitor.

& so piquant, so companionable. While I have full possession of this little lover I can never wish for any other.

I need not tell you the name is Minny. I find my idolatry increasing sadly now that I begin to feel such an influence over her. The interest of managing her is so intense. She is so very sensible & reasonable & full of feeling that is like playing the most deeply interesting game & so far thank God, I have been able to play the winning part, for I am certainly mistress of her little heart & of her spirit. We had several battles, but none lately & her affection & obedience increase in equal proportion. G loves her as well as I do but she has never taken so much toil & trouble about her & consequently has not her mind occupied with her so much & the child, of course, feels the difference & tho' very fond of Aunty "Doudina", it is in a different way.

Wednesday 16th. We had a very pleasant party at V,[316] at least we met very pleasant people. Mr & Mrs Scudamore whom I knew before, Lord & Lady Hood, such a nice amiable young couple & his mother Mrs Hood, who has been a beauty, 2 Mr Holmeses & that was all. I must however tell you the sad news that there was a marked change from our last meeting with Mr H, such as convinces me that the old bachelor had felt himself in some danger & he's determined to recede. But all the little ins & outs of the case I must never tell his secret. When will it be comfortable to pour forth such thing into your sympathising bosom?

I have thought as much of Mrs Cunliffe's wise speech, but it's all turning upon whether he was wishing to marry or not & this is just it. I am more than ever convinced by the symptoms yesterday that there was a scratch, but the experience of 49[317] would soon set all right again if it were an inconvenient one. I must not write more now, for I have another letter to send by this post. I am glad there is a prospect of our seeing Henrietta. We hope Papa or Mamma will come here about the 10th of Sept & we shall, I believe, return with them, about the 20th. Farewell dearest. With best love to Mrs Cunliffe.

Ever your most affectionate, Ellen Tollet

---

[316] Were they with the Archer-Clives?
[317] Uncertain to what the number 49 refers, since 1849 has not yet arrived.

21. Minny with pet rabbit

Letter 50 [*cat: 161*]
Unexpected visit to Welshpool; Joseph Sykes, the Philosopher; visit to Royal Academy

[*probably sent from Welshpool*]

May 14th 1847

My Dearest Annabel,

What will you have been thinking of me for not writing sooner? What more will you think when you hear my history of where I have been at Welshpool. I had a most rapid & prosperous journey from London & found a pleasant, cheerful party here on Thursday, but there was the damper of a letter from W Clive giving an account of Minny being very poorly with inflammation of the chest - leeches etc. You may fancy I felt uneasy, but Friday's account was good & I staid quietly telling Georgy & Mary (Wicksted) all my London news to their great edification.

Well, on Saturday the carriage was at the door to take the Wicksteds to Crewe Station on their way to Shakenhurst when a letter came from William written in so nervous & uncomfortable style that I ran & put on my bonnet & shawl, had my brushes & night clothes thrown into a bag & snatching up a book & a roll got into the carriage & went off, taking our footman as escort as far as Ruabon - got to Welshpool by 7 o' clock & found all going well, but the sweet pet was much reduced & her cough still bad. However on the Monday her doctor said, "Take her off for a change of air as quickly as you can," & we sallied forth on Tuesday & I came on here, dropping William & his child at Styche [*his brother's residence*].

They follow me here on Saturday. I need not say to you what a hurry this has been to both mind & body but, thank God, I am pretty well at ease now & can begin to feel something like the repose which I have for some time been longing for. Dearest G is very well & quite lively with the excitement of my return & with hearing all I have to say.

The A[*rcher*] Clives come next Wednesday, but I am sorry to say the Philosopher [*Joseph Sykes*] will not join them. He has written me his reasons for not coming after leaving the verbal invitation unanswered for more than a week. He is most strange but alas! most interesting & I will, I think, tell you all when we meet, but don't expect anything romantic, only one of those sad bits of real life which perhaps it is well for us to know – if we are strong enough in our faith & hope to bear them.

Have you read an article in the January *Edinburgh* [*Review*] on Pascal? Try to find out for me who wrote it. I don't consider it as anything very powerful but extremely interesting & written in a good spirit & the subject of it is one of overflowing interest - I mean the character of Pascal. Did you ever read either his *Pensées* or *Lettres Provinciales*? I am reading *Modern Painters* with greatest delight.[318] You must read it. It will help you to read Nature better.

You can't think what a sweet invalid Minny makes - so sweet & gentle & loving. Her cold was quite accounted for by a most imprudent expedition in an open carriage to the W of the [*Powis*] Park. It was exactly like one of your attacks & the same system pursued - bleeding first & then bitters. The fever soon went but I fear the cough would be rather obstinate.

I got to the Academy on Wednesday. I don't delight in *Joan of Arc*. Landseer's big picture is very striking; & a fine Stanfield made it. Mulready's[319] full of beauty & a Danby[320] I delight in a very simple subject of trees & reflections with a heron in the corner. Look at it. I am most anxious to hear from you, dearest A.

I find Mr Reeve is the widower of a great friend of the Nightingales of whom I have heard them talk eternally by her maiden name. She was a most charming woman & has one little girl. Mamma is very comfortably well & takes Dr Holland's stuff. Farewell, dearest A. My pleasure at the Hill St dinner[321] & evening was seeing how nicely you did the honours – so polite & yet so dignified. I admired you.

It is most pleasant to adore what one loves.

Your most affectionate,

EHT

Richard Monckton Milnes has been referred frequently previously in these letters: his first mention was in Letter 9 (1835) with regard to his poetry. He became a witty, literary politician. From the mid 1840s, Florence Nightingale had been attracted to him through his kindly attitude to the ordinary man, and his support for the emancipation of women. After many proposals of marriage, he finally proposed to her at Whitsuntide in 1849 but she rejected him. Perhaps it was because she was ambitious for herself and could see no future in being too involved in his social life.

---

[318] *Modern Painters*, Vol 1, (1843) by John Ruskin (1819-1900).
[319] William Mulready (1786–1863), Irish painter.
[320] Francis Danby (1793–1861), Irish painter.
[321] Another house of the Crewes in London, often used by Henrietta.

The letters that follow refer quite often to the couple, and from Letter 52, Ellen implied Annabel's interest their relationship.

Letter 51   [*cat: 160*]
Capesthorne; Charles Cotton; Annabel's relations; bluebell chain; reading, whist, drawing; 'Modern Painters'; Minny better

28th

May [*1847?*]

My Dearest Annabel,

I flatter myself you will be glad to hear from me again as my last letter did not give a very prosperous account. Thank heaven, I can now say that Minny is quite recovered her usual fine spirits & with them some peace of mind to me. It is not that I am given to harass myself with ungrounded fears but there is something peculiarly affecting in seeing the child ill & I suppose no one who has suffered much can help a sort of feeling as if sorrow has got into the habit of coming & therefore would come, but this is only at dark moments. I feel as if I had a good deal to tell you of my quiet sobs.

We had the A(rcher) Clives last week & most agreeable they both were & they seemed to enjoy their visit. We had beautiful weather & I must say the place did look perfectly lovely & they liked the Wilbrahams & Mrs Delves Broughton[322] who were here & the dinners were quite astonishingly good (which I think he appreciates & she admires). In short it was a good hit. As we agree she really wears her happiness so agreeably that we can quite forgive her for it – but it is marvellous. He is a thoroughly good, useful & pleasant domestic article with looks that win upon you, I think, & a most pleasant evening, not half so interesting as a less earthly healthy well-to-do person but just one who in this world makes & enjoys happiness. I think I never felt anything of this kind more striking than Mrs Davenport[323] coming here - just after she left us. She is looking handsomer than I ever saw her. There is a cold parity in her beauty & a mere simplicity in her

---

[322] The Delves Broughton lived at Doddington Hall near Woore.

[323] Now a widow, Mrs Davenport was formerly married to the owner of Capesthorne. She appears often in later letters.

character & manner which makes her a person entirely different from all other women. She is even more unlike other beautiful women than plain ones & it seems so strange that in her the absence of charmingness seems to be her great charm.

The contrast of her fate & C [*Caroline?*] Clive's was really a thing to haunt one! She carried dearest Georgina off to Capesthorne yesterday which I was very glad of as old D[*avenport?*] is left at Wiesbaden so they would enjoy their friendship most comfortably. G continues most cheery & looks quite beautifully well- long may it last! Mrs D told us that Manoni? is Jenny L.......'s servant & mentioned some nice anecdotes of her. He was chosen as being trustworthy, not to be bribed by her visitors!

It was strange that you should meet the Philosopher [*Joseph Sykes*] & I wish you had been next to him at dinner. I am glad you agree with me in liking his looks which is certainly a very remarkable one.[324] If you will expect a history of romance you must be disappointed. Georgy being away, I was left alone with my meditations only interrupted by Minny & her sweet ways. I have been reading *Modern Painters* & am perfectly delighted with the first part of the 1st vol. I read some of it aloud to C Clive & she meant to buy it. I have also got the next section of Pascal & am reading much that is new to me of his. I have also got Coleridge's friend to crack my brains over & all this with drawing makes me busy enough.

We play whist at night. I really hardly like to tell you of the beauty of this Spring above all others. We have had no east wind & hard cloudless skies but the most glorious clouds & soft south winds & sunshine & the expression of nature has been quite different. There is no beauty of Summer or Autumn the least to be compared to it & I certainly never remember being so much enchanted with its loveliness before. Perhaps you will say my own perceptions are quicker than is hardly likely –Yet we know that "Nature never did betray the heart that loved her"[325] & therefore I am prepared to believe that our enjoyments of her may go on still increased to

---

[324] This was a different opinion about Joseph Sykes. She called him an ugly youth in Letter 8. He had stayed with the Tollets for a long time before Eliza's death in 1836.

[325] Quotation from Wordsworth's *Lines written above Tintern Abbey*.

the end. But still this spring is not like former ones. I have just been interrupted by Minny begging to help to make a bluebell chain, which is now happily completed.

I see in your letter that you ask me about Mr H V's[?] health. It has been a little ailing but he is very fussy about it. I believe his great object in life is some great metaphysical work about his writing & he is always anxious to be well in order to be able to work at it. Everything is to give way to it! I saw Sir V's name somewhere in the newspaper.

We go to Shakenhurst on the 16th. Penelope is off to the Nightingales in Hampshire tomorrow. Are the Delameres come to London? Were you disappointed in Jenny[?].

You have heard me talk of the Charles Cottons & their romantic history. After 6 years of great happiness only clouded by bad health she is going to be confined & is perfectly well! A second miracle! You remember that he was constant to her for 15 years!

Farewell, dearest of A's.

Give my love to Mrs Cunliffe.

Ever your most affectionate,

E H Tollet

The letter below is by far the most important; it is two letters pushed into one tiny envelope with an additional comment on the flap. The problem is that the second part of the letter seems to relate to a royal event which took place in Crewe at a later date than the first. So far we have not resolved this contradiction. Certainly Ellen would have enjoyed writing the childish play dialogue at the end, just as she enjoyed charades.

Letter 52   [*cat: 264*]
Holiday in Towyn; news from France; present Archbishop; Darwin's thoughts about Sumner; Florence Nightingale; Mr Milnes; Cheshire gossip; Miss Martineau; Queen's stopover in Crewe; visit to Atherstone Hall; Poor Law Officer

Towyn
Monday, July 10 & Wednesday, July 12, 1848
Postmark: Machynleth
To: Hon Miss Annabel Crewe, Marsh Gate, Richmond, Surrey

My dearest Annabel,

I will make up for my long silence last time by a quick reply to your long & delightful letter which was even more than usually acceptable in our present state of retirement. I think it may amuse you to hear a little of our way of life at this most unheard of place. All our friends talk of looking us out on the map, but perhaps you have more Welsh geography. Towyn is a 2nd rate [?] sort of Welsh town half a mile from the sea, but immediately on the shore are 2 or 3 new houses one of which we rent. It is very a good house & clean.

22. Painting by Ellen or Georgina.

The sea is magnificent – a wide uninterrupted expanse of ocean which never retires far, even at low water. There are good sands but no rocks or any particular beauty in the shore itself but on turning our backs to the sea we have before us a nearby plain with herds of cows grazing & a river winding through it; beyond this plain about a mile off, lies the lovely wild bare hills, which stretching on each side of a narrow valley, lead the eye on to Cader Idris which rises above them all in the distance & is really a grand object.

You will easily believe that here are materials for sketching & as we have William's open carriage here, we are able to penetrate into the country all round us which is lovely - full of valleys & rocks & brooks & every perfection of Welsh scenery. So far all sounds Elysian but then our weather has been very indifferent, sometimes frightfully stormy & the time of year is not the best for drawing. Still we have amused ourselves very much with our drawing & the best thing is that the sea has worked wonders in G's health. She now looks quite robust. Minny too is more blooming than ever but I have not been so well as usual, strange to say. Our fatigue & anxiety, I think, had previously knocked me up & I am only just now beginning to get right. We leave next week.

On wet days we have been rather dull as you may fancy with only a small supply of books & such horrid hard horse-hair chairs & sofa. Then our mutton is necessarily either tough or high, having only a damp cellar to keep it in. The butcher is obliged to get our 'go' order before he can run the risk of killing a sheep! We get 30 delicious eggs for 1/- which is a comfort & of course brought all our own groceries & the butter & bread are excellent so superior to what they would be at Newcastle! The people are so nice, honest & simple & polite. I forgot to mention, when on the eating subject, delicious salmon at 4^d a lb! I am afraid you are hardly housekeeper enough to care for my details, but I know who is.[326]

We have not been so destitute as not to have the *Times* every evening & how deeply interesting it has been. How horrible. What a gallant death did that noble Archbishop die.[327] It appears to me one of most touching events of modern days. The hireling Louis Philippe[328] ran away because he was a hireling but Arch[*bishop*] followed his master's example & gave his life for the sheep as he said himself. I wish I thought the Archbishop of Canterbury would do the same.[329] I hope he would tho' I don't wish him to have the opportunity. I rather should have liked to have heard Sumner's lectures tho' a sentiment of his filled me with horror – he says: "Prayer is a disease of the Will". Do get Maurice's *Sermons* on the Lord's Prayer, only

---

[326] Mrs Cunliffe comes to mind, or one of her servants.

[327] The Archbishop of Paris was trying to negotiate peace during the riots in 1848 but was killed by insurgents on the 27th June.

[328] King Louis Philippe ran away, abdicated and was exiled to England in 1850.

[329] John Bird Sumner (Archbishop of Canterbury, Feb 1848–Sept 1862), previously Bishop of Chester and probably known to the Tolletts, was chosen by Lord John Russell.

2/6. Mr Darwin said Sumner's *Lectures* were more than he could understand but he delighted in listening to them, as he would to good music.[330]

I have had a charming letter from Florence [*Nightingale*] since I came here. They were come to London & she had seen Mr Tremenheere.[331] There was not much to tell of course but she could not resist writing to me about their interview. How I wish I knew whether he has the slightest feeling for F. beyond what every intellectual or moral being must have great admiration! She really is, in heart and mind, <u>perfection</u>. I think her even improved since you saw her - certainly handsome & I think more perfect in manner & if possible raised in mind by her Roman life. It is quite natural it should be so. Such people must improve & grow nearer & nearer to Heaven. I think religion is more than ever the great object of her thoughts, as it is I am sure the main spring of her conduct.

She does not mention Mr Milnes having been at Embley,[332] but of course he meant there by "Hampshire". I am glad to hear "The Crescent"[333] is shining so brightly in domestic life & I trust there is no fear of his wife hiding the cross. I have seen your name at the Q[*ueen*]'s Ball - very gay indeed! Penelope went to dine with my Lord but Pugin [*the architect*] did not come but she did not care for that & seemed to hear Cheshire gossip from L[*ad*]y De Tabley. I think the death of poor Mrs Cornewallis-Legh's unexpected baby is a sad thing.

By the bye, I sifted the *Jane Eyre* report & feel sure she is not Jane Evans. Immediately on our return to Welshpool, Mrs Davenport is to visit us there. It will be a droll change seeing her there & alone instead of at

---

[330] After giving up the study of medicine at Edinburgh University in 1827, Darwin decided to become a clergyman but fortunately abandoned this career also. However, Darwin recorded his views on Sumner's *The Evidence of Christianity*.

[331] Seymour Tremenheere (1804-1893), barrister, schools' inspector, poor law officer and a government officer, was a friend of Miss Martineau. Florence Nightingale was in the public eye for her literary work before her fame as a hospital reformer. She had been to Rome – hence the reference.

[332] Richard Monckton-Milnes was Florence Nightingale's suitor at this time, and Florence Nightingale often stayed at Embley Park in Hampshire. Note that Ellen was telling Annabel about it, a useful source of information about the man she later married.

[333] A soubriquet for one of Annabel's friends?

Capesthorne & with Mr D, but I expect to enjoy it extremely. You know how very much I always admire her. If her visit affords anything amusing or interesting I will give you the benefit.

I suppose Henrietta will be coming to Hill St on her way North. When are you coming to Madeley? Do say before long. I have not read Miss Martineau but long for it. FN did not speak of Archd(eacon) Manning.[334] She did not approve at all of the effects of his fascinations on young ladies she says he encourages them to religious confidences which are most dangerous to them. You ask about where Mr Trevor lives. [335] He is ambassador to the Mining Districts to poke out about Education, & so he is either travelling or in London or occasionally in Cornwall as the case may be.

Farewell now, dearest A, I have chattered on about O [*nothing*]. All well at Betley but a distress about the hay, a noble crop, spoiling. You must direct your next to Welshpool, but of course, I don't expect it yet.

Your most affectionate,

E H Tollet

According to Queen Victoria's diary this event below took place in September, 1848 **after** *the date on the main letter. It must be a later letter. Hinchliffe wrongly states that it took place in October.[336] Also the days are not consistent with the postmark. The letter continues:*

Saturday evening 8 o'clock. Weather dark & rainy. Scene the back parlour at Betley Hall. Time tea.

Ellen: There's a carriage.

G: So there is . . . .

Mother: I'm excessively frightened.

G & E: How very foolish – we are not frightened at all . . . .

---

[334] Henry Edward Manning (1808-1892) became a RC Cardinal and later Archbishop of Westminster.

[335] An associate of Mr Tremenheere.

[336] In his more respected book *Barthomley*, to add to the confusion about this event.

Father: How excessively wrong of you not to be frightened. It's very odd you can go on in that way. It must be something serious.

G & E: Well let's go & see.

So saying they rush to the front door where they find Fox already holding up a lamp to the features of Mr Willott the clergyman who sits at the door on our horse chay[337] & both[338] are exclaiming, "The Queen's at Crewe Hall - Yes & P. Albert & 3 children, & dinner is ordered at 8 o'clock dead."

"Oh dear," cry the Ladies, "only think! No one at home to enjoy the fun it is too dreadful! How did it happen?"

"Oh I can't tell exactly but all of a sudden the 2 determined to stop at Crewe Station & asked if they could be put up" & Edwards said, "Yes, perhaps then & at the Hall. I met a carriage going from the Hall to fetch her!!!"

This, dearest, is all I can tell you at present but tomorrow we may hear more. The paper announced her intention of sailing from Aberdeen. If so she could not have got on this railway but we suppose she never embarked but came by land all this way. Of course there must have been some contretemps to account for the 2 storming an Englishman's castle, but what a strange, wondrous, delightful event for the said castle to afford a night's lodging to a benighted Queen.[339] How I wish you & I & a few more select guests had been there to enjoy the fun & to hand down the remembrance of it to our posterity!

---

[337] Chay probably means chaise (carriage).

[338] Was this Wilmot?

[339] Here are the crucial dates from the online *Queen Victoria's Journals*. On Monday 10th July 1848 Victoria visited the Zoological Gardens from Buckingham Palace, and still the Palace on Wednesday and so could not have been at Crewe. On Friday 29th of September, the Queen and family decided to return from Scotland by train from Perth rather by sea. They reached Crewe on Saturday. From the journal: "At ½ p. 7, we arrived at Crewe. After some discussion, we remained there, & found the rooms of the Inn, very good, & quite sufficient for our words. We dined downstairs." They left for London at 6 on Sunday morning. These dates are later than the letter. The source of the story in the letter remains a mystery.

Sunday. I have heard that the dinner was to be at the Inn not at the Hall but I hope that she went there to sleep that there may be a "Queen's Bed".

On Wednesday G & I are going to Atherstone to visit Mrs Bracebridge.[340] It is a visit of F Nightingale's making, she being anxious G & Mrs B should make a friendship. The address is: C.B. Esq. The Hall, Atherstone. He returns on Saturday, I believe. Poor dear Henrietta, I fear she is very poorly & I long to hear what Dr Rigby says to her.

Ever Dearest A, your affectionate,

EHT

[*Inside the flap*] W. Clive has been to Bradfield to the reopening of the beautiful church Tom has built. The Bishop of Oxford preached & 100 clergy were present.[341]

Letter 53   [*cat: 267*]
Apologies to Mrs Cunliffe; society news; Henrietta; reading Lamb; Florence Nightingale's beliefs; rain in August; Annabel's picture for Dickens

Betley,

Monday Aug 28th 1848

My dearest Annabel,

At last here is quiet day to write to you which I have long been thinking of. I know Henrietta wrote to you as soon as she arrived, so you know something of us all.

Let me begin by acknowledging the receipt of a note from Mrs Cunliffe. I never dreamt of including My Lord among the friends whom I would ask to call upon the E C[*lives*] or [*Lord Powis*], taking it for granted that he was certain to do so. I only alluded to the Twemlows & Wilbrahams & Mainwarings.[342] My Lord has called I know, but I know nothing of any further civilities & will take care not to interfere in any way in the matters.

---

[340] Mr & Mrs Bracebridge took Florence Nightingale to Egypt.

[341] Tom Stevens' church was designed by G G Scott. After Carry's death he never remarried. He also rebuilt a Church of England Community College in Bradfield.

[342] The Mainwarings lived at Whitmore Hall.

It was rather hard on poor Henrietta coming into a week of company in spite of many advance circumstances. I thought her decidedly better than last [*time*]; she was most agreeable & affectionate to us. Lady Morley was quite distressed at the alteration in her but no wonder, not having seen her since she went abroad! Time enough to alter any one. She certainly does look very delicate, all eyes, but she was elegantly dressed & looked remarkably nice, I thought. Lady M was rather a moveable [?] feast, as she was last year & did not arrive late Thursday, her leaving on Friday did not have much of her & of course she was very different person[?]with no intimate friend like Mrs Cunliffe to draw her out. But I always like her, independent of her fun[?] she is such a nice, natural character. The de Salis[343] family paid great court to her. The old Countess is very goosey[344] & sent off in an agony to Chester for a doctor because she had a bad night. [*illegible*] forgives her, but I really believe she had designs on My Lord for her daughter. She said to Georgina that she believed him to be "a man of first rate intellect, a master mind only clouded by shyness & eccentricity!"

How long she means to stay I don't know, but we, like H[*enrietta*], think it will be a good while, for we heard the young gentleman talk of <u>hiring</u> a poney[345] during his stay. Lady Williams was to come on Friday & leave for Capesthorne today. On Saturday Mrs Davenport came to us & is just gone home to receive her beloved sister-in-law. It is her first visit to Capesthorne & I should think it would be very painful, tho' a good deal less so than [*in*] her brother's life time. How far Mrs D & she will ever hit it off, I don't know, but it is wise to try this experiment for only 3 days at first. It shakes both my mother & me that Mrs Davenport[346] does not seem so happy as she did in the days of her slavery. I really believe she feels lost for want of her master. Georgy & I are to go there on 15th or 16th to meet the Hortons & there are hopes of Mr Leitch,[347] the artist, but the niece has threatened to have him in Scotland which puts us in a fright. I shall be so glad to meet Mrs Horton's son! D alas holds out hopes of Mr Felps[?] which would be

---

[343] A wealthy European family.
[344] Meaning *nervous*.
[345] Alternative spelling of *pony*.
[346] Mrs Davenport was formerly the Lady of the House 'in her slavery'.
[347] Artist to the Queen.

too delightful. Nothing can be can be more open or affectionate than she is with me as well as G, as I look upon it. Mr D disliked me which made her so exclusively G's friend in his lifetime. I am so very glad you read & liked Maurice's *Sermons*. I will do your bidding about Stanley's & I know where I can borrow them.

We have had a great deal of interesting reading lately. The Final Recollections of Lamb are deeply interesting. I forgot whether you are an admirer of *Elia*.[348] I am thankful to say G's health continues to improve & her spirits are conspicuously better. Mr T has actually been at Lea Hurst, the N[*ightingale*]'s place in Derbyshire, on his way from Scotland. Florence wrote to us to go – but of course we would not. I fully believe he is a little *épris* with F but that will never do him any good. As to her taste for Romanism, she has it in a philosophical & religious way. I think no abstractions or errors would blind her to the beauties of their faith nor deter her from enjoying the associations with the days of early Christianity, which Romanism is so full of. I know she said Christian Rome interested her more than Pagan Rome - she was always joking over the Basilica with Lord Lindsay so now I think I have explained to you how she gave people the notion of learning that way. She formed a friendship with a g[*ood*] f[*riend*] of Henrietta, Mr Collyer & R C. I need not, I am sure, say what a sad disappointment it was – not that because we had long expected it – but sad was your giving up Madeley this year.[349]

Oh, the sweet pleasures of August you have not lost much, for the eternal gain has made everything of this kind impossible. The dripping state of every [*illegible*] & here the sponginess of the earth – nothing was ever so destructive to all enjoyment! I can't help thinking how lucky we were to be able to make so many drawings at Towyn, otherwise this summer would have passed a blank in that time.

I hear you are doing another Dickens picture.[350] Indoor models are bad this year. I am copying a drawing of my own, an odious occupation. It is for

---

[348] Published in 1823 in book form.

[349] Implying that Annabel had not been to Madeley that year.

[350] Uncertain what this drawing refers to. According to Annabel Crewe, Charles Dickens visited Crewe Hall where his grandmother was housekeeper (see

Mrs Nightingale but really I believe it will be a failure. We are going tomorrow to Peatswood to meet a good artist a pupil of De Wint.[351] So I hope we may see something good.

Penelope is gone to Welshpool; she says Minny is most satisfactory both in body & mind. They are going to have the B[ishop] of Madras there, [352] which P[*enelope*] will enjoy. I suppose you know your friend Mrs Levett is married. I hear she is a pretty, pleasing person & it is a great marriage for her. H(enrietta) is to come here next week. How we shall wish for you, dearest Annabel. What should you think of steaming[353] down to us some day? Would it be so great an effort? Only from life, do you know?

Farewell for the present. I wish you would write rather before the regular allowance & then I could write again after H's visit.

What a sad loss that Daga's wife has to every body.

Ever with best love to Mrs Cunliffe. Your most affectionate,

E H Tollet

Letter 54 [*cat: 263*]
Henrietta's poor health; the Hensleigh Wedgwoods; amusing Darwin visit; Punch; Florence Nightingale and Monckton Milnes; Wicksted's house near the Queen; writing letters; gossip

Capesthorne
Sept 19, 1848

To: Hon Annabel Crewe, Marsh Gate, Richmond, Surrey

Dearest Annabel,

I have not done exactly as I would – *viz* write after Henrietta's visit to Betley. I have waited till I came here which after all will not make my letter any better. I daresay now you have seen H[*enrietta*] herself & know all about

---

Letter 33). She was a wonderful storyteller, and may have influenced the writings of Dickens. These encounters must have occurred around 1820 (*Cheshire Archives and Local Studies*).

[351] Peter De Wint (1784 – 1849), an English landscape painter.

[352] Probably the Rt Rev George Spencer (1799–1866). He was the Bishop of Madras between 1838 and 1849.

[353] Ellen's term for travelling by train.

her. We called at Crewe a few days before she left & I was grieved to see her so poorly. Indeed I was quite anxious to know what you think of her – she seemed to me so very weak & likely to be weaker still, unless some remedy could be devised. I am afraid tonics do not agree with her yet she seems to require them so peculiarly. While with us she was, if not very strong, still what I call, very comfortable in far better spirits than last year & I really did not feel once as if she were shocked at any thing anybody said, which was a great blessing. Dear soul, I was glad her last week at C(rewe) was one of perfect repose. It would, I hope, give her strength for her journey.

We had the Hensleigh Wedgwoods and Mr Darwin with us. It was quite odd to see the latter in a country house & he declared he had never been in any but suburban ones before. He is very invalidish[*sic*] & I was afraid it would kill him, but when he once took to lying flat on his back on the library sofa, I began to think he might bear it.[354] I want him to write "A Week in the Country" for *Punch*. One of his general remarks is to be that we have lean venison for dinner every day.

The Wicksteds are having great fun in Scotland being next door to the Queen. Before her arrival the steward came to beg leave to bake at Abergeldie [*Castle*][355] & also to ask for room in their coach houses. They sit close to her in Church & they were expecting her to come to see their house when they wrote.

A great disappointment awaited us here. Mr Leitch has been commanded by the Queen to stay & give lessons to Miss Eliza of Hoherlahe[356] so has come not here. Lady A & Miss Horton & Teresa T arrived by the 7 am train. Miss H is very, very nice. She is quite enthusiastic about Florence. She was going to see them in Derbyshire but they are all suddenly gone off to

---

[354] After his world expedition, Charles Darwin returned home with a permanent undiagnosed illness. Darwin had known the Tollets for many years. He had corresponded about cross-breeding of cattle in 1839 with George Tollet and on fox-hounds with Charles Wicksted (F Burkhardt & S Smith, Correspondence of Charles Darwin, Vol 1, (1985), Cambridge UP, and other references in Vol 2 & Vol 3).

[355] Two miles from Balmoral. (see earlier footnote on Abergeldie.)

[356] Half-sister of Queen Victoria.

Frankfurt. What as bait did you throw at your aggravating woman? What have you heard about Mr M M?[357] I thought it must all have been over by this time. F[*lorence*] is extremely conscientious about ever revealing any of those affairs, so we are certain not to hear anything from her & my head was so full of other things whenever at Embley that I did not question Parthe[*nope Nightingale*], as I intended. Do pray tell me anything you hear. The N's are coming back for the winter in Embley. There are many things I could tell you if we met that I can't write.[358]

Do you remember how you angered me once by admiring that strange sentiment of Emerson's about a letter being as good as an interview![359] It is only the shallowest part of one's mind that our nibs run out on paper. There is besides in letters an entire absence of those involuntary disclosures which make our friends talk so charming, those little betrayals of oneself & others which slip out unawares & which both wisdom & principle remind you to withhold when you are writing. I believe some reserved people find it more easy to reveal thoughts through the medium of pen & ink but for my part I never found it so except when touching on some very painful subjects in which agitation is apt to interrupt in conversation.

Mrs Holland & Emily are here so we are many women & only a few dull men. Arthur D is not at home. He is growing very handsome & is tolerably pleasing. He has his father's mouth precisely. Lady Williams seems to have approved of everything here, but the fall of Trinker. I confess there appear to me to be some dead bodies where living forms could not be well spaced, but it is all done (with) the agent's advice & is no doubt generally right.[360]

---

[357] Mr Monckton Milnes has been rejected by Florence Nightingale before.

[358] Was Ellen giving information about Monckton Milnes? Ellen, it seemed, had been to Embley.

[359] This sounds like Emerson but we have been unable to find an exact quotation. The same sentiment was expressed in a letter of recommendation for Walt Whitman. Ellen seemed to be making a number of 'involuntary disclosures' in these letters.

[360] Difficult to make sense of this rambling paragraph. Who or what was Trinker? What are the dead bodies?

Offley was very lively & pleasant; he seems to like his lovely Muxton life.[361] Tell Mrs C, with my best love, I did not misunderstand her note in the least.[362] I understood it just as you say, & think it very possible that I might have done unintentionally what she guarded me against – at the same time I should not like to do anything the other way – you understand now don't you? The E C's asked us to dine to meet the W Egertons but we could not go. Our little Dr told us he had been to see him as he had been a little ailing. Mrs T is looking beautiful & people report she is going to (be) married to the Archbishop of Canterbury, Major Gordon or Mr Tollemache, all equally true. Farewell dearest A.

Your most affectionate,

E H Tollet

Letter 55   [*cat: 265*]
F Nightingale; religion; Papacy; Ellen's reading; Hungerford & marriage; Chair at Oxford; George Tollet gave up farming; Mrs C

Welshpool
Dec 26, 1848

Dearest Annabel,

> Tho' Christmas may not be to us
> The merry time it once was ages ago
> Though I like our old heads in the right places
> & a friend is a pleasant thing I think of.
> Oh, like me I get ever a friend
> Though a friend I am seldom to see.[363]

And so I am thinking of this dear woman this Xmas Day sitting alone, as I am during afternoon Church which my prudent care for my health prevents me attending.

---

[361] The Offley Crewes were at Mucklestone.

[362] Has Ellen fallen foul of Mrs Cunliffe again, or was she still referring to the same note as in Letter 53 [*cat 267*]?

[363] Seems an embarrassing piece of doggerel!

Minny is just scampered out with her old nurse. I am a governess, the real one being invalided & gone home on sick leave. I came here a fortnight ago leaving the Great House for domestic purposes & Fanny had been proving herself mortal by being ill for the first time in her life[364] & so it was sad to leave G behind for a time.

All is now quite well at B[*etley*]. On my arrival here I found the governess very bad & Minny not well, so I was of great use & thank goodness, my darling is now blooming. Having satisfied your friendly anxieties about health & I proceed to express my own which are great to hear, that dear Mrs Cunliffe is quite well again after the serious ailment you mentioned. Where are you I wonder? Still in London, I guess. Whenever you don't know where people are exactly, always conclude they are in London & 9 times out of 10 it is right. I am really glad to hear that you warned my Lord against those horrid people. "The Cunliffe Hobby" is on call - Miss [*D*] is really the very boldest girl I ever saw.[365] After I wrote to you I saw sense & searching but a midnight meeting at Madeley can suffice to make me do justice to the subjects. It is all the worse in her as she affects the religious character – fasts on a Friday etc.

My Lord really talked so much about the Miss Waldegrave; at last asked our opinions of them so often, that we begin to hope he might really be falling in love but from the last accounts I had, he still goes on asking the same questions so I fear he will never get any further & he seems so happy & will [*be*] content now, that I believe after all, matrimony would be an experiment & with such a wife and mother-in-law as the old countess meant to give him a most dangerous one. Do pray tell me what he said to your warnings. He called on us & said he wanted to see Annabel & was going to London! Since then P[*enelope*] & G[*eorgina*] have dined there & met the Vyses.

---

[364] Fanny, who had been treated as an invalid most of her life, seemed to be dismissed harshly by Ellen.

[365] Ellen was discussing advice on suitors for Hungerford. It was guessed that arranging a marriage for Hungerford was the "Cunliffe Hobby".

G has had a very clever letter from F[*lorence*] Nightingale about the Pope.[366] She can't in her heart justify his running away. I am quite distressed at its merely considering him as a fine moral character. Besides even if we thought it symptomatic of this fate of the Papacy, this would be no comfort. For every one who knows anyth(ing) of foreign religious matters, says that if Papacy goes, this is nothing better than infidelity ready to rise up in its place & bad, as tho' the spiritual dominion of this life may be the State of Strauss[367] would be worse.

You may imagine how quiet my life is here – the dinners at P(owis) Castle have hitherto consisted of 4 souls by Lady P. & her daughter, W[*illiam*] & myself, but now Lord P. or George come home for Xtmas (Christmas). The married event[?] has been stopped happening[?] by the illness of a baby. I suppose Lord P. is looking out for a wife, as he had taken to visiting so much.[368]

I am so glad you like Maurice's sermons. I think it is very interesting to see the infinite variety of thoughts which (are) deep, tho' simple words suggest to thinking minds - like his Divine truth is a well of endless depth, tho' happily his water at the surface is as wholesome as that beneath is & I confess I like to be helped to dive a little.

Did I rave to you about *Guesses at Truth,* 2nd series published in 1848?[369] It is such a book! I forgot too whether I mentioned the Regius Professor of Modern History. Of course you would hear of it. I hope the appointment may be of use by drawing him away from metaphysics or solitude.[370] Sir F Doyle[371] would rejoice in the event I know, indeed I believe Dr Liddle & he had fingers in the pies.

What a melancholy end of *Talents & Knowledge* of the right without victors is poor Mr Smythe! I am very thankful in my heart this Christmas

---

[366] Pius IX.

[367] Was she referring to *Strauss: Life of Jesus* published in 1835?

[368] Presumably Lord P is Edward, 3rd Earl of Powis. He succeeded to the title in January, 1848. He never married (*thepeerage.com*).

[369] By A W & J C Hare (two brothers).

[370] Sir Henry Halford Vaughan.

[371] Sir Francis Doyle (1810-1888) was a British poet.

for G's health is so wonderfully restored & with it her spirits much improved.

Papa is going to give up his farm.[372] At his age it is no pleasure, only expense. He will let for £370 per annum. The tenant will supply us with butter & cream – we share beef, sheep & pigs. Do pray tell me when you write whether dear Mrs C is out of her Harper [*court case*] yet[373] - we never hear a word about it now.

Farewell with best love, your most affectionate,

Ellen Tollet

Letter 56 [*cat: 299*]
Some humour & dinner at the Vicarage in Betley

[*1848?*]

My dearest Annabel,

I return *Repudiation* with many thanks. Well, our dinner party went off very well. The moment I saw Mr Farquhar, I felt as if I had seen him before, so exactly had my mind pictured him & his conversation & manner were both just what I expected. He is so very like Mr George Clive & Georgina & I say he is the hero of a French novel with whom the heroine (a married lady) is very much in love. Nothing can be more frivolous than

---

[372] George Tollet's farm was the original medieval building across the road from Betley Hall, where he had built his much praised model barn. The listed barn with water mill still stands and has been recently undergoing renovation. According to the 1851 census, Old Hall Farm was tenanted by Charles Timmis with a household of 12.

[373] Referred to in a letter from Henrietta. This seems to refer to an earlier case brought Mr Harper in July 1847 for various expenses incurred by the plaintiff, who, at the time, worked for his father, Mrs Cunliffe's Land Agent. Mr Harper was claiming £100. At the time Mrs Cunliffe's income was stated to be £6000 pa. The jury returned a verdict for the plaintiff; damages £185 (*Staffordshire Advertiser*, 24 July, 1847). The dispute continued in May 1848 where Mr Harper now claimed £1000. The court case involved 100 witnesses and barristers from London and Oxford. It was described as "a most tedious affair". The case was adjourned until October (*Staffordshire Advertiser*, 24 May, 1848). This is presumably what Ellen was asking about but the editors have been unable also to find the outcome of the case.

this character appears, but there is a sort of gay, good humour about him that is rather amusing for a very short hour. I sat next to him at dinner & he told me 3 French stories which, after what you had said, was rather overcoming. He talked a little of you & said he liked you very much & thought you would marry Hugh Cholmondley – but he was on his guard, knowing we were friends, as I could not draw much out. I should not have thought him at all worthy of your agreeable dinners. For a ball he would be valuable, or whenever you had an infliction of very young ladies.

23. The home of the Rev and Mrs Henry Turton.

Yesterday Mrs T(urton) could not persuade him to go twice to church, so she wrote a note to G(eorgina) to borrow *Proverbial Philosophy* for him.[374] This note he brought himself to our back door, where he found the cook – every other soul being at church except Mamma - the cook came to Mamma & got the book!!![375] Picture to yourself the scene in the kitchen

---

[374] *Proverbial Philosophy* (1848), a book of thoughts and arguments by Martin Tupper, mentioned previously (Letter 35, *cat: 295*).

[375] Their mother would hardly approve of a suitor, who would not go to church twice on Sunday. Has Ellen been trying to find a suitor for her sister in the past years?

when he revealed himself but denied her to preserve his incognito! A propos the dinner - Mrs Turton's little dinner was so nice – everything so well cooked, that if Prince Albert had been there she need not have been ashamed. Only fancy my laughing about a friend of ours who was disappointed at her brother marrying the grand daughter of an apothecary & the gay Mr F[*arquhar*]is the grandson of Sir WT whom Papa remembers, an apothecary tho' he afterwards rose so rapidly. I hope he did not think I meant any malice.

If you have any communication with my Lord of Crewe will you mention Charles coming here this week, as I want him to be asked for Saturday, tho' if I fear he would not thank us for any pains, but we should like him to go with us![376]

Your most affectionate,

EHT

Letter 57   [*cat: 266*]
A party at Crewe Hall with the Crewe family; Ellen wanting a chat with Annabel in private; Welshpool; cholera

Betley

Aug 17, 1849

My dearest Annabel,

I was going to write to you the early part of this week but when I found I was going to dine at Crewe I thought I'll just wait & see if there is any news, having mentioned the event of yesterday. I will not go back to what happened 3 weeks ago till I have told you the more recent details.

Charles & I went to C[*rewe*] yesterday & found the Grevilles, Palmers, Blackburnes, Mrs Brooke & Lady Morley & Mr Lattrell who were just arrived. I had not seen Mr Brooke Greville for years & years & should not have known him & he asked who I was! He seemed vary amiable. I was sorry to hear that tho' Mr Willoughby's health seems pretty good, that tumour increases & must be operated upon some day. Dear nice Mrs Blackburne, I was so glad to see her again & Fanny looked pretty with her

---

[376] Charles was probably a sporting companion for Hungerford and knew him well.

long black ringlets & red carnations. Of course we spoke of our mutual anxiety to hear a better account of dear Mrs Cunliffe. I felt rather hardened with your secret because I felt that Mrs B attributed the excessive retirement of the last year entirely to a cause which gave her more uneasiness with regard to health than she otherwise would have felt. I heard a very amazing story of Miss de Salis from Capt Greville – but I will keep it until we meet.

Do come to Madeley & let me come & see you! I could sit in my own room half the day or only come out when wanted, but I should so like once more to be with you for something more than a morning visit. How are you, dear? Here it is very cool & suited to you. How I should rejoice to hear your kind comforts coming to an end.

I shall now go back to Welshpool & send an anecdote for Mrs Cunliffe. I was calling one day on a good soul in the town of Welshpool & in the room I saw a fattish, amiable-looking elderly lady – but she never spoke at all till just as I was going away she seemed to make a great effort & to my surprise said, "I think ma'am you are a friend of the Honourable Mrs Cunliffe?" You can fancy my surprise & she went on to tell me how she had lived near her for years at Llangollen – how she loved the remembrance of her & of all her kind, good pleasant doings at Dyn Bryn – how her Friendly Club had prospered – in short she had tears of affection in her eyes & I felt quite delighted with the warm-hearted creature. She spoke of Price as a girl.[377] It was Miss Hughes, the dau[ghter], of the late clergyman at Llangollen & I promised to convey her best wishes to your Aunt. I am sure you would have been delighted. I have heard the way in which she spoke of the love she had won from people about Dyn Bryn.

The Powis Castle people returned before we left Welshpool. They were quite alone except for Dr W Graham. Lady P[owis] is wonderfully recovered & seems much the same as usual; her strength of body is something marvellous. We had a much less melancholy parting from Minny than usual. She was so much less tearful which I attribute to her being happy with Miss Miller. She is going with her father next week to Oakley Park where there is a little Victoria Clive of her own age.

---

[377] Mrs Cunliffe's lady's maid.

I have felt rather nervous about the cholera coming to Welshpool but hitherto there is no appearance of it although it has been for some time at Shrewsbury tho' not severely.[378] It is subsiding at Nantwich & beginning at Newcastle. It is very odd that 4 of the servants at Crewe have been ill the last day or two. I don't believe any one of them had anything of the nature of cholera. However no place is safe for 3 servants have died at Vaenol.[379] Mr Ap……. Smyth's place in Wales, a lone house, no cases at Caernavon the nearest town, except that of the doctor who attended these servants & died.

Lady Morley is looking as well as ever & seems quite equal to her métier. Poor Mr Lattrell looks rather past his & has too many of the infirmities of age to look comfortable as a visitor but his mind seemed fresh & lively. I am sorry to say my mother has been poorly lately but is better again. Oh, the rest is status quo. Farewell for the present, my dearest A – a bulletin will be welcome too.

Your most affectionate,
Ellen Tollet
P.S: We came home last Monday.

Letter 58   [*cat: 268*]
Mrs Tollet, Mrs Cunliffe & others ill; Ellen was the nurse; news of Parthenope & Florence Nightingale

Betley
Oct 1st,1849

Dearest A,

A thousand thanks both for your letter & its plots. What quantities I have to say! First thanks to dear Mrs Cunlifffe for the prescription – but

---

[378] Cholera was a worry to the population in Great Britain. In Newcastle-under-Lyme, with a population of about 10,000, over 200 people died and 1700 were taken ill during the outbreak which lasted from 19th June 1848 to 30th October 1849 (E A Underwood, The History of Cholera in Great Britain, *Proc Roy Soc Medicine*, Vol XLI, 165-173). The Brampton Museum in Newcastle has obtained a grant (2017) from the Heritage Lottery Fund to research the cholera epidemic map which annotates the houses in Newcastle where someone died of cholera.

[379] Near Towyn.

which my mother did not try for this reason, that she has no ailment but mere nerves. She has no irritation to soothe & even any small quantities of mercury lower her & act on the bowels. You see the cases are so different. I have no doubt that my mother's is in some way bodily ailment still in her present state; it is quite impossible to trace her discomforts to any bodily cause. A mental exertion will give her a bad night & these said mental exertions are caused by the most trivial things you can imagine – no real cause of anxiety, tho' I am sure she might have many / or at least one nightly one/ seems just now to affect her. In the beginning of this attack no doubt a derangement of the liver existed but that has long since passed away & I know that nothing but air & time can do her nerves any good so we must be patient & as long as there is no disease, I doubt not she will always rally from these attacks, even tho' her age is so advanced.

Fanny came back from the sea only to be laid up for a week with one of her gouty attacks & when I tell you that Minny has been having her liver out of sorts you may imagine that I, who am supposed to be & certainly am the soundest of the set, have had a good deal to do. But what are all such bodily fatigues compared to the weight of weariness which G's state causes me & yet she thinks me the happiest of women, I believe, & certainly I have the happiness of being free from any violent discontent about myself & I really begin to think one had better spend over life in fretting about other people than spend one week in bewailing oneself. I believe nothing but knowing how close a community of feeling that is between the sick & anxious & their brethren could have made me write to you in this way. If you had been all well & prosperous not a word of this would have been written. My dearest love, you know how deeply every word of your bulletin interests me.

The effects of the Brighton move have rarely on the whole been good – for how could the good aunt have been made worse more effectively than by anxiety about you & I know you were suffering from that horrid London? If the air has been a little too stimulating for her perhaps that effect may go off. If not & you are obliged to make another move. She has at least, you say, a little more strength than she had to bear it. I am sorry Dr Holland could not come. I think he would have been a comfort to you, tho' I daresay the dear patient herself had almost rather be left to nature. Every thing that is nourishing & nothing that is stimulating must be her systems. I should think I am convinced that in most cases of general derangements the kidneys sympathize & I have no doubt it is difficult to distinguish between sympathy & original sin in any of our organs. Does Mrs C. like sago – if she does, did she ever try it boiled to a perfect jelly & eaten cold?

I have not slept out of this house for two months but I have [*dined*] at Crewe several times. Don't laugh at me when I tell you I thought Mrs Vyse almost pleasant the first ½ hour. She is so very pretty & good humoured but I soon found her wearisome indeed – so full of herself, so brimfull of long stories of the merest trifles which could only be interesting to herself. Dear Mrs Blackburne – what a jewel she is. I know her very little but I can't help loving her. I did contrive to escape Lady Charlotte & heard a great many stories against her. Mrs V declares that most of her sentences begin "If we get Ashridge ......" : this Mrs V. took care to forward to Lady Marian Alford!![380] who is her great friend & who gave her a splendid pink gown which Lady C E sent her maid to beg the pattern of!! Kate Greville's staying on at Crewe H[*all*] was a fruitful topic For Lady C's comments which Cap[t] G might have foreseen certainly – tho' I am certain nothing could be more innocent - My Lord & he never exchange words & as to other young men no woman can be so safe, for I plainly see, my dear, it will end in future petticoat parties there – it is evident that his Lord would like that & the last time I was there 4 ladies sat in a row at dinner most contentedly!

I had a long letter from Parthenope Nightingale the other day. They were staying at Mr Stuart Mackenzies with the B(isho)p of Norwich just before he died. They liked all the family so much. Have you read Maurice's *Sermons*? I strongly recommend them. One vol. *Lamestiner Recollections* in 1848 is very exciting, but so vain!

I have had an invitation to the Hinckers to meet Mrs Henry Coleridge, STC's daughter.[381] I must go but only for 2 nights. I wish I may meet Mr Cheney. I should like to see him again –still more his drawings. Florence

---

[380] Marianne Margaret Egerton (1817-1888), Viscountess Alford, was an artist, art patron and author. She was interested in needlework.

[381] Samuel Taylor Coleridge, the poet.

goes on as usual working hard at doing good & happy in her wisdom & goodness & a vast number of other blessings added!

Farewell dearest A. We are expecting Tom Stevens today for a few days which I am so glad of.

Your most affectionate & faithful friend,

EHT

Letter 59   [*cat: 269*]
Illness; nature of lumps; telescope; more about Florence Nightingale

Betley,
Nov 7, 1849

Dearest Annabel,

Thank you much for your report of your journey & for the subsequent bulletin via Henrietta. It is a great comfort to think of your having so kind & safe a friend & doctor as Dr Holland close by you. What he says about the complaint is precisely what I expected. I had always thought it was connected with that old pain, tho' I have never heard you say whether the pain she now has is very like the former one or not. Have any external remedies been tried, such as stimulating ointments, or anodyne plaister[382] or medicated baths to sit in? It seems as if medicine could barely reach the last & so far it is well to think that her constitution will not be damaged with the violence of the remedies, but that nourishment & gentle treatment will give nature every chance of acting & act she does most wonderfully sometimes in such cases.

We have an instance close by of a man who was given over by several D(octor)s having a mysterious internal tumour. He at last went to Bickerstaff who said, "You have one chance but it is a poor one, that of its bursting but I fear it is not of a nature that will." However it did & he is recovering fast after an illness of 2 ½ years & he says he knows it had been coming for 12 years. I am so glad to hear that the sickness is a little better and you, my dear love, to think of yours again having been ailing.

---

[382] Anodyne plaister comprises: red lead, 4 ounces; oil of lilies, half an ounce; Venice turpentine, 2 drams; opium, camphire, sugar of lead – all mixed together.

I daresay your bilious derangements proceed from not being able to take your most usual exercises. Pray use if possible a great deal of <u>friction</u> as a substitute. Before I leave the subject of health I must tell you that I am better in all respects except the power of taking exercise. My back rebels against it & I sometimes fancy that my weak point is in the bowel tho' some of my symptoms have led D(octo)rs to a different opinion. Lady Halford is wonderfully better & grateful beyond expression to Packman. It is indeed a wonderful triumph to him.

I liked my visit there very much but I had a horrid journey home - many obstructions on the <u>line</u> which kept me out till ½ past 10 at night – missed our carriage, etc.

Have you read *Evangeline* by Longfellow?[383] It is very pretty. Of course you will read *Shirley*,[384] a stupid name I think.

You will be glad to hear my mother is a great deal better in nerves & spirits. Georgy & I are going to Welshpool in a fortnight. P is coming back from Ireland very flourishing having seen Lord Rosse's telescope but not <u>through</u> it.[385] Did I ever tell you what a taste Minny has for the stars & she names her chickens "Arcturus", "Capella" - after favourite stars!

We have had quantities of rain here & today is a most winterly one, cold & wet to the worst degree. I grieve to say I think ours is a horrid climate in Autumn. In Leicestershire they have not half the rain.

You will I know rejoice I hear that I think G a shade better in mind tho' I fear not in body. I have a scheme but must wait till I get to Welshpool to practise it. Arthur Davenport is to go into the 1st Guards. Only that Florence N. is gone to Egypt with the Bracebridges.[386]

---

[383] A long epic poem about a girl in search of her lover (1847).

[384] *Shirley* (1849) a feminist novel by Charlotte Bronte. Ellen was quick off the mark to read it.

[385] 36 inch reflector telescope at Birr Castle, Ireland.

[386] Florence was taken by her friends as she was probably depressed after rejecting Monckton Milnes. It was a period for her of self-examination, and thoughts about what the future held for her. After his marriage to Annabel, Florence wrote about herself to a friend stating she was "the idol of the man she adored" (Bostridge, pp 128, 130).

Farewell, dearest A, I am more than ever thine,
Ellen Tollet

24. Main entrance of Betley Hall.

The relationship between Ellen and Annabel was complex. The former was assuming that she had some power to influence Annabel in her judgment and choice of suitors. The correspondence of the 1840s shows the increasing obsession of Ellen towards Annabel, which was not reciprocated. It is often assumed that women tended to share secrets and probably write in an affectionate manner. It seems probable that Annabel confided in her sister about Ellen's excessive familiarity, because Henrietta wrote in an undated letter (cat: 351) about the "Tollet affair", which was resolved without "a scene". She further commented that she was certain from what she knew of Ellen's disposition that Ellen did not know the terms on which the mutual friendship was based. The reader will have observed the increasing warmth of feeling by the writer from the mid 1840s, as illustrated by their mode of the endings "Your affectionate" changes to "Your most lovingest" or "Ever, dearest Annabel, your attached friend" or "Farewell, dearest Annabel" or "I am more than ever thine". Perhaps Annabel had always decided to meet Ellen in company or with Mrs Cunliffe or Mrs Blackburne to avoid any possible embarrassment. She had also suggested that they should not write too frequently. This could have led to Ellen pleading desperately in Letter 57, "Do come to Madeley and let me come to see you. I could sit in my room half the day or only come out when wanted."

The next three letters reveal the developing relationship between the two friends. They continued to confide in each other. Ellen discussed her prospects of life as an unmarried woman with strong religious beliefs, and showed her concern that Annabel should choose a suitable husband. She confessed that she dreamt about her. At some point Annabel had disclosed her true feelings for Richard Monckton Milnes, described as Annabel's 'idiot'. (This is a term Ellen also used in writing to Parthenope Nightingale about their romance.)[387]

Letter 60   [*cat: 218*]
Illness and religious views on suffering; Ellen to go to London

Betley,
Monday 6th [*1849*]

My Dearest Annabel,

I must disobey you for once & write to you before I have a letter to answer for I cannot bear to think myself a fair weather friend. I must judge by my own feelings & think you will like to read a few lines from me, your faithful, loving & sympathising friend. You have indeed suffered sadly, dearest, & it would be in vain to tell you how every hour of every day I have thought of you & wished good wishes of all times for you. I cannot wish you more patience than I know you have had, nor more alleviations in tender nursing & affectionate doctoring.

Active bodily suffering is one of the chastenings of which I have least experience <u>in</u> <u>myself</u>, but I have seen too much of it in others, not to know that it is a discipline which God is pleased to bless with peculiar effects in purifying the hearts of His children & one under which He supports them with large gifts of heavenly comfort. What you have been enduring, my dearest A, will, I have no doubt, give an additional value to the many years of health which, I trust, are in store for you – I really believe health is one of the blessings that requires a temporary privation of it to make us thoroughly appreciate it – more than any other of our gifts.

---

[387] Claydon House Archive, bundle 245.

I am certain there are some uninterestedly strong people who can neither understand their own privilege nor the suffering of others. The enlarging of our sympathy for fellow creatures is a great gain from our own pains. Not that you seemed to require this, dearest A, for I know too well the tenderness of your feeling for all who are in trouble, sorrow, need or sickness – but it is better to have a virtue increased than a fault corrected.

Surely this dreadful weather will prevent Mrs Cunliffe's journey even if she can leave you, which I hope & trust she can. I am going to London to A Vaughan & other friends the end of next week. I need not say all that you will know so well of the happiness of seeing you. Each day is I trust bringing improvement. That blister[388] must have been a very effectual one, tho' so unusually painful. My mother thanks Mrs Cunliffe warmly for her trust to her friendship to let us hear more. Perhaps we may hear more tomorrow of her arrival at Madeley!

There never was so much sickness in our village as now. Everyone has an inflammation! My mother's cough is obstinate & will be so till summer comes. In other respects she is much better. God bless you, my own dearest Annabel.

Your ever most affectionate,

Ellen Tollet

Letter 61   [*cat: 354*]
Visit to Olton & the Archer Clives; British Association; comments on being an old maid; Ellen unwell; stays at Trentham

Solihull [*Olton House?*], Monday
[*1849*]

To: [*A, Upper Brook St*]

Dearest Annabel,

According to orders I write from the ocean of domestic felicity in which it is difficult for me, an old maid, to feel like anything better than the serpent in Paradise. I don't think these lives a woman with the commonest degree of attraction who could help feeling rather aggravated at seeing such a proof of the inconsistency of Fate.

---

[388] Blistering was a common method off curing ailments.

I know you & aunt don't agree as to the charms of the man[389] – tho' I defy anyone not to think him one of the pleasantest husbands possible, as cheerful & nice in his manners to her – so fond of his children. The only fault I can find in him is his being too fond of Paul de Kock[390] & indeed his very refined mind he cannot have - that is conceded. The children are perfect – boy sensible & good – girls pretty & full of fun. I can't reckon the last new £7000 a year as any gain (tho' they don't think so) for this place is to me all that one could want of worldly goods. She is as much in love as the day she married & acknowledges that every time he comes into the room is a fresh *accès de bonheur*! The Harcourts are pleasant enough but not violently agreeable. I rather wish them gone than not to have some quiet talks with C[*aroline Clive*]. She is very kind to me, not tender like some of our friends, that charm is wanting & that after all is the real sunshine of a visit, but she rather likes my company & is glad that I should like hers & her husband's.

There are lots of pleasant books & nobody ever works; they only read, eat, & talk. I suppose you have seen the Staffs Paper with all the speeches. It was really wonderful what good speakers they were. Not me who was not fluent. It was rather fatiguing because the room was hot but otherwise I liked it.[391]

I had a very pleasant dinner & breakfast at Trentham Parsonage [*The home of Rev Thomas Butt*] – very clerical Mr Wilbraham was there & he & Mr

---

[389] She was referring to Archer Clive, V's husband.

[390] Charles Paul de Kock (1793-1871), prolific French author and popular reading throughout Europe.

[391] The British Association for the Advancement of Science meeting returned to Birmingham in 1849, and she was at Olton House again. Perhaps Ellen attended the Association meeting for a second time. By 1849 ladies were being admitted as Associates. In the Address, the speaker says that this is "exciting the surprise and perhaps scorn of those who think women fit only for household cares or showy accomplishments." He continues there are some "whose proficiency in several of our departments might have put many an FRS to shame" (*Report of the 19th meeting of BAAS* (1840), p xxxv).With her husband Charles, her long-time friend Emma Darwin also attended the conference but there seems to be no record of their meeting there (see reference in Appendix 3). Whatever meeting it was it appears that Ellen might have been a speaker.

Edward foil each other so well that I have seen neither of them so pleasant before. What an odd thing that is when 2 people happen to have the knack of making each other agreeable. Mrs E is rather disagreeable & they are not a happy couple.

I was knocked up [*ill*] & sent an excuse to Crewe. I was sorry because I fear it would annoy Lord C[*Humgerford*] but really I was poorly & the thought of Lady Charlotte E appalled me, I shall go home on Thursday. Welshpool,

Journey fixed for the 4th. Meet we must before that. Do you think you could so far be devoted to Friendship as to finish up the season with another day or 2 (audacity) at Betley? It would be charming. With best of loves from G. I was going to say but I must repress the rising falsehood & say <u>my</u> beloved Mrs Cunliffe.[392]

Yours most affectionate,

EHT

Letter 62   [*cat: 185*]
Looking after Minny; reading Dickens; dream about Annabel being married
[*Welshpool*]
[*before 1850? (see below)*]

Sent to Rome, Italy

Dearest A,

It is impossible for me to know that you are alone at M[adeley] without a wish to present myself before you. If it cannot be in the <u>body</u> let it be in the paper. But you must not feel yourself put into debt by this gratuitous letter. If G[eorgina] brings any news I shall very likely write again. First I enclose Mr N. It was droll enough his discovering such need of cleansing the outside of the Lloyd platter, you must let me see the other letter.

Strange to say, we have had another inspection here, a Mr Brown who does Workhouse Schools – very agreeable & good. He knows & likes Mr N. No, my dear, it is this week G is at Capesthorne, she took care to ensure no party. She says she is better for the sea. The Powis people have been

---

[392] Ellen seemed to be acknowledging that Mrs Cunliffe had made criticisms of her. Many of the references at the ends of the letters to 'dear Mrs C' were ironic.

visiting Cheshire & met Mrs D[*avenport?*] with whom Lucy was much struck & they went over to C[*apesthorne*] & heard the school children sing. I have only seen them once. Tonight William is again there & I am as much alone as you for my sunbeam has set beneath the counterpane.

I was delighted with the lad Copperfield[393] – how good the shipwreck ship scene was & Mr Micawber was really very rich at last tho' I had before got quite tired of him.

I am very glad to hear the much improved account of Miss Wynn.[394] I daresay her sharp bodily pain has done good in the end by making rest appear bliss – whereas before she was feeling as if rest were idleness. She has great possessions still & I trust will be able to enjoy them.

You will be sorry to hear Blue eyes (Minny) was naughty today very pert to Miss M. I was summoned & ordered a punishment which told dreadfully - all the dolls to be shut up all tomorrow. She has been perfectly charming in her penitence, which is always the case.

I really think I must tell you how tormented I was last night by a dream about you. I thought Mr Bullock had come unexpectedly & married you - & all my ingenuity went to prove to myself it was not unkindly meant in you not telling me till it was all over.[395] Don't you know the restless discomfort of that kind of argument? In my dream I thought it no bad thing. Now it was once done only it was hasty certainly!!!! It was a relief to wake & in half an hour after to see a very decidedly unmarried letter. I can't get the view right at present but we shall try again.

I am charmed to hear of your damson success. It is always my first idea when I order a dinner here. I believe W[*illiam*] C[live] is rather tired of it before the end of the season.

You will be glad to hear that the money for the juvenile offender is all promised & I am writing to ask how he is to go.

Dearest & ever thine,

---

[393] *David Copperfield* by Charles Dickens first published in 1849.

[394] Charlotte Williams Wynn (1807–1869) was a friend of Annabel; her mother was, before she married, Mary Cunliffe, the sister-in-law of Mrs Cunliffe. She was also related to the Clives of Powis. She was a letter writer and diarist (Milnes–Coates archive, University of York).

[395] Ellen feels she exerted a strong influence over Annabel's choices.

Letter 63   [*cat: 183*]
Visit to Crewe party; sharp wit; puns on "cast"

January 23, [*1850*]

Dearest A,

There are some things which are only good hot & I think my *Crewiana* is one.[396] The party was very cheerful & pleasant not intellectual but so very easy that only a cross person could be dissatisfied. I only staid 2 nights as I did not like to deprive my mother of her whist & myself longer & I was not very strong. Sir G Cast is such a great friend of mine, he is quite

25. Crewe Hall from the east [from Hinchliffe's 'Barthomley'].

affectionate & so merry & open & kind to everybody that he always makes a party feel genial.

I fell to Mr Brooke's show at dinner both days & liked him very much. The young ladies say he was a dreadful puppy before he married but that I did not see much trace of & I am sure he has a heart, tho' how he came to give it to that plain, uninteresting little wife is a mystery. He is amiable, I

---

[396] Another invented word by Ellen for a party or festive occasion at Crewe Hall.

daresay, & certainly unaffected. She is evidently pleased with her good clothes & on the ball night she was quite excited by her diamonds which were really very handsome for the Nantwich Ball!! I mean handsome for any ball but what a treat for Nantwich! Her sister, Mrs Ricardo, was then a pretty woman. Mr Littleton was very solemn as usual but did his best to talk. I suppose you have heard of the flirtation (it can be nothing more) between Lord Hatherton[397] & Lady V Talbot. I really expect he will marry again from all I hear of his good looks.

I have had an account of the Tollemache wedding[398] & of the bride; she was draped & her bridesmaids too in grey/mourning for the 1st wife. She is not at all pretty with a cast in the eye. Between ourselves, Julia T says that when they lunched at Dorfold he appeared [*illegible*] more as the widower than the bridegroom but he is a very nervous man.

We have got a very nice new curate who is going to bring us a bride next week.

Our nephew George has got prizes for an essay on English History – a Tutor's Prize not a College one, but he is so young it is a credit.

This is only an "*Hors d'Oevres*". I must add an anecdote tho'. Lady Cast has not done yet. Sir G. C[*ast*] told me he was dining with Louis Philippe[399] & he asked him to read an article in the *Times* which he did & came full stop on the sentence "As to the Orleans Party" – "that is quite insignificant."

A great want of tact & almost sent poor dear widow into fits both days by asking him when she should retire from dessert & also when she should go to bed. On the latter occasion I came to the rescue & he really grew quite witty & said, "I can tell you the hour for every thing then, Lady C" & so it was laughed off. I have nearly finished the casting: the first Vol[400] is delightful.

Favourite dearest, ever thine,

---

[397] Edward John Littleton (1791-1863), Baron Hatherton, politician.
[398] The wedding fixed the year of the letter in 1850.
[399] For dating purposes Louis Philippe died in August, 1850.
[400] She meant her letter.

EHT
PS: 100 congrats to your idiot.[401]

Mrs Cunliffe died on 15ᵗʰ February, 1850 in London. In the following weeks Annabel was desolate and under the constant care of Dr Holland. She wrote the following heart-rending letter to her sister dated 21 February, 1850 [cat: 470].

> *Dearest Henriett,*
> *You would like to have some tidings of your poor A. You are now the only one to call me by that name! –that name which she so fondly spoke & wrote. How [to] understand it all, my dearest dear, and sound my misery in all its depths – thus it is with those who have suffered as you & Ellen have. She has written me 2 touching letters, full of love and sympathy. …. tomorrow my own darlimg leaves[402] –but yet not that, for she is ever present - & I often repeat*
> *"Not to the grave, not to the grave,*
> *Follow thy friend beloved,*
> *The spirit is not there"*
> [*She went on to complete the poem by Robert Southey and then she explained that, "Dr H had watched and tended me so carefully, so carefully ……. ." He thought her pulse a little stronger.*]
> *The letter continues:*
> *I sometimes think how much, how entirely I enjoyed her which is a comfort. I can remember often dwelling upon it at the time & being fearful of letting the happy days slip by unnoticed. The last summer at poor Madeley when we lingered amongst the roses & honeysuckle surrounded by the doggies & when she [Mrs Cunliffe] drove me around the lovely Bryn, the air perfumed with lilacs & seringa or when we sat watching the evergreens being cleared, crashing about our eyes & ears, I can look back to it ….. to recall such happiness has gone forever…*
> *Were the following two letters from Ellen, the ones Annabel was referring to?*

Letter 64   [*cat: 184*]
Soon after Mrs Cunliffe's death

---

[401] Ellen was hinting that she realises Annabel's love for Richard Monckton Milnes is reciprocated.
[402] She is to be buried.

Friday [*Feb 1850?*]

[*No greeting; probably incomplete*]

The line from me, my Dearest A, to meet you on this most trying day when you will be inclined to exclaim, "Behold my house is left unto me desolate."[403] Thank God you are stronger & better able to bear up. So dear soul, I have no constant duties to prevent my answering to your call at any moment after Tuesday. My dear mother does not require constant watching as Minny. We are many.

This morning my dear child is gone leaving my heart like a bird's nest filled with sorrow but I bear up & think my hardening process goes on flourishingly. How nice of Mr Milnes sending you that lovely book. I was saying the other day that, tho' I spend my own time trying to forget all I feel, yet I am glad there are some people who feel & don't try to forget but can write it all down so beauteously.

You will expect from what I say to find me turned into a sphinx. My Lord has been here yesterday. What a very curious & interesting history it is of Mr G Clayton's self sacrifice. He must be a saint or very near it. Well, dearest, one cannot often in a life go through all you are going through. Now let us hope the worst will now be over & that after this last great exertion, time may bring peace hourly & insensibly – but still lovely.

Ever dear love, your most affectionate,

EHT

Letter 65 [*cat: 182*]
Sympathy for Annabel; after Mrs C's death on 15th February, 1850

Welshpool, Ash Wednesday, 1850

Yes dearest A,

I had heard of Mrs Blackburne's[404] going almost as soon as she went. I am sure she will be as much comfort as any human being can be. For this last week you have been hardly ever out of my thoughts. How well I know

---

[403] Matthew 24.2, more or less.

[404] Annabel's relation, Mrs Blackburne, now became her companion.

what you say of living only in the present moment - with a future that she dare not look at, yet supported from hour to hour by Him who will not desert us in almost need whenever that is. Oh! Who, who knows what ever suffering some earthly trials can bring or could even bear to think this world were all? I believe there are many who go through life without ever feeling intense misery either from peculiarity of temperament or circumstance. Those who have felt it may recover but they can never forget. They have passed through the fire a "the smell of fire is on their garments" it never leaves them as it found them. God grants to us (who can but have felt it) all its purifying effects. I can do nothing for you but feel for you & pray for you, beloved A.

It seems to me that everyone I love is in some trouble except Minny. Her constant enquiries would touch you I am sure. She said the other day, "Oh I am so dreadfully afraid of breaking that glass cup, Mrs C gave me." These little spontaneous traits are very sweet to our heart.

God bless you for He can bless ever more,
I evermore, your faithful friend,
E H Tollet

The following letter was sent after Mrs Cunliffe's death in 1850 by Georgina [cat: 187].

Dearest Annabel,
I cannot express how grateful I am to you believing me worthy of possessing the dear little pins in remembrance of one for whom (you thus prove) you knew my affection and admiration and whose affection, kindness and sympathy I can never forget. None can know better the loss you have had, nor more earnestly desire consolation for you than, your very affectionate,
G Tollet

Ellen seems to have written few letters at this time. Annabel's friendship for Richard Monckton-Milnes had grown into romance. Henrietta had to be convinced that this was a suitable match for her. Ellen very unwisely also voiced her doubts.

It appeared that Richard Monckton Milnes in most respects was an ideal suitor for Annabel. He was admired in society, a clever, witty speaker and thoughtful. But he did have a darker side, which was well-known. Was this acceptable by aristocratic men in

Victorian society? Among his collection of books at his home in Fryston Hall, there was his cache of erotica, a library, of great fame in Europe. The poet A C Swinburne wrote in 1869, they were "unrivalled upon earth – unequalled, I should imagine, in heaven".405 How Monckton Milnes' suitors, Florence Nightingale and now Annabel, tolerated this acquisition is unknown, although they were not prudes. Is it likely that Henrietta and Ellen had been deterred and found him unsuitable for Annabel.?406

Annabel continued to have ties with Madeley through the building of the monument to her beloved aunt. There was considerable correspondence about the design and the time spent in having the expensive Caen stone delivered. It was completed after her marriage.

Letter 66   [*cat: 181*]
After Mrs Cunliffe's death; opiates; Ellen's mother very ill; maid by bedside; Florence Nightingale in Egypt

Wednesday, 29th [?] 1850407

Dearest A,

As you shall hear all that is to hear this very day. The sending for Mr Bickerstaff was just one of those things one does because other people may think it right without any wish for it, or hopes of good. But all was well, for my dear mother liked seeing him: this she thought it a "sad extravagance"! & he was so very kind & feeling he comforted her. I must tell you that the great wonder is that her pain has not (been) intense & constant – if you could see her soon you would think the pain would be dreadful. Mr B approved of all that had been done & really gave no new advice except that he begged she might have as much opiates as would agree with her.

He said her pulse was very weak but that she might either live for weeks or if any new ailment comes on her, end might be rapid. That was last Thursday being every day since then she has been better, more easy & sleepy & appetite strength are all wonderful. Dear creature, her mind is a perfect normal. She always had great enjoyment of life & now she really seems to enjoy death. She speaks of everything attending her death in a view that is positively lively. The worst of it is that tho' we have got a very

---

405 From *A C Swinburne: A Poet's Life*, by R Rooksby, Routledge (1997).

406 Bostridge, p 129.

407 Date check: F N landed Alexandria, 18 Nov, 1849, in Cairo 27 Nov & in Athens in April 1850 (see *The Life of Florence Nightingale* by Tyas Cook).

nice nurse, her valuable maid who has been everything to her is getting worn out being a weakly person, tho' the attendance is not half so arduous as it often is. I am delighted to find her better.

I can do without great pain in back & legs & one or two days of agitation & standing up at the bed. I am now much better in the day. The poor maid fainted away by the bed side, but that was from an accidental cause.

Chas & Mary & Mab (their daughter) are gone & W Clive, & Minny only is left. She is perfectly enchanting & helps me on, as nothing else could. I am so glad to hear of Miss Wynn profiting by Tunbridge, it must be very nice you 2 being together.

Did you ever read Dewey's *Lectures on Human Life*? He is an American. I like them very much. Speaking of the beauty of this world he boldly says: it is not any particular consolation however that it is all so fine, if life itself be a misery; a magnificent prison does not console a prisoner – of course he argues (& so do I) that life is not a misery except in a few rare cases but to these I grant the external beauty is poor comfort. Just now his place looks lovely & my garden – Oh! it is divine with the grass just mown & M[inny] drawing 6 dolls in a cart over it!

I have just got one of Flo N's Egyptian letters. Thank goodness it all sounds very ugly tho' very clever & all that, but I think you and I need not go. Carnac (Karnak) & Luxor are neither tempting to be sure that such a painful sight, the remains of ruins of the temples all glorious & the ruins of the human race so wretched around them.[408]

Farewell, you seem to delay your coming. It is a great comfort to get your notes.

Your ever loving, EHT

Letter 67 [*cat: 180*]
Mother's imminent death; bereavement

13 May 1850

My dearest A,

I can't help writing a few lines to tell you about us & to thank you for sending these very nice notes. I think the first is really as feeling & sensible

---

[408] Note their sympathy for the poor.

an expression of sympathy as I can read. The man has a heart, I am sure.[409]

My dear Mother has been worse the last week. I suppose her complaint increases & must tell more on the general health. She is now up stairs in 2 rooms. She has still has not violent pain but general discomfort & increasing helplessness. Her mind is very clear & still full of energy. She has, I think, every possible attention & support both to mind & body. She likes one Clergyman very much & he comes often to read to her & she reads a great deal to herself & seems full of quiet & calm preparation for the close of a long & well spent life. I think the thought of this last suffering & of my father's sorrow which distresses me most in this event - you can understand it all I am sure, dearest.

Yes, my Minny is here - more really delightful than ever more real comfort than ever. She is so good & sensible & loving. Oh yes dearest, you are far, far more lovely than I am tho', as you say, you are rich in friends – I think all the friends in the universe could not make up one quarter of what you have lost! I think duties can't alone do anything towards filling up the void. You must try to make a work for yourself to do it. I know the love of your friends can sweeten your cup but it cannot prevent having to drink it. Active usefulness is the only remedy for desolation. You, who performed your appointed duty so properly & lovingly, will not fail to find some task (though none so sweet) though at present as you say *all* appears "as vague & uncertain."

God bless, your beloved ones, ever of most affectionate,

EHT

P.S: I must get the *Edinburgh Reviews*, but have so little time to read.

As indicated previously no letters from Annabel to Ellen are known to exist at the present time. The following letter [cat: 482] from Annabel to her sister Henrietta (often shortened to Henriett or Hen) shows the style of Annabel's letters. Also the letter described events which Ellen was also writing about. It is undated but clearly was written between the deaths of Mrs Cunliffe and Mrs Tollet. Annabel spent a week at Betley

---

[409] Ellen was perhaps thinking of Monckton Milnes and the book he sent to Annabel after Mrs Cunliffe's death.

Hall, and descriptions of the Ellen's garden suggest a date in May or June, 1850. There are references to relatives of her family.

Madeley Manor, Monday

My dearest Henriett,

On Wednesday, I cadaired to Betley, & did not return till the Tues after, so yr letter greeted me there & was enjoyed also by the Tollets.[410] It was nearly 3 yrs since I had slept under their roof & I enjoyed much my long talks with them & the sitting out & idle saunter in E[llen]'s garden. Mr T was uncommonly well, full of old stories of my Gr father,[411] but it was a bad week with Mrs T[ollet] more cough & weaker & I did not see her. However she has improved again since & on Friday E[llen] went for a few days to Welsh Pool.

Poor little Fanny has had a narrow escape of the jaundice and Emma & she went to their own little home. She is well, only weak, so Saturday (the day before yesterday) Emma returned.

Thus I have an experiment of the _solitary system_ from Tues to Sat & found I got through it exceedingly well. However, in summertime, with the house full of workmen & a morn visit on one day from E[llen] & G[eorgina] & "my Lord" [Hungerford],[412] it was hardly a fair trial! Every thing takes so much longer than one expects that the rooms are still in a chaos, & it is impossible to fix a day for the sale, until I can place & arrange the furniture I am thankful to hear you are better, but can understand your not feeling equal to Crewe.[413] I am told, that you say you are "_not invited to Madeley_" which I take in the light of a joke! With your hay fever, & then your lumbago – it would have been more than useless to _invite_ you, & I fear in its present state you would not find the poor house, very comfortable – painting, etc, still going on but _invite_ yourself, dearest Hen, _whenever_ you are inclined so to do, & you will have the best welcome, that A can bestow. My _schoolboys_ return today, & we must hope this continual rain will cease. Fanny &

---

[410] In Welsh cadair means seat. Is it also a name for a carriage? There is evidence that Annabel preferred not to stay in Madeley Manor under these circumstances by herself.

[411] Both Annabel and Hungerford enjoyed anecdotes about the first Baron Crewe.

[412] Like Ellen, Annabel also referred Hungerford as "My Lord".

[413] After Mrs Cunliffe's death, Madeley Manor was no longer required by the Crewes, and presumably the sale was of contents and furniture. Subsequently the Manor was let.

Henry have not fixed a day for coming back, the Dr at Chester wishing to watch her a little longer. Henry seems very well.

I think, H[ungerford] is gaining "golden opinions" from his new tenants, by visiting amongst them in his Gig – it is very wholesome for him thus driving about, & such an interest that I don't think at present he will need company at Crewe. He does not seem to expect any before October when the Carletons are to be there. E[llen] came back with me Tues to make a sketch in the village, dined with me, & returned to Betley in the evening.

Awaiting me was a drawing from Mr Poynter so I was able to learn E[llen]'s opinion.⁴¹⁴ Between us, we discovered, various objections, although parts pleased me greatly. One idea I take much too, having sundials on the structure, which will really be useful. So I despatched a long letter the following day to Mr P[oynton] stating my wishes & have received a very amiable reply, & a promise of another design forthwith. I am panting to begin!

Poor Mr W Wynn has rallied considerably & I should think now may last many weeks.

I am really better – they all tell me I look so, & Betley dolce far niente (enjoy being idle), seems to have been of great service. They were very kind & let me walk before breakfast & then have it alone, so that I had plenty of repose.

Tell me about poor Mrs Morier – I was grieved at your bad account, & can she be worse in consequence of the sickness having (as Mr Carleton told me) stopped? How is your tooth? I hope all put to rights. Now remember, you are to offer yourself to Madeley when so disposed & believe me ever dearest Henriett.
Your most affectionate,
A[nnabel].
PS 'Little O' is settled at Astbury & Henry with him – in England for a few weeks.⁴¹⁵

At some stage after Mrs Cunliffe's death Annabel wrote to her sister Henrietta an extract of which is printed below [cat: 479]

---

⁴¹⁴ Ambrose Poynter (1796–1886), a British architect, was commissioned by Annabel to design a fountain in Madeley as a memorial to her aunt Mrs Cunliffe, and that is the drawing referred to. A description of the final design accepted by Annabel can be found at the beginning of Part V.

⁴¹⁵ Little 'O' the artist is mentioned in Letter 14.

"….. Monday was a very hot day, but I drove over to Betley and had a talk sitting out with E and G, and found the garden in great beauty. Mrs Tollet has rallied decidedly and liked to see me for a few minutes, so I went up and found her in a beautiful airy apartment; 3 rooms opening out of each other. She asked after your hay asthma and was altogether less changed than I expected – nothing to what I witnessed! But then Mrs T from always having looked older and thinner could not alter as my darling. Ellen will be able for a night or two soon ….." [to keep Annabel company in Madeley].

The next letter [cat: 486] from Annabel at Crewe Hall to Henrietta carried the news from Georgina that Mrs Tollet had died. She commented on the previous week's short visit:

"…… I saw Mrs T for a few minutes. She was very kind and showed something of her interest in things about my sale, being amazed that some of the Betley inhabitants had bought the fine champagne. But I perceived a great change and felt more aware than did her daughters how near the end of life she was. There has been abundant cause of thankfulness that has not been prolonged with the certainty of such dreadful future sufferings. But there is always sorrow, whatever has been the preparations for these events. I have lost another kind, old friend of childhood. Ellen would have joined the family group here, but for this loss, which would have cheered us up. I believe….."

Mrs Frances Tollet, George Tollet's wife, died on the 11th September, 1850, aged 75. The family were in deep mourning for a long time afterwards. There are few existing comments about her death. Later Minny and Mab, the two granddaughters wrote how, "Dear Grandpapa walked at Grandma's funeral when he was 83 years old."

Before Mrs Tollet's death Annabel had told Henrietta [Letter, cat: 471] that, "Poor Mrs Tollet has undergone an operation in the arm which will give temporary relief."

Letter 68 [*cat: 186*]

After Mrs Tollet's death; confusion of Hungerford about dates; Ellen helping in school matters; Duke of Sutherland; Ellen pays Mrs Blackburne's bill at chemist; Saturday night

[*Nov/Dec 1850?*]

To: Hon Annabel Crewe, 16 Upper Brook Street, Grosvenor Square, London

Dearest A,

I did see My Lord & relieved his mind from a horrid idea that Thursday was the 11th, tho' he said very patiently, "I should very much prefer Wednesday certainly, as I only go to Teddesley, Monday."416 He quite understands his date now, I assure you. So, my dear soul, we shall all 3 meet under his hospitable roof on Wednesday. I long to hear more of poor Mrs Morier417 & still poorer Henrietta.

Your slates are here but I have watched in vain for the cart today so will keep them till I hear more.418 I hear the box is very heavy.

Lord Hatherton was in immense form & told them he had been 82 days in London & had dined out 80 times.

This morning I was alone in the library having a chat with the schoolmaster when up rushed a carriage & out came the Duke of Sutherland dreadfully deaf, of course, but very chatty & affectionate to my father. His D(uche)ss he has left to preside over the D(uche)ss of Argyle's 5th confinement.419 He was on his way to Lilleshall & had slept at Crewe Station & had had a call from my Lord already this morning. Their interview must have been rather sick as the D[*uke*] said, "He had hanky tied over his mouth, so I got a pencil & paper. Then we found that we had not much to say." Tell dear Mr B, the druggist tenderly enquired after her health when I paid the bill.

---

416 Teddesley Hall was a large Georgian Country House near Penkridge in Staffordshire, but has since been demolished. It was the home of the Hathertons.

417 On the 30th March, 1851, census date, Mrs Morier was living at 26 Bolton Street, London with Henrietta Crewe and her son Greville.

418 What were the slates for? Could they be for the monument?

419 The birth of the 5th confinement of the Duchess of Argyll was on 25th Dec, 1850 (*thepeerage.com*) which confirms the likely date of this letter.

[There is a continuity problem here which we have been unable to resolve satisfactorily. It seems that either some pages are missing or have been misplaced.]

…..at stake in reality than you have, I am so sure that for you she will be for the really best, dearest love, God bless you![420]

The Wicksteds have been here. Charles still came but looking well. M[ary] brought me *La Tulipe Noire*[421] but I don't think it looks attractive. Only think of what my previous dinner party led to! – a correspondence between Mr Maurice & Mr Burkin on religious subjects – Mr M is very much shocked at sheepfolds & they have hit hard at each other but Mrs W[edgwood] says two such good men can do each other nothing but good. She has actually read the letters & says she longed for me. Don't speak of this as they may not like it public.

Poor dear Henrietta, I am so grieved at her having been ill again. There is something melancholy in this proof of the frailty human affliction that we should all be inclined to think these 2 devoted friends have been "long enough together" but we know Mrs M[orier] has faults of disposition & dear H has some little ones of temper. How different these two are. Give me the latter tho' neither are pleasant! You will I know write again soon. I dream about you. Best love [to] Mrs B. Surely the house must let with those lovely carnations.

We are moving some furniture to make ourselves look better, I have discovered. I am so glad you felt cheery at last, dearest A.

Your most affectionate,

EHT

Letter 69   *[cat: 188]*
Black edged; a sad year has passed; Mrs Cunliffe & Mrs Tollet died in 1850; marriage prospects but not for Ellen

13th January 1851

My dearest Annabel,

---

[420] Difficult to determine the context of this sentence.
[421] By A Dumas (1850).

I was going to write after the December visit at Crewe but as that was not to come off why should I delay telling you with 1000 thanks what a pleasure your last letter was to me? To feel that as you say, "We are more than ever to each other," is indeed a great blessing left behind by the sad year 1850. For you I am sure the year of sorrow has left so much that is good behind; you are, I am more confirmed & sure & strengthened in all goodness. Your sympathies for the sufferings of others are deepened & enlarged by your own, & therefore if we judged as Angels, we should speak of the blessings of 1850. I only hope that in some degree having also suffered, I may also in some small degree have been blessed, tho' indeed I fear one has sad ups & downs in the growth of the spiritual nature & I grieve to say honestly I feel rather cold & dead [as] to what I need to do.

Dear old Henrietta wishes Georgina "*une sainte hereuse année*" or so do I to you, dearly beloved friend. Since I wrote we have had our Etonians here - so good & pleasant they were amused us by their beginnings of observations about men & manners. George has actually begun to say that "*une belle*" awfully ugly; another laughs so "awfully loud". I always encourage him to say just what he thinks because it gives him an opportunity of knowing what our opinions are & where they differ from those of the 5th form!

We had Julia Tomkinson & Harriet Tayleur[422] to meet the Wicksteds, but the latter never came on account of Charles's leg. The 2 ladies were both, I thought, very agreeable, but they did not like each other. We talked about 11 hours in the day & I was quite exhausted - never, my dearest A, let us spend a whole day together. Humans can't stand it. Still, as our ladies only came for 2 nights, it was all very well & nothing could be more highly edifying than our conversation.

We did read aloud one half hour that exquisite bit of *Mary Barton*'s[423] and *The Well of Pen-Morfa* in *Household Words*.[424] I suppose you have read it. *The*

---

[422] The Tayleurs lived at Buntingsdale Hall is near Market Drayton.
[423] Mrs Gaskell wrote two novels *Mary Barton* and *The Well of Pen Morfa*.
[424] A weekly magazine edited by Charles Dickens from (1850) which included fiction and journalism with the intention of encouraging more writers.

Moorland Cottage we sent for. I have bought *The Ch: a Family*[425] but have not read it. I am reading *Alton Locke.*[426] I think it is very clever & interesting & if you can stand Chartism & Socialism you should read it. There is a chapter on Emersonism which is admirable. Thank goodness I never was taken in for a moment to admire him. I mean his Eulogism. I agree with you in not liking Mr Bennet's letters at all –but I think he had the active spirit of doing good which our Church wants[427] & therefore I grieve to love him.

Your account of the curate at Mr Brookfield's Church was truly astounding. I wonder what could be done for our Parish by a really perfect clergyman. There is no other hope for us & that is a forlorn one certainly.[428] Our people are not poor, not wretched, but the best are so worldly & the worst so profligate. The new curate comes this week. Charles Wilbraham[429] called & stayed [*for*] dinner the other day. He gave a sad account of his brother's sufferings from his leg. He was very pleasant – I mean more so than is usual   If you can keep him off his anecdotes & off his civilities, all is well, but I am tired of the first & provoked by the second - that is a critical point in one's acquaintanceship with a man when one has heard every one of his anecdotes. I am convinced many people are thought agreeable as long as their anecdotes last, & for society the old set will do for years, but to be agreeable to your friend you must forget all your stock in trade & originate, or the poorest bit of original novelty will do little than your most splendid wares that have been laying by.

This figure reminds me of your new carpet, not 3/3 a yard which I rejoice to hear of.[430] That anything so pleasant as my treaty upon it should come to pass, I can hardly believe. William Clive has been rather tantalising me with talking of glasshouses & taking Minny – but I fear he will back out

---

[425] Unable to trace this title.

[426] A novel by Charles Kingsley published in 1850. It was written in sympathy with the Chartist movement. Thomas Carlyle appears in it.

[427] Ellen was advocating Christian values.

[428] In her *Journals* Ellen has stated that there is too much worldliness and drunkenness in Betley.

[429] Was this the vicar from Audley?

[430] Annabel must be refurbishing Upper Brook Street.

of it. [431] You have never mentioned Mr MM - so I suppose he is in town. What did Miss Wynn say to your not going to sister Galway's?[432]

Ever believe, me dearest A, your most affectionate,
  Ellen Tollet

Clearly Ellen was advising Annabel about marrying Richard Monckton Milnes in the following letter.

Letter 70   *[cat: 179]*
Black edged; Annabel confiding in Ellen; before proposal of RMM: Punch cartoon

[probably February 1851]

My dearest Annie,

I feel that I have a great deal to say & that is the best of all possible reasons for writing. Thanks first for your nice letter. I am so glad to think that you have got dear Mrs B(lackburne) with you now but I hope she will not wish for a very long season in London & that soon I shall hear you are coming to Madeley where everything will soon be looking springy.

My garden is already quite gay & the weather is like April very showery but bringing everything forward. I am thankful to say G is better than when I last wrote. You had a good supply of news. I suppose Miss D .....'s Mr Skellern is the man who bought the island of Lewes [*Lewis?*].[433] I wonder whether he was a tall man with a large nose when I was with her at Mrs Martin's.

Your account of the Clive dinner I could quite understand at least about the Drawing Room & no room could ever be pleasant with a fire place at one end, & the door opening upon it, but the dinner might have been agreeable if all the party had come; those vacant places ruin everything.

---

[431] Ellen was most anxious to see the Great Exhibition and William Clive seemed unwilling to please either Minny or his sister-in-law.

[432] This refers to Richard Monckton Milnes' sister, Henrietta, who married Viscount Galway.

[433] In 1844 Sir James Mathieson bought the Island of Lewis.

It is not at all true that Walter Cooper is *Alton Locke*.[434] He is a much more sensible man I am sure than ever poor Alton was. Oh yes, Mr Kingsley wrote yesterday. I hope he has altered & improved it since it came out in prayer when I read it. There are nine passages. I dined & slept yesterday at Peatswood & that Mrs Moore, who was enthusiastic to praise the character of Sandy Mackay, should be thought worthy of Scott.

What you said of Mr MM of course deeply interested me & I shall speak to you on the subject just as openly as I should to a beloved sister. The idea of Mrs B[*lackburne*] or any one speaking to him would indeed horrify me because I conceive that, what would induce you to accept him, would be the conviction that he was in thorough earnest in seeking you. Now if any one said a word to him that conviction you never could have. I certainly honestly think there is no good reason for his delay – at any rate beyond the period of your stay in Town. He has all fair & reasonable opportunities & if his own mind is as decided as it ought to be, speak he will, and worried I fear you are & must be. But my faith is strong not only in all things being ordained for the best but in your being able to think so. Still I can't help feeling anxious to know how things go on & I hope you will write often.[435]

I have had a very good natured note from Lord Hatherton saying that Mr T's want of private fortune would put him out of the question for the present, as he should try to find some one with a little Independence. It will be a pleasure having Charles & Mary on Saturday tho' only for a few days. Have you seen the capital picture in Punch of the naughty boy who chalked "no popery".[436] Shall be very good in writing after.[437]

Love to Mrs B.

Your most affectionate,

Ellen Tollet

---

[434] *Alton Locke*; see previous letter.

[435] It sounds as though Ellen was resigned to the fact that Annabel will marry.

[436] The cartoon referred to was one which represented Lord John Russell "as a naughty boy chalking up the words `no popery' and dodging round the corner" published in early 1851. It caused a crisis in Parliament. (*The Life and Works of the Seventh Earl of Shaftesbury* by E Hodder (2014), Cambridge UP).

[437] Meaning after Annabel has married.

Correspondence between the Nightingales and Tollet family further confirmed Ellen's views about the marriage. On 10th March 1851 Ellen wrote to Parthenope to inform them of Richard Monckton Milnes' proposal:

> *".... Yes, my dear, she is going to take Mr M Milnes for better or worse – I think the two are always united & therefore prefer the conjunction instead of the disjunction. We have each been from home for a few days so I have actually not seen her since the great question was asked and answered. (It was last Tuesday morning – the hour I don't exactly know.) Of course, I am & ever shall be most deeply interested in this marriage. ...."*[438]

Later on 10th April, Ellen commented:

> *".... I dine with the Milnes a second time on Monday & am promised C Dickens, but I don't much care, for I believe he's dour ...."*[439]

This letter expressed her concern about the marriage also.

Letter 71 [*cat: 189*]
Georgina's improving health; Ellen to go to London; suitor for Lord Hatherton; Ellen's comments about Mr MM a few months before Annabel marries him

April 5, 1851

My dearest Annie,

Won't I keep my promise about writing often when you assert so peculiarly that it is a pleasure to receive my letters? I hardly feel as if we were separated. You are so constantly in my thoughts & you are really almost the only subject that interests G. About you she will sometimes begin of herself which is a great event. However, thank god, I have a better account to give after both as to body & mind. Her throat is got well at last & she is certainly better than when I came home.

---

[438] Claydon House Archive, bundle 245.
[439] Claydon House Archive, bundle 245.

My Lord called on Thursday & brought in such beauteous flowers which are filling her room with fragrance at this moment. I do quite long to hear the F Kemble's readings. After a nice read I am just ready to go back to London for a little more amusement & the Shakespearian line would exactly suit me. Mrs Wedgwood writes most tempting accounts of their doings but they are going to Paris very soon.

How I long to have you back in Madeley & yet today an east wind is not exactly the one to make one think of séances in gardens![440] Will you return to me as you went I wonder! I am prepared for anything I assure you & I am proud to say I don't feel the least selfish.

That Mr MM is a puzzling man is certain: he may have peculiar notions as to the degree of friendship that may exist between men & women. That a man who lives his sort of life should feel a difficulty in staging his flight & fixing himself for ever is most natural. At the same time I must own he never can have by any possibility a better opportunity of doing so than he has now. I am quite sure he has more of that by a merciful law of nature when personal vanity ceases – house beauty begins in the female head.

Your most faithful,

EHT

Another letter showing Ellen's concern about the marriage was sent to Parthenope on 15th June 1851:[441]

"*Of course, if I had chosen for her it would not have been a man so in and of the world, but I really believe that (strange to say) his heart is still undestroyed. Though I hope – and is not that all one can ever say about this world's happiness? – dearest A[nnabel], my childhood's friend, so closely connected with every most tender remembrance of past happiness – I do indeed pray that she may be kept safe. My thoughts are full of this subject, and I would give much to talk it over with you. What wonderful luck is Mr Milnes in. He must have been a great saint or martyr*

---

[440] Was Ellen thinking of the oak circular arbours on the lawns at Madeley Manor, where they could sit sheltered from the wind?
[441] Claydon House Archive, bundle 245.

in a former state of existence to have such a fair thing given him – – love to all,
EHT".

The Great Exhibition of the Works of Industry of All Nations opened on the 1st May 1851 at Crystal Palace. It closed on 15th October 1851, and Ellen was not taken there.

PART V: Marriage of Annabel, 1851 onwards

"I am taking cod liver oil which agrees & I am looking quite handsome"

"I want him [Charles Darwin] to write 'A Week in the Country' for Punch"

26. Madeley All Saints' Church.

The marriage of The Honourable Annabel Crewe to the Honourable Richard Monckton Milnes in Madeley, All Saints Church, took place on 30th July 1851. The wedding party assembled at Madeley Manor and then proceeded to the church where there were 24 guests from the peerage and upper gentry from this area, including Ellen Tollet, Miss Duncombe and Mr & Mrs Hinchliffe.[442]

They moved to Crewe Hall for their wedding breakfast whilst the Madeley villagers had decorated their houses with "rustic solemnity",[443] and celebrated with food and drink

---

[442] George Tollet, now very deaf, joined the wedding reception at Crewe Hall (quoted from Hinchliffe (1856), p 332).

[443] Monckton Milnes' description.

for two days. The honeymoon was spent at Hatherton Hall and then in Devon. Later they travelled to the Continent. Their future homes were at Fryston Hall in Yorkshire and Upper Brook Street in London.[444]

Earlier Henrietta had written to Annabel saying that Mr Milnes would not have enjoyed living at Madeley Manor, though it would hurt Annabel to leave *"your Bryn, your low window room and your memorial above all."*[445]

In Madeley before her wedding Annabel had spent considerable time planning an elaborate monument in memory of her charitable aunt, Hon Elizabeth Emma Cunliffe Offley. It was a fountain 33 feet high built of Caen stone. It stood on a large, walled, gated base and appears, some say, to have a Middle Eastern look.[446] From the letters to her sister Henrietta, the reader realises that the monument should be of the finest quality, and be designed well. The fountain supplied water to 3 acres of land donated by Annabel for use by the people of Madeley. The gift cost £2000. The allotments on Manor Road are still in use, but the memorial (a listed monument) is in need of repair and no longer supplies water.

Life for the unmarried Hungerford, after Aunt Cunliffe's death, changed by having other relatives as his hostess at society events, such as Emma Blackburne.

The correspondence between Ellen and Annabel continued but to a lesser extent.

Letter 72 [*cat: 190*]
The Monument & the letting of the Manor; servants mentioned; sadness that Annabel is no longer in Madeley

Betley Hall, Oct 15 1851

Madame RM Milnes,
Poste Restante, Leipsic [*Leipsig, Germany*]

My dearest Annabel,

I was so glad to receive your delightful letter & as you are so complimentary to our English epistles, I will instantly favour you with

---

[444] Williams, Jean M & Williams, L, *The New Madeley Manor House.*
[445] Quoted from Letter from Henrietta to Annabel [*cat: 256*].
[446] "The monument [*has*] ….. lead spouts and carved shell-like basins on four sides; the top is an ornamental crested parapet in Jacobean style" (Tringham, Nigel J (1014), *The History of the County of Stafford, The Victoria History, Vol XI*)

another. Your last Danube trip I do envy you. We have still wonderful weather & the heliotropes still untouched & yesterday G & I were sitting on the well-house garden seat for an hour – our feet quite warm but we are now become liable to rain, which we were not [at] all [in] September.

I must tell you of a droll visit to Crewe Hall. We were sent for in a hurry to meet Sir A & Lady Gordon & there was no one else but Miss Duncombe. I know, my dear, that all the precepts of Christianity could not make you do anything but hate Lady G. Still she is so amusing & he was particularly pleasant. I have discovered that if a husband & wife contradict each other, it allows of other people doing the same & gives great ease & freedom to conversation so pray that I don't ask you to be quite Lady G – do decidedly differ from Mr M sometimes. She began by telling me she hated your husband, but as she spoke quite as well of her enemy as most people do of their friends, he has no reason to complain. Her 2 dear friends are Lord Landsowne & Mrs Norton.

We drove by My Lord's drive to Madeley – so much to see & I was glad I wanted so much to see the Memorial. I was greatly surprised at its size but the proportions are different from what I fancied. I had thought that

27. Annabel's fountain in memory of Mrs Cunliffe.
(photographed in 2018)

beautiful ornamental work about the coats of arms would have been perforated - I daresay you understand me. The small texts are very nice & "the flower withereth" etc, very nice. The water was not in it. It was a lovely day & the woods looked their best. I saw Mrs Markells[447] but only for a moment. It was quite miserable to look at their rooms; still it is best as it is.

You were not intended for such a lonely life. Yes, thank you dear, I am very well, rather fat, but I have not been to London & the G(reat) Ex(hibition) is gone for evermore. If I had had anyone to say "Come" or "Will you" or "Do come to me & see it"- all very well but I was not eager driven enough for the pleasure to make me continue the plan for myself. I think all pleasures & amusements should be forced upon one – the seeking them destroys their charm.

I don't at all expect Col Stanley to take Madeley, tho' perhaps my reasons for this opinion would not be particularly reasonable.[448] I don't want people who are in such a hurry.

G has just had a nice letter from Henrietta – very full of the Miss Wells & their clothing. She seems much better.

How very pleasant your Mr Thompson sounds. I do like picking up chance acquaintances in that way. One often gets to know them far better than neighbours. I like strangers –there is a freedom in the beginning of intercourse which often wears off - at first people have no impression about each other's characters – only care for each other's opinions which is so pleasant. However the next best thing to a stranger is a real old friend. We were pleased with the other day at meeting up an old friend, Mr E Butler –he is so peculiarly agreeable & he & Miss G[*eorgina*][449] - it would have done you good to see –she is certainly much better, thank heaven.

Did I tell you our good servant, Lewis, is going to be married & tiresome of her & also one of your flower *madchens* is married to our clerk's brother, Miss Barker – now Mrs Warham – I suppose a Minton's dessert service

---

[447] She was the house-keeper in Madeley Manor.

[448] The Hon Col Stanley did become a tenant of Madeley Manor until 1856 (see Williams, p 213).

[449] Ellen was still trying to find a husband for Georgina.

will be a sort of propitiatory gift to the Emperor –whether to induce him to look upon the poor little Princess Royal or to forgive England & the Mayor of Southampton for selling Hogarth, I don't know. I only hope V&A are not so worldly as to think of Matrimonial Alliance yet - tho' why?

I have not mentioned your brother. He is well but I confess very nervous - but he talks of having had such a pleasant evening when no one could think he enjoyed anything. I should say so when I have actually detected William Clive is discouraging the visits of 2 young gentlemen already!!![450] We have heard of the Powyses paying a visit at Badger that would be so suitable an alliance –surely the father must intend it.

Ever thine,

EHT

Letter 73 [*cat: 227*]
Marriage; politics

Dec 31, 1851

My dearest Annabel,

On this last day of this old year I must write to you. What a year to look back upon it must be to you. May the next be not less happy though more peaceful, more of the deep waters & less of the torrent – or rather I ought to say whatever it brings of joy or sorrow may you possess your soul in patience or thankfulness.

My Lord was here yesterday in very good spirits & he had the pleasure of telling of this famous marriage which has excited us all beyond measure. Thus [*Caroline*] D[*avenport*] wrote a mysterious note to G the very moment of the proposal.

Lord H[*atherton*] followed it up with a very lively letter next day. I know you will be surprised to her accepting him but <u>we</u> heartily agreed knowing her to be set in this midst of dangers - knowing also how very few people she could have married without offending her son, who in this case is quite pleased. Then I think to a woman who once upon a time married Mr Davenport, Lord H will appear so amiable & pleasant & Teddesley will be

---

[450] Marriage prospects for Minny; she was only 10.

the very place for her to exercise her benevolent inclinations;[451] in short I rejoice for her & for him it is luck indeed. I know how provoked you will be at his being in love (which depend upon if he is) & will not bear to hear of the masterly manner in which he conducted his affairs – no tedious doubts did he inflict on the widow but carrying the attack straight onwards – nay asked all & gained all! My dear A, if you had not married, don't you think he would have given you a chance?[452]

Mrs D. writes very happily & insists on G going over to hear all about it & I cannot describe to you how lively & amused G has been already, advising her friend & calculating all the pros & cons. I fancy Mr L & Lady M, are pleased because they knew he would marry & dreaded something foolish. I suppose they will have to leave Teddesley.

Our Christmas Party came safe to hand. Minny, not looking very strong, but very happy with her cousins. We go to Welshpool on the 8th.

I long to hear what you say to the marriage & also your Palmestoniana.[453] We think it is Austria & not France that has shipwrecked Lord P. Are we right or wrong? How very exciting French affairs are. I don't like L.N. [*Louis Napoleon*] but I am all for his dictatorship or whatever he calls it, as I think it is a necessary step that must be gone through before they can get a constitutional government.

I am very busy with the children. Minny requires a great deal of superintendence & just now I am father, mother & governess.

Farewell, dearest.

Love to MM.

Your most affectionate,

EHT

---

[451] Annabel and her husband spent their wedding night at Teddesley Park, the home of Lord Hatherton.

[452] A tactless remark by Ellen.

[453] Lord Palmerston was the controversial Foreign Secretary, later becoming Home Secretary.

Letter 74 [*cat: 225*]
A short, witty, kindly letter to Annabel when she is expecting her first child
Welshpool, Friday, 23 Jan 1852
To: Annabel at Fryston[454]

Dearest A,

It is very flattering of you to wish for a letter from me, surrounded as you are with wisdom & wit. I wish the fates had allowed me to be with you, both when I find myself regretting what I have missed. I have only to look at Minny to be perfectly convinced that there is no spot in the inhabited world where my bodily presence is worth so much as here.

You seem to be going on very well & will soon be safe from fear of mischance. Fryston must feel more like home than any place you have yet been in since you were married & you must enjoy any approach to feeling settled. Not that you are, like me, fully convinced of the blissfulness of rest. I am not always in that frame of body & mind but each year I have a little more foretaste of it & if I am to live to old age, I hope it may please God to make me satisfied with it. I look upon the repose of old age to be far from useless; its soothing influence upon the young is so precious.

What a nice letter from Aunt Caroline,[455] thanks many. I have heard Mrs Coleridge, & Mrs Lawrence talks of Speddings[456] - do you remember the 2 children at L's? I suppose D Bacon is not their father & perhaps uncle.

We had a native dinner party last night & a clergyman brought a cousin – unknown. We were struck with surprise at white gloves buttoned – with a little pleated frills round the wrist & other signs of dandyism. He proved to be an able London lawyer, a collector of coins, an antiquarian, had been lately in Paris, spoke French in a distinguished manner, vanquished Georgy neatly in an argument. In short performed rather brilliantly & consequently I hope liked his audience.

So Sir Watkin is going to marry. They say no one who had ever seen him

---

[454] Letters were being sent to Annabel at Fryston Hall where she now lived.
[455] Sister-in-law of Mrs Cunliffe.
[456] Near Bassenthwaite in the Lake District.

as a bloomer[457] at Vale Royal ever could have accepted him. I have a longing to see a Paris letter if you get one that will do. Mrs Davenport is to be married the 11ᵗʰ at Lambeth – dress white terry velvet.[458] I have a good account from Shakenhurst but the boy is still languid. Who wrote *Physiognomy* in the *Quarterly*? Did I ever tell you how completely Julia has set me against Lord Ward? My love to Mrs Blackburne & Fanny.

Ever your affectionate,

Ellen Tollet

In her first season as hostess Annabel "had to preside over twenty-six dinner and twelve breakfast parties." Perhaps that is why she preferred country living at Fryston Hall in Yorkshire, and one of the reasons Florence Nightingale had rejected Monckton Milnes, because she craved for independence.[459]

Letter 75 [*cat: 226*]
An amusing letter about politics

Welshpool

Feb 24, 1852

Dearest A,

I really must have a word with you about public affairs which are just now so exciting. I am sorry that Lord John[460] should be or rather appear to be driven out by his old colleague & hope Lord P[*almerston*] did not mean it out of spite & revenge. It is altogether such a strange mess. Lord P chafed countenancing L N[461] & then chafing Lord John by his anxiety for an efficient militia! I cannot bear the thought of a Derby & Disraeli government but I am sure it can't last more than one session unless it can get the Peelites. I see your "*Poeta*"[462] was at a Palmerston dinner. Lord

---

[457] Bloomer: a person who matures or flourishes at a specified time.

[458] The marriage of Lord Hatherton to Caroline Davenport (neé Hunt) (1810-1897).

[459] Bostridge, p 129.

[460] Lord John Russell.

[461] Louis Napoleon III.

[462] Spanish for poet - describing Annabel's husband?

Powis was not violent against New Reform Bill because why? He thinks £5 renters more manageable than £10!

Another happy letter from the Hatherton pair. We go home on the 8th. I think you might come & rest at Betley on your way south – one night would not be too severe for Mr Milnes & he could leave you a few days & fetch you – do think of this. I saw Mr M voted with Lord P. but I am sure he did not mean to drive Lord John.

Oh, I must tell you that the jury of ladies have awarded my father a Prize Medal.[463] He is so pleased.

This nice bright weather will do you good. Mrs Hensleigh W[*edgwood*], has been dining at the Tennysons & says he earned quite as well as any proser could.[464] G's bed came from Welshpool. Don't you like the name of *Bleak House [1852-3]*? It sounds rather like *Wuthering Heights.[1847]*.

Greatest affection,
Ellen Tollet

Letter 76 [*cat: 224*]
A cheery letter about news from Betley; George Tollet's heronry

Betley Hall
June 10, 1852

Dearest Annabel,

You say you wish to hear from me & in this wet weather there are leisure moments, even with the Wicksteds & Minny in the house. We saw My Lord who told us you had not been quite well at Lord Ashburton's, but I trust it was only one of the ails your state is heir to & that you are still as you have been all along - as well as can be expected.[465]

We have become busy & rather gay in our intensely quiet way – one of our guests was Offley & you will be glad to hear he went to Madeley & saw the schools – he reported very well of the boys & Mr Holt. I don't think he examined the girls. He heard that the Stanleys took no interest in these

---

[463] For George Tollet at the Great Exhibition of 1851, using the feathers from his rare breed of birds. The feathers were used to decorate ladies' hats.

[464] Proser – A person who writes prose as against a poet, thus insulting him, because he could obviously write well.

[465] Annabel was expecting her first child.

affairs – I suppose It would be very difficult to take to other people's charities & and when a woman has 6 children she has 6 good excuses for neglecting every other duty, which I must say, she seldom fails to avail herself of, to keep a fair balance amongst ones duties & affections is as difficult as to do it with European Powers & Russia & Austria representing Husbands & Children. It is very difficult to prevent friends, neighbours as coming badly off like the small states.

We went with Offley to our Boys' School & they did very well & I was amused at the Master saying, "He was so glad because Mr Crewe would tell Mr Wade," plainly showing how much they prize the education of each other than ours [*in Betley*].

Georgy & I are reading Margaret Fuller.[466] She was the person you would have hated much & I a little, but the book is I think very interesting. Have you come across a little book called *The Influence of Poetry, 2 Lectures* by Mr Robertson of Brighton?[467]

How you must have enjoyed buying your 2nd trousseau – the little things are so pretty & though the most hopeful person cannot look at them without some anxiety mixing with the pleasure yet they must ever have a charm which no other lace & cambric can possess. I am sorry to tell you that one of your flower showers has been confined a good while![468]

In fact on the 20th of April, my Father is wonderfully well & amuses himself with fowls by day & herons by night. On these long evenings he sits at the Drawing Room window with a telescope watching the herons who really seem as if they performed for his amusement. Three young ones standing on the top of a fir tree in every possible attitude, while grand old birds soar about. It is a delightful thing to see the power of enjoyment of nature at 85.

Halford Vaughan is very anxious to have to do so as old as possible & he is always asking about my father with a view to his own future prospects. I wonder you had some land of the Cleveland Horses & now at last they are

---

[466] Margaret Fuller (1810-1850) was an American journalist and critic, and also a women's rights advocate. Ellen was a feminist.

[467] These were two lectures on the influence of poetry on the working classes, implying that everyone should be educated in the arts and sciences.

[468] A clever pun. Presumably Annabel had given Ellen some plants.

offered to the D[uke] of Norfolk for 1000g[*uineas*], and then sold by auction for 1100guineas. Charles & Mary stay on Saturday. They are very pleasant active guests. The Archer Clives are in Ireland but coming to London the end of the month. We shall go to Welshpool very early in July. Before then I hope for good news of you. May every blessing attend you & yours. I ever am, your affectionate friend,

Ellen Tollet

PS: I am taking cod liver oil which agrees & I am looking quite handsome.[469]

PS: I am sure writing must now be troublesome so pray don't think of it.

The following extract is from a letter to Parthenope revealed how Ellen would miss the company of her childhood friend:

15 July 1852

".... It has been a great pleasure having the Milneses at Crewe [Hall], though it is a sort of farewell visit & there was a party in the house last week which made it rather a stately meeting in our best clothes. I suppose I may some day by some happy chance get acquainted with MM. He has a sort of manner which frightens me & stiffens men & strikes me dumb (how marvellous), then there comes a flash of friendship which surprises me, so I am quite unable to respond. As to anything like a comfortable talk with him I have never had it..."[470]

Letter 77   [*cat: 223*]
Heartburn remedies for Annabel; life for unmarried, educated women

Betley

June 27, [*after 1852*]

Dearest Annabel,

I was very glad you disobeyed injunctions & wrote to me & that you are able to send so tolerable an account. I hear from others that you are

---

[469] Ellen was joking we suppose.
[470] Claydon House Archive, bundle 245.

looking very well, just when most people look hideous. I am sure your heartburn is very disagreeable [and] Mrs Turton is [in] a similar state coming into the room saying "I have just taken my 5th dose of magnesia,"

28. Hon Mrs Monckton Milnes (Annabel Crewe). Photograph by Camille Silvy, 1861.

which I think proves alkalis did not do her much good.

I was at Dorfold yesterday after leaving my wife & child[471] at Crewe Station. There I had a long chat with Julia & a short but very spicy one with Mr Norris.[472] He and his sister are bitten by the Deaconess scheme & are actually going on a pilgrimage to Kaiserswerth.[473] I have a personal horror of living in a community & would never advise any old maid to enter one

---

[471] As in her *Journals,* Ellen referred to Georgina as her wife and Minny as her daughter.

[472] Rev J P Norris, H M Inspector of Schools in the Betley area.

[473] The Deaconess scheme in Kaiserswerth near Düsseldorf was founded by Pastor Fliedner in 1833. It was a training scheme combining medical, social and educational needs to achieve better nursing in hospitals. Florence Nightingale wrote a document about it, showing her mid C19th feminism. It had been the institution where she gained much knowledge about hospitals. (Bostridge, p 97)

who had a remnant of a home to stick to, but there are some few widows
…… who might be useful & happy in an institution & in large towns these
might have a supply of ladies as day scholars who might be taught to teach
school & make Grace, keep Penny Club accounts in a right way instead of a
wrong, as is their usual mode at present. When people propose these
institutions as remedies for the wretched state of the lower classes, I listen
with the greatest interest but it is only when they are suggested as offering
work & consolation to higher women that I am fired with indignation.
What! Because we have neither husbands nor children and are therefore to
have no armchairs & books of poetry on our own firesides & then forget[?]
to hear how the married women especially those who have been married
twice like Lady Hatherton talk of the blessed privileges of Nuns &
Deaconesses!

Even you & your Richard are announcing that your duties are not "so
easy" & your responsibilities are heavy! No doubt it is so, but they are those
which you chose for your selves & those which it is generally supposed face
the duties & responsibilities most connected with the affections &
consequently the lightest & easiest. By the bye, does it not sometimes
make one rather more doubtful in one's admiration of duty, when one
reflects that the only duty one wishes to perform is towards oneself is their
cook: even her patties had better be made light because she loves Master &
Missus. In all the relations of life the only duty we care to be done to us is
that which is done because people love us so they can't help it.

However it would not do to act upon this doctrine & I make Minny
come & say Good Morning every day, tho' perhaps now & then she is too
busy with play to wish it herself. She is as great a duck as ever overflowing
with happiness & affection. She has all the knowingness of the fountains
but we hope she may have the depth of this well also. I am glad for G. to
have a life without me at Welshpool. It will bring her & Minnie closer
contact. Henrietta gives but a poor account of herself, how kind she is to
poor Mrs Cockshutt & she says how kind Mrs Symons & Mr B G are to
this poor girl at Paris. We shall stay at Welshpool till our school
examination brings us back. I hope I may find you & a certain other
individual at peace. How welcome will he or she be! Of course I depend on

Mrs Blackburne for writing to me. May God bless you in every possible way.

Your Affectionate Friend,
Ellen Tollet

In a letter to Parthenope,[474] Ellen disclosed information about a visit to Fryston Hall. She wrote from Betley on the 18th December 1854:

"...... I have perhaps been, as you know, staying a week at Fryston where Annabel and I took sweet council together on all that concerning Flo and her affairs ...... & RMM is very nice though he must be odd about everything ..... Do you know I was actually decoyed to write to dear Flo about a poor captain. I felt quite ashamed. I often dream of her ...."

Florence Nightingale through her work in the Crimea became a legendary figure in Britain. In December 1855 the Nightingale Fund was set up for the training of nurses. Richard Monckton Milnes was a founding member.

The Nightingale family were inundated by letters of adulation for Florence. The elderly George Tollet wrote to his friend William Nightingale on the 13th December 1854:[475]

"....It is impossible for you to have afforded a greater solace to my old age than by sending me the letter I have just received – I had every reason to feel the greatest interest for your excellent daughter under the usual circumstances of friendship, but from the extraordinary efforts she has been making out of pure love to her fellow creatures. The anxiety of friendship is merged in loftier feelings & my heart has rejoiced at the accounts I have received ..... For an English lady so connected in the bloom of beauty and in the prime of life to take upon her this Labour of Love under all its frightful circumstances is one of the extraordinary Events of the World –that she should arrive with her Suite just at the time of that most sanguinary

---

[474] Claydon House Archive, bundle 245. Florence Nightingale and her nurses were in Scutari in the Crimea in November 1854. There was extensive coverage in the newspapers.

[475] Claydon House Archive: bundle 226.

battle gives a foretaste that she will be supported by that aid which will bring her safe through her arduous undertaking and restore her to you and Mrs N again…..."

29. Marianne (Minnie) with her father Archdeacon William Clive.

Life for the Tollet family was greatly disturbed by George's death, five years after his beloved wife. In his obituary he was described as a *Whig of the Old School*, and respected by all who knew him.

The hall was inherited by Charles Wicksted, whose main residence was at Shakenhurst. The surviving daughters were wealthy, having inherited from their maternal grandmother, and having kept a share in Betley Hall. From this time in the 1850s they visited friends and family and stayed in London at various rented addresses, as well as visiting Betley.

Penelope and Frances seemed to stay together, as did Ellen and Georgina. The latter pair spent time mixing in literary circles and, of course, continued to be attached to Minny.

Letter 78   [*cat: 793*]
About Annabel's children; they met in London

May 24, [*late 1850s*]
To: Annabel in London House Upper Brook St

Dearest Annabel,

I fully meant to have written to you yesterday but somehow the day slipped by. On Wednesday your two darlings came to dinner. They were most sweet & good. Amy [*Amicia*][476] a little bit shy when W Clive & his brother were in the room but both were as happy & loving as ever with Minny & very flattering to me in wishing to stay long with me after the rest were all gone to the Botanic Garden. It is so pretty to see them together, Florey[477] asking Amy at dinner whether she might accept my offer of more rice & custard.

I hope better news of dear Georgy. Her pain really got worse instead of better until yesterday when her doctor determined to try large doses of quinine, thinking it had taken a neuralgic form & certainly this experiment has had some success for she is easier today. Her general health is surprisingly good. I have kept up very well. P[enelope] & F[anny] leave town on Thursday. We are rejoiced at your account of Robin who is, I trust, now quite safely over his soapy tendency.[478] What a success the Dr D'A…. had done to the Miss M……

Ever your most affectionate,
EHT

From time to time after her marriage Annabel returned to the north Midlands area with her children. From Crewe Hall, she visited Madeley and sat by the monument to her aunt, where once Ellen passed by in Mrs Turton's pony carriage. "They got out and had a few minutes' talk".[479]

---

[476] Amicia Henrietta, Annabel's first daughter.

[477] Florence Ellen, Annabel's other daughter; note the two names, friends of her parents. Ellen must have been very flattered by this.

[478] Did this mean that Robert, called Robin, her son is dribbling or cutting his teeth?

[479] From *cat: 833* (Milnes-Coates archive).

Annabel wrote a letter (dated 27*th* January, possibly 1863) before Richard (Richie) had been made a peer, to Henrietta from Crewe Hall [cat: 581] part of which is quoted below:

"…. I have had a charming letter from E[llen] (now <u>Mrs Minny</u>) saying how <u>she</u> had enjoyed the fortnight – one bit of amusement was that on the 18*th* in marches Ellen with triumphant smiles embracing me as I sat at the gallery breakfast table: 'I have the news' etc, and is as I poetically described it, 'She was the first to place a coronet on my brow'. In plain prose that Lady Rich had written to tell her there was to be a batch of peers made and RMM to be one …… but certainly nothing is really settled and Richie is full of doubt whether Lord P[almerston] will create any peers. If he did I should suppose there is no doubt he would be one. Meanwhile Ellen and I had some laughs and jokes and you can fancy her humorous way with two friends……"

Annabel said she would feel very shy about a change of name and Richie would miss the House of Commons.

The following letter is from Minny to Annabel after a visit by Amicia.

Letter 79   [*cat: 878*]
Black edged; from Minny to Annabel, Lady Houghton; about Amicia

St Fagan's Castle Cardiff[480]
*Aug 10*th *[1864 or later]*[481]

Dearest Lady Houghton,
You must allow me to write a few lines of thanks to you for allowing us such a charming visit from darling Amicia. I have enjoyed her company so very much & she is quite a companion to me. In every way, I think hers is a particularly sympathetic nature & I have never found sympathy come from one so young who has been as free as she has from any great sorrow, I trust she may long be spared

---

[480] The summer home of Lady Harriet Clive.
[481] Richard Monckton Milnes became Lord Houghton on the 20th August 1863.

this, though it is, alas, a refining fire that seems necessary to most of us. We are quite delighted with Amicia's playing - she has such a good touch & her feeling comes out there too. She is immensely improved in music since I last heard her, but 3 years in her life make a great gap.

We accomplished our journey very successfully yesterday & find this a charming old house full of lovely old china etc & the country very pretty & being only 4 miles from the sea, it gives us sea air as well as hill air - we go on to Tenby on Monday. I hope you are feeling better, dear Lady Houghton. Pray don't think of answering this - I only wanted to thank you so much for the loan of such a darling. Ever your very affectionate,

M C Bridgeman[482]

Letter 80   [cat: 1008]
Black edged; Minny's friendship with Amicia

[*Possibly after 1870*]

My dearest Annabel,

Was so glad when the luggage went off in good time, but I was sorry to hear the train had been altered to 3 o'clock, as that made you have such a long waiting at the station. I know you will like to hear of dear Amicia [*b 1853*] from me. She is indeed very charming, so very modest & sweet yet with a great deal of character & much natural dignity. She & Minny are quite devoted to each other & are delightful companions in their reading & in every way. I am quite amused at their industry, not only in going thro' everything in the *Times* about present affairs, but working away at Lord Stanhope's *Queen Anne.*[483] Today Sir Ed & Lady Blount[484] came in unexpectedly & then M[inny] & A[micia] & Willy[485] went to Shrewsbury.

---

[482] (Minny) Marianne Clive had married in 1862 the Rev Hon John Robert Bridgeman. Their son William was born in 1864. Their daughter died in infancy.

[483] *The Reign of Queen Anne until the Peace of Utrecht* was written in 1870.

[484] Sir Edward Blount was a Paris Banker living in Rugeley. The Blount family eventually inherited Betley Hall in 1922.

[485] Willy (William) became a politician.

My own dearest A, how I wish I could have seen you better, but you & I must rejoice in what pleasure we can see in those around us & I think the affection between our two daughters is a sort of carrying on of our friendship & which is very, very pleasant to see.[486] I consider it has been so much your doing & that you had the wisdom to foresee it would be a success. Dearest of friends, I feel sure you will soon be a little better again - perhaps even before you leave dear Mrs Blackburne. <u>She</u> will not give you high or tough meat!!![487] Shallow thing.

Your loving,

EHT

"I look upon the repose of old age to be far from useless; its soothing influence upon the young is so precious"

---

[486] Ellen often referred to her niece as her daughter.

[487] Ellen was noted for enjoying very rare mutton. She ended on a joke.

Postscript

Afterwards

Ellen spent more time in London after her father's death in 1855. Betley Hall was inherited by the Wicksted family, who were living on their estate in Shakenhurst. For a time Betley Hall was let to a succession of tenants until Charles Wicksted's son George and his wife Margaret moved in. After George's death Margaret remarried but continued to live there until her death in 1922. The Betley Estate was sold in 1925.

30. This is a group photograph taken at the Welshpool Vicarage. Of the three women, Marianne is recognizable on the right. In the centre is Georgina identified by the sling supporting her disabled arm. The woman on the left could be Ellen. The men and boy have not been identified.

In 1862, Minny married the Hon John Robert Orlando Bridgeman, the second son of the Earl of Bradford of Weston Park in Staffordshire. Their son William Clive Bridgeman was born in 1864. He corresponded with his great aunt Ellen, but ignored her kindly advice not to enter politics by becoming Home Secretary (a Conservative) in 1922, and the First Lord of the Admiralty, and Viscount Bridgeman in 1929.

31. *Georgina in later years. The sling on her arm mentioned in the previous photograph is just visible.*

Ellen's closest sister and companion Georgina died in 1872. Ellen occasionally returned to Betley and once went to Betley Church in 1872 to dedicate some choir desks. She was accompanied by Minny (now the Hon Mrs Bridgeman) and her father the Archdeacon William Clive. No doubt it was a nostalgic occasion for them, since William previously preached there in 1836.[488]

32. Ellen Tollet, the only photograph we have been able to find.

---

[488] *Journals*, p 122.

Ellen died in 1890 in her house in Harley Street, close to Minny's residence. Apart from interests in the Betley estate, which were bequeathed to Charles Wigley Wicksted, the bulk of the remainder was left to Minny. The personal estate was valued at £10,728-4-0.

At the end of her life Henrietta, a devout Catholic, enjoyed the company of her immediate family with a wide circle of friends. She died in Prior Park in Bath in 1879.

Despite his eccentricities, Hungerford had exceeded all expectations by being an efficient and caring successor to the first Baron Crewe, his grandfather. He had the loyalty of his tenants and good advisers. His generosity was exemplified by the quality building of estate property, schools and churches. Crewe Hall was refurbished in 1837. After a disastrous fire in 1866, Crewe Hall was redesigned by E Barry with impeccable Victorian taste, and appears as it does now.

When Annabel took her children to see Hungerford, he showed positive dislike of normal childish ways. However, age brought tolerance, and he seemed later to show real care for the children of his nephew Robert. He outlived his two sisters and died in 1894. He was succeeded by his nephew, Annabel's son, who became the first Marquess of Crewe.

Annabel enjoyed a quiet life in the country, where she fulfilled the expected role of the lady of the manor at Fryston Hall. She preferred this to the busy social life in London of her husband, when they stayed in Upper Brook St. There were three children whom she adored. She enjoyed being responsible for their early education. They were: Amicia (1852-1902), who married Gerald Fitzgerald in 1883; Florence Ellen (1855-1923), who became a novelist and writer of short stories, once collaborating with Thomas Hardy; lastly Robert (Robin) Crewe Milnes (1858-1945), who became a Liberal peer. He had an illustrious political career.

However, Annabel did not have the best of health throughout her life, needing to be often within reach of a doctor. She died of pneumonia in July 1874, a gentle, agreeable, kindly person, as once described by Lady Palmerston.

Afterthoughts

Without doubt Ellen Tollet's correspondence has provided a rare insight into the lives of two marriageable young ladies. They both matured from inexperienced twenty year olds to more experienced women. By 1855 Ellen was wiser and less playful in her manner; she had experienced the deaths of her parents and three sisters. What did she have to look forward to? She still had her immediate family, and she had sufficient income to be independent with a companion or housekeeper, near her beloved niece Minny. She was able to mix in London society in the literary set of the Gaskells, Cloughs and Nightingales and she saw her friend, Emma Darwin, more frequently, often to discuss religion. She was now "the letter-writing old maid," as predicted in her letters.

Ellen emerges from the letters as a strong-minded woman, whose views had changed during the course of the writing. She thought she had some influence over Annabel's decisions, but not in the matter of love. The friends still continued to confide in each other about marrying Richard Monckton Milnes, despite warnings from Annabel's relations.[489] Ellen had to admit defeat by saying about his proposal, "He can never have any possibility of a better opportunity of doing so than now." At the age of 20 Ellen was lively, witty and could be the heart and soul of a party. Much later Annabel had commented on two occasions that Ellen would have enlivened her group at a gathering in Madeley after Mrs Cunliffe's death.[490] She also joked about the 'coronets' when Richard had been made a peer.[491] At the end of her life Ellen, as a spinster, had gained the respect of her family and her influential society friends.

Early in her adulthood Ellen had suffered the loss of a close friend the first Mrs Turton, her delightful sister Carry, and her respected older sister Marianne, all in childbirth; she had suffered with the latter the agonies of miscarriages and stillbirths. It is not surprising she felt that marriage was not for her. She also tried to dissuade Annabel from an early marriage, probably because she feared for her life too.

Ironically the birth of Minny fulfilled Ellen's wish to look after a child. In Betley there were other members of her family also needing attention – her invalid sister Eliza and her aged parents. Thus was her dilemma to remain single or to marry – a problem for many other women at the time.

Strangely the Reform Bill of 1832, when some men gained the vote, was not mentioned by Ellen in these letters. However she was totally unhappy about the role of women in society, as her writing here and in her *Journals*

---

[489] Letter 70 [*cat: 189*].
[490] [*cat: 486*].
[491] [*cat: 581*].

showed. Mary Wollstonecraft, Fanny Burney and Jane Austen had paved the way for the writers she was conversant with, including Miss Martineau, Mrs Marsh Caldwell and V (Caroline Clive). Ellen seemed to hold the sociologist and feminist Miss Martineau in awe, and would have shared the views of her illustrious forebear, Elizabeth Tollet (1694-1754), the poet and an early feminist. The inequality of the sexes was a matter concerning the unmarried sisters mainly because as women they had little power to make any changes in society.

As a single woman Ellen complained that there were few occupations open to her and she would have shared the views of progressive women who were trying to change the lives of others less fortunate. She was aware of the social changes being made, and while talking about them she was frustrated that any positive actions she took would have been ineffective. Ellen attempted to use her influence by writing to men of influence about such matters as providing a better education for girls. The Deaconess Scheme she had rejected because her talents would not be fully used. The possibility of entering a convent she had not accepted, perhaps through her lack of calling and commitments to her family. On religious grounds she would not have become later an active member of the suffragette movement – possibly a suffragist. Surprisingly she did not become a writer. Her ability to turn the dullest idea into a humorous statement was a real attribute that was practised in her letters and diaries.

Religion was a fairly common topic included in Ellen's letters and here she demonstrated the prejudices of the time. Ellen belonged to the Anglican High Church, attending the Sunday services in Betley and helping at the Sunday School. She could account for her sisters' deaths through the doctrine of Predestination. Her letters to Annabel were totally tactless when she discussed Henrietta's conversion to Roman Catholicism, and the latter's attempt to convert her brother Hungerford and Georgina to her faith. Ellen had no time for the Catholic belief in miracles. However the Methodism and Unitarianism of her friends were tolerated.

The modern reader has probably been surprised by the way in which Ellen had discharged her thoughts on philosophical topics, such as the meaning of life, the role of women, religion, birth, marriage, and death. It seemed as though it was self-analysis, and a means of communication with friends she did not often see. Perhaps she really felt the need for greater intellectual stimulation.

This was a time when privileged women were given some freedoms. As discussed in Appendix 3, the British Association for the Advancement of Science was gradually, rather grudgingly, allowing accompanied women to grace their meetings. After all, there was a young Queen on the throne in 1838.

To write is to select. In Ellen's daily diary (*Journals* from 1835 to 1836), she had written reminders to herself of her thoughts and happenings in her life as they occurred. In her letters to Annabel she selected parts of her life which she wanted to share with her friend.

The letters were written not for publication, but for Annabel, and they revealed Ellen's personality in a way to impress Annabel, whom she rarely saw. She was hardly likely to comment on her customary visits to the Poor House or to the local schools or Sunday sermons as she does in her *Journals* and it seems a pity that she did not elaborate her views about the political scene. She had time on her hands to write about her prolific reading, her relatives in higher places, and society gossip. How frustrated she must have been!

Why were these letters kept? They obviously had a value for Annabel, and the reader realises that Ellen enjoyed her friend's responses. It is regrettable that we do not see them. Ellen's letters were often amusing, sometimes heart-rending and occasionally disturbing. That some of the letters survived was surprising, since they had reached their destination, often abroad as in Part I. The addresses often were minimal with just the name, poste restante and the name of a major continental city. The letters must have been valued by Annabel because they were then transported back to this country. Perhaps Annabel treasured them to recall past memories, or, of course, she may have just put them in a box and forgotten about them.[492]

The epistolary novel became a highly successful art form in the eighteenth century, mainly through Samuel Richardson's novels *Pamela* and *Clarissa*. Later Jane Austen's early novel *Lady Susan* followed the same trend of fiction. The letters of Ellen to Annabel are read as a narrative but are fact. Their story exemplified a real image of life for two wealthy women who were bound by the conventions of the mid–nineteenth century.

---

[492] Also surprising since Annabel spent her married life mostly at Fryston Hall in Yorkshire, which was demolished in 1934.

These letters of Ellen Tollet to Annabel Crewe and Ellen's *Journals*, together with previously published work on the Tollet family, are building up a detailed picture of nineteenth century life of a privileged, upper-gentry family in Betley in North Staffordshire. It seems ironic that the large family of eight children of George and Frances Tollet in the early 1800s should have only one surviving great grandchild, the son of Minny, and he did not inherit the estate.[493]

Appendices

Appendix 1: The Houses of the Writers

Below are brief descriptions of the country houses occupied at various times by Ellen, Annabel, Hungerford and Mrs Cunliffe.

Crewe Hall, South Cheshire

The original Jacobean hall was built in the early part of the 17th century by Sir Ranulphe Crewe. It was a very large house but it was extended by

John Crewe, the 1st Baron Crewe in the 1780s and 1790s with many interior changes. By 1832 when the correspondence started between Ellen and Annabel, the main building appeared substantially as in the first illustration (p.7). In 1837 Hungerford Crewe, having become the 3rd Baron Crewe, employed the architect Edward Blore to make major interior changes and improvements to the house. This work continued until 1842. During the period of the letters the hall would have remained visually Jacobean. After the main hall was destroyed by fire in 1866, Edward Barry, son of Sir Charles Barry, was commissioned to take charge of the rebuilding of the hall. He

33. Hungerford's Coat of Arms.

---

[493] From the family tree, Margaret Blount married George Wicksted who died in 1895. Subsequently she married Colonel MacDonald who predeceased her. She died in 1922, and the Betley Estate passed to her side of the family to Sir Walter Blount.

retained the Jacobean façade on the front of the hall, but there were many additions including the tower. The hall contains many reproductions of the original woodwork. At this time the Crewe family were extremely wealthy and during all renovations before and after the fire, spared no expense on the work, as can be seen in the present hall. Hungerford always commissioned excellent designers for his property. However this story takes us beyond the period of the letters. For a comprehensive account of history of Crewe Hall, consult *Come and Build It Again*, by Ray Gladden, edited by Jerry Park.

Betley Hall, North Staffordshire

The Hall where Ellen was born and lived in her early life was a typical Georgian three-storey mansion as shown on the cover of the book. It was built in 1783 by Charles Tollet on the site of the previous half-timbered hall. It contained about 30 rooms. There was also a walled garden, and its grounds and lakes extended to a park as can be seen on the book cover, engraved in 1820. On 26th October 1835 William Gilpin, a landscape designer of the Picturesque Movement, advised on further improvements that could be made.

The Betley Friendly Society (established in 1762) had annual public festivals to raise money on Whit Tuesdays. On these occasions the improved grounds of the hall were opened to the public to see the ornamental lakes, the well-kept walks, punctuated by grottoes, flower beds and impressive trees.[494] The main approach to the hall was an imposing drive with its entrance in the centre of the village of Betley.

George Tollet's other important addition to the estate was the construction of model farm buildings, including a mill near the black-and-white Old Hall in about 1807. These listed buildings are being renovated. Betley Hall was finally demolished in the 1940s. (See N Tringham, Editor, *The History of the County of Stafford, The Victoria History, Vol XI.*).

Madeley Manor, North Staffordshire

In 1823 Foster Cunliffe-Offley, the son-in-law of the 1st Baron Crewe, built a house in Madeley for himself and his wife Elizabeth (or Emma if her second name is used). This was on land bought by Lord Crewe in 1822.

---

[494] From *local newspaper reports.*

The building described as a manor house was an extension of an existing property and built in regency style with a fine classical frieze. During the

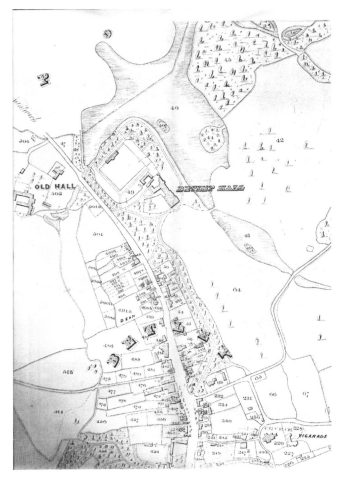

34. C19 Estate map of Betley village showing Betley Hall, the drive into the centre of the village, the Church and Vicarage, the farm at Old Hall, the walled garden and the lakes.

period of the letters Mrs Cunliffe lived in Madeley Manor which was mostly a new property. The house has had various tenants over the years and is now a care home. A lake to the east between the house and the M6 road remains. Accounts of the estate, Madeley Manor and the frieze, and its past residents can be found in J M Williams & L Williams, J Kennedy and N Tringham in the General References.

Appendix 2: Census Returns

The census returns from 1841 to 1881 provide spot checks on where the main individuals in these letters were living at these dates, and the size of their households including the number of servants.

On the 6th June 1841, Ellen was living in the Vicarage at Welshpool with William Clive, Georgina and Marianne Caroline (Minny) who was listed as aged 4 months. The household had 7 servants, including one man servant.

In 1851 on the 30th March, Ellen was living at Betley Hall with a very full house. On this date the household included George Tollet, Penelope, Frances, Charles Wicksted, his wife Mary and his daughter also Mary, a Swiss governess, Sophie Howder (aged 26). These were supported by a substantial number of 13 staff, including a housekeeper, butler, coachman, two footmen and various maidservants. George's wife Frances had died earlier in 1850.

On the 7th April 1861, Ellen, then aged 48, lived at 30 Queen Anne Street, London. She was described as the mortgage holder. Penelope (63) and Frances (60) were described as visitors and there were 5 staff. Ellen and Georgina lived on the census date in 1871 with 5 servants at Bilbrook House, Codsall, near Wolverhampton. It is not known whether they were visitors at Bilbrook or renting the property at the time. Ellen had sufficient private means to rent a succession of houses over her life. In 1881 she resided at Portland Place, supported by four servants. However, she died in Harley Street. By this date all her siblings and most of her friends had died.

On the 1841 date that Ellen was in Welshpool, Annabel (20) was staying in Upper Brook Street, London with her aunt Mrs Cunliffe, and a household of 9 servants. At the same time, Hungerford Crewe resided at St George, Hanover Square, London. Henrietta was living at the other Crewe residence, Prior Park in Bath.

In 1851, before she married, Annabel was still living at the same address with Emma Blackburne (aged 55) and 5 staff. On this census date Henrietta Crewe lived at 26 Bolton Street, London with Harriet Morier (60), who was described as the Land Holder, and Greville Morier (25), a Clerk in the Foreign Office. Subsequently Henrietta lived in Tiverton in

1861 in a house with a walled garden (next to a Roman Catholic Chapel), and also in 1871, with just one companion/servant on both dates.

In 1841 the population of Betley was 884 and declining, whilst that of Madeley was 1492 and increasing quite rapidly, according to census returns. On the other hand Crewe was very small with a population of 295 in 1831 but around 2000 by 1841 caused by the construction of the railway works.

Appendix 3: British Association for the Advancement of Science and Women

In Letter 20, dated 31st August 1839, Ellen casually mentioned that she attended the British Association for the Advancement of Science for a week, whilst staying at Olton House which was six miles from Birmingham. In August of that year the BAAS meeting was held in Birmingham, which is why, presumably, Ellen arranged for a visit to Olton. The first annual BAAS meeting occurred in 1831, and the question of whether it was appropriate for women to attend was a matter of debate from the beginning. Very few women presented papers in the early years. However, wives often accompanied the 'gentlemen of science' as they were often called, and they were allowed to accompany their husbands at social events and dinners. William Buckland, who is also mentioned in the letter wrote pompously in 1832 'Everybody whom I spoke too, on the subject agreed that if the Meeting is to be of scientific utility, ladies ought not to attend the reading of papers.' He felt that it would no longer be 'a serious philosophical union of working men.'[495]

Women were expected to sit in the gallery or a fenced-off section of the seating although these restrictions were largely abandoned eventually due to practical difficulties at some venues. At the 1838 meeting, women could attend all sections except Section D which included botany and zoology: the latter subject was deemed to be inappropriate. However this restriction

---

[495] Information about women and the BAAS has been taken from 'Science and Sociability: Women as audience at the British Association for the Advancement of Science, 1831–1901' *Isis* (2008) 99, 1-27, by R Higgitt & C W J Withers. This essay is the source of most of the comments in the Letters. For readers interested in this aspect of women and science the paper is available online. See also Letter 21 for more of Buckland's eccentricities.

was relaxed for the 1839 meeting.[496] Ellen revealed in Letter 14 her interest in Geology which, no doubt, accounts for Ellen and Penelope attending the geology section.

Ten years later the BAAS meeting returned to Birmingham, and again Ellen was staying in Olton and refers to meetings (Letter 61). It seems likely that she attended for a second time, and spoke

.

Appendix 4: Preparation in Betley for the Queen's Coronation

"The inhabitants of Betley being desirous that some public rejoicing shall take place on Thursday the 20th June 1838 the Coronation of our blessed Queen. It is intended amongst other rejoicings that there shall be a procession of the children from the Sunday Schools, headed by a band of Music and Banners & that cakes & wine be given to them.

That a tea drinking be given to the females, particularly to the Poor Widows in the School Rooms at 6 o'clock

That a dinner of beef and potatoes be given to the working class at 2 o'clock in the afternoon at the different inns and ale to drink the Queen's health

That the bells ring at intervals the whole of the day

That the inhabitants are requested to meet at the school room at 3 o' clock in the afternoon to join in the procession when the National Anthem of 'God Save the Queen' be sung & that a subscription be opened to defray the expense

That persons joining the procession are requested to wear white favours

It is proposed the girls of the National Sunday Schools will have tea at the Hall at 5 o'clock that the boys only shall have cake and wine at the school at 2 o'clock

A dance on the Lawn in front of the Hall & fireworks afterwards conclude the festivities of the day.

List of Donors

Rev H Turton £1, George Tollet £5, Frances Twemlow £3, Miss Fletcher £2, D Rathbothham £1, Christʳ Robinson £1, Chas Robinson 10/-, Thomas Wilson 5/- ,George Harding 10/-,William Salmon 5/-, James Shufflebotham 5/-,Thomas Dean 5/-, James Twemlow 2/6, William Salmon 2/6, William Lloyd 2/6, Thomas

---

[496] A report of the Birmingham meeting is available online. It is the *Report of the British Association for the Advancement of Science*, John Murray (1840) London (available online at Princeton University Library).

Wrench 5/-, Wilkinson Grantham 10/-, John Brows 2/6, James Palliser 2/6 not paid, George Mountford 5/-, Philip Morrey 2/6, Mrs Jones 2/6 not paid, Joseph White 2/6 not paid, William Hodgkinson 2/6, William Shaw 2/6. Thomas Latham 2/6, Mrs Southwell 2/6, Mr Short 5/-, Miss S 3/-, Mr Parks 10/- not paid, Charles Leighton 5/-, Joseph Markam 5/-, John Warburton 5/-, Mr Shufflebotham 5/-. "

(from BLHS Archives, George Tollet's Album)

Index

*The correspondents Ellen and Annabel, and Minny and Hungerford (also known as 'My Lord') have a large number of entries and are listed separately here. It is a list of letters denoted by bold **L45**, for example, and pages by 125.*

*The index is not exhaustive. We have concentrated mainly on those with several references and well-known individuals. For example, the large number of novels referred to, and their authors, are not itemised. As above letters are referred to by **L34** or **L13,332,56**, and pages by 125, for example.*